Food & Soul

Recipes and Inspiration for Gathering, Growing, and Handcrafting Real Food

by Ellen Arian

For Pat,

Wishing you all the pleasure and comfort that good food brings.

Ellen Arian

Copyright © 2016 by Ellen Arian

All rights reserved.
No part of this book may be copied, transmitted,
or reproduced without permission.
Printed in the United States of America on
SFI®-certified, acid-free paper.

Designed by Lisa Vega

ISBN 978-1-937650-78-0
Library of Congress Control Number: 2016953403

SMALL
BATCH
BOOKS

493 South Pleasant Street

Amherst, Massachusetts 01002

413.230.3943

smallbatchbooks.com

*With my whole heart,
I dedicate this book to my beautiful daughters,
Kate, Eliana, and Rebecca—for whom I first learned to cook,
and with whom I savor my most enjoyable meals.*

*And to the memory of my grandparents—
Ernestine and Leo Greenberger and Helen and Max Lester—
and my great-aunt Evelyn Friedl. My happiest childhood
memories took place around your tables,
where I came to know good food and unconditional love.
You have been among my greatest blessings.*

———— ♦ ♦ ♦ ♦ ————

*The heart of this book belongs to Carol Kenney
for encouraging me to teach what I know and write what I live,
and for helping me do it in more ways than I can number.
You have my deepest gratitude for your friendship and
for so generously sharing the work we both love.*

"A book is like a key that fits into the tumbler of the soul. The two parts have to match in order for each to unlock. Then—click—a world opens."—Brad Kessler

"No one who cooks, cooks alone. Even at her most solitary, a cook in the kitchen is surrounded by generations of cooks past, the advice and menus of cooks present, the wisdom of cookbook writers."—Laurie Colwin

Contents

- xiii   WITH THANKS
- xv   FOOD & SOUL/Preface

1   STOCKING YOUR PANTRY

- 3   The List
- 7   Food Thoughts/Raising Hens for Eggs
- 23   Does Organic Matter?
- 26   Notes on Ingredients

28   MILK AND CREAM

THE BASICS:

- 34   *Yogurt*
- 39   *Cultured Butter and Traditional Buttermilk*
- 46   Food Thoughts/Keeping a Family Cow
- 49   *Quark Cheese*
- 53   *Maple Vanilla Ice Cream*

USING THE BASICS:

- 56   *Yogurt Cheese*
- 59   *Compound Butter*
- 60   *Herbed Buttermilk Salad Dressing*
- 62   *Amaranth-Buttermilk Corn Bread*
- 64   *Delicate Whole-Wheat Pancakes*
- 66   *Cheese Soufflés with Maple-Sweetened Berries*

69	FOOD THOUGHTS/A Path to Gratitude
71	*Quark Puff Pastry Dough*
74	*Quark Twists*
76	*Quark Rugelach*
79	Bread and Plenty
82	**SOURDOUGH**
85	*Sourdough Starter*
95	FOOD THOUGHTS/Brotform
97	*Sourdough Wheat and Rye Bread*
109	FOOD THOUGHTS/Boule
110	FOOD THOUGHTS/Crispy Eggs
112	*Sourdough Fruit and Nut Bread*
117	FOOD THOUGHTS/A Memorable Loaf
121	*Rosemary-Parmesan Focaccia*
126	*Sourdough Challah*
130	*Sourdough Pizza*
134	*Herbed Parmesan Bread Twists*
137	*Sourdough Biscuits*
140	Using Sourdough to Lower the Glycemic Index of Everyday Baked Goods
143	*Sourdough Banana Bread*
146	*Sourdough Cocoa Cake*
150	Bold Baking

153 WHOLE GRAINS

FOR BREAKFAST:

155 *Morning Muesli*

158 *Breakfast Porridge: Variations on a Theme*

161 FOOD THOUGHTS/Heirloom Grains

163 *Oatmeal with Warm Fruit Toppings*

165 *Prune-Orange Compote*

166 *Warm Maple-Glazed Apples*

167 *Maple-Nut Granola*

AS SOUP AND SIDES:

169 *Barley and Mushroom Soup*

171 *Basic Brown Rice*

176 *Ditto the Bean*

179 *A Pot of Soup That You Can Make with Any Lentil, Pea, or Bean*

184 *Corn Polenta: Variations*

187 *Quinoa in Shiitake Mushroom Stock*

IN BAKING:

189 *Buckwheat-Oat Scones with Orange and Currants*

191 *Apricot Upside-Down Skillet Cake*

193 *Apple Crisp: Variations*

197 *Coconut Carrot Cake*

199 *Miniature Chocolate Cupcakes*

201 *Cocoa Brownies*

203 VEGETABLES

205 *A Light Touch*

205 *All-Purpose Vinaigrette*

IN SOUP:

212 *Golden Star Soup*

214 *Zucchini Soup with Buttermilk and Fresh Herbs*
216 Food Thoughts/Inspiration
219 *Cauliflower and Leek Soup*
221 *Butternut Squash Soup*
223 Food Thoughts/Crafting a Salad

IN A SALAD:

224 *Sourdough Bread and Roasted Summer Vegetable Salad*
226 *Traditional Greek Salad*
228 *Tomato Salad with Chive Oil*
230 *New Potato Salad*
232 Implicit in Vinaigrette
234 *Rebecca's Everyday Vinaigrette*
235 Caesar Salad Two Ways
238 Food Thoughts/Homegrown

ON THE SIDE:

240 *Sautéed Ramps*
242 *Tamari Green Beans*
243 The Allure of Summer Pickles
244 *Making Pickles*
248 *Italian Broccoli*
250 *Crispy Potato Rösti*
253 *Creamed Spinach Gratin*
255 *Roasted Sweet Potatoes with Thyme*
256 *Maple-Glazed Brussels Sprouts*
258 *Butternut Squash Gratin*

260 **PURE WATER**
263 *Cucumber Water with Lemon Slices and Fresh Mint*
264 *Pink Raspberry Lemonade*

265 *Sparkling Sour Cherry Lemonade*
267 *Rosemary Lemonade*
268 Food Thoughts/Sun Tea
270 *Iced Hibiscus Tea*
271 *Green Tea*
274 *Ginger Tea*

275 BY YOUR OWN HAND
277 *Vegetable Stock*
280 *Shiitake Mushroom Stock*
281 *Rich Chicken Broth*
285 *Fish Stock*
288 Food Thoughts/Poultry, Red Meat, and Fish
291 *Ghee*
293 *Gomasio*
294 *Tamari Toasted Pumpkin Seeds*
295 *Mayonnaise*
298 *Pesto*
300 *Ricotta-Almond Spread*
301 *Olive Spread*
303 *Mongolian Barbeque Sauce*
305 *Creamy Hummus*
307 *White Bean Spread*
309 *Elderberry Syrup*
311 *Red Wine Vinegar*

315 Gathering Ingredients and Supplies

WITH THANKS

It would be impossible to individually thank everyone who contributed in some way to this book because nearly all those I know have shared an insight or a cooking tip or healing wisdom or a meal that mattered. I offer collective thanks, then, to my family and treasured friends for your cherished support and encouragement, and for taking time out of your busy lives to read my work and share it with your friends. I'm grateful to each one of you.

Food & Soul owes its completion to a few who deserve to be singled out. I offer my thanks to:

Judy Craig, for supporting me as my cooking career evolved and offering practical help when this book was a work in progress. Mimi, our shared Jersey cow, is recent evidence of your big-heartedness and your willingness to jump all-in if it means helping me and sharing an adventure.

Megan Sager, for helping launch my culinary career, creating the name Ellen's Food & Soul, and generously offering food thoughts, writing thoughts, and much-needed support.

The Natural Gourmet Institute in New York City, my culinary home. Over decades, I learned from your chef instructors, who taught me to more deeply understand the culinary and healing properties of whole foods. And to the memory of Dr. Annemarie Colbin, my most influential teacher, who modeled how to question and inspired me to use my training to improve people's lives. Your work made everything possible.

Small Batch Books, and especially to Trisha Thompson, for embracing my imaginings and helping me transform those imaginings into reality.

More than anything, a cook needs appreciative diners—and so to Mark Arian, for the high value you placed on my learning and cooking, and to the brightest lights along my path to writing this book, Kate, Eliana, and Rebecca. Thank you for eating my experiments and enabling my learning.

FOOD & SOUL

PREFACE

I offer these recipes not as the definitive last word on handcrafting foods at home, but rather as my own love song to a particular way of inhabiting the rich realm that is the kitchen, with happiness and caring devotion to detail. Take these pages, then, as a beginning, as my own variation on a theme that, if you give yourself to it fully, will occupy your hands and imagination for years to come.

When taken in its fullness, the kitchen can be a wondrous place, a realm of mystery and surprise that has the potential to engage you, harness your intelligence, and nourish you well.

I came to handcrafting food in a roundabout way. As a young mother I had children to care for, but I knew little about cooking, and the kitchen was not where I wanted to spend time. Finding a way to make food preparation interesting became necessary to my survival as both a mother and a cook.

My natural inclination was to throw myself into the task of sourcing pure, nutritious, local ingredients long before it was fashionable to do so. I somehow believed this was a necessary beginning, and I was then left with the task of figuring out how to turn these ingredients into meals. Once I found dishes I liked to prepare and serve, I might have to wait months for the same ingredients to come into season again so that I could cook and learn some more. But because making food artisanally, which was where my efforts took me, is so engaging and so much fun—and because it's perfect when there are children alongside you—it held my interest as waiting gave birth to anticipation.

If you already enjoy spending time in the kitchen, or if you are determined to enjoy spending time in the kitchen, artisanal home cooking might be a path you want to wander. It is endlessly interesting, the results are nearly always delicious, and if you're not afraid of an occasional mishap, you will appreciate making discoveries of your own.

Contrary to what you might imagine, cooking artisanally is not about a fancy presentation or clever tricks. At its best, it is an uncomplicated and traditional way to cook, and there is an elegance to the process. Artisanal cooking is about crafting foods using ingredients and approaches that have integrity, rather than about cooking in a stylish way or with an ingredient-of-the-moment. The technique is to use your own two hands in the same way a craftsman does: offering care and loving energy, and relying on a time-honored process and ingredients that are far removed from the industrialization of today.

> The journey toward this way of cooking, once you begin it, will lead you down a road that becomes joyously endless, with twists and turns, and a path that happily circles back onto itself. For some people, cooking will remain an unavoidable necessity, if they do it at all. But for the home artisan, it can become a cherished and abiding passion, and the kitchen can be a refuge in a world that often feels without order. The cooking will nourish you physically, and when approached with care, it will nourish your spirit as well.

You will want to begin with real food that is fresh, pure, and close to its source, and this, to my mind, is where the thrust of your effort belongs. Ingredients like these are not hard to find; for most of us they are available from farmers' markets, small farms, home gardens, online sources, and even the grocery store. They are also available from others who approach their pursuits artisanally, growing their own produce or raising their own livestock with care and attention to detail. The key is to begin with ingredients that are as close to harvest as they come and then to let those ingredients shine. You should be able to taste them, always, in the finished dish.

It feels important to assure you, here at the outset, that handcrafting foods has more to do with humility than with showmanship. Your own learning will never end, you will never "arrive," and most of the time those you cook for will never know what went into preparing a particular dish; they will only know that the taste is incomparable. Handcrafting foods, then, is not about garnering praise or recognition—it is about giving pleasure and finding pleasure in the process.

It's true that opening a can is safe; what's inside never changes. But isn't that part of the problem? It's so ordinary, predictable, and tasteless, and it's so little fun. As the chef Paul Bertolli wrote, and as the artisanal home cook should adopt as his or her mantra: "The trouble you take will also be your enduring pleasure."

• •

What you will find on these pages, as abundant as they may seem, is merely a sampling of the many ways you can handcraft memorable food in your own home kitchen. There is far more for us all to learn. And while I have no easy means to grant you, immediately, the ability to glance at a bread dough and know how the rise is coming along, reading these pages, experimenting with these recipes, and paying attention to detail will, over time, put you in touch with your own inner artisan. And so begins the pleasure of getting from here to there.

• •

STOCKING YOUR PANTRY

"Have nothing in your house that you do not know to be useful, or believe to be beautiful." —William Morris

Take a good look around your kitchen. Now ask yourself how it makes you feel. Does it relax you, or make you feel uneasy? It's an important question to consider, because one way to keep cooking front and center in your life, and to maintain your enthusiasm for approaching it as a craft, is to make sure your kitchen is exactly the kind of place where you like to spend time.

Over many years spent cooking in all sorts of places, I've observed a few sure marks that are common to well-loved kitchens. Countertops usually bear an abundance of fruits and vegetables, all fresh and in good form. A vase of flowers often adds beauty, fragrance, and a bit of the outdoors. And there are special touches, a lot of them: crocks and jars filled with favorite ingredients, gifts from friends and family, or treasures picked up on travel. The impulse to spend time cooking is nurtured by these ingredients, tools, and mementos. They need not be costly; rather, they need only mean something to you.

In my own kitchen, a cherished favorite is a sky blue pitcher from my grandmother. It sits on the countertop next to my stove and is filled with cherrywood spoons. Among them, I have my well-worn favorites, the one or two that fit my hands just so and respectably handle many jobs. I also have a drawer full of aprons, some with stories behind them connecting me to the people I love, and a few whose origins I cannot trace. Regardless, no real work in the kitchen is possible without the reassurance of one of these aprons wrapped around my waist. Without it, I am simply not up to the task. The point of these tools, and others like them, is the comfort and familiarity they offer and the utility they provide. They enable my culinary wishes, helping me transform ideas and imaginings into food on the table. They feel good, set the mood, and help get the job done. They never let me down, and there aren't many things in life I can say that about.

Equal to, or perhaps more important than, having the right tools is having ingredients readily at hand, which brings us to the pantry. There is something deeply satisfying about a well-stocked larder. When you're ready, you'll want to look with a critical eye at what you already have—items you may have relied upon for years—and think about whether or not they still pass muster. While there's no firm rule for predicting the shelf life of pantry staples, it's a good idea to check any herbs and ground spices that are more than several months old, and any whole spices, flours, or grains that have been on your pantry shelves for close to a year. Evaluate other ingredients for freshness as well. Smell and taste them, because some of what determines shelf life is your own sense of what's palatable.

As you're sorting and restocking, take a look at the following list of items that, as you move through these pages, you will begin to call on as ingredients in cooking. Having them at arm's length, while it may initially seem like work to accomplish, will make handcrafting delicious food much easier.

············ **THE LIST** ············

This list is by no means exhaustive. There will be other pantry items you may want to have on hand to satisfy your tastes and desires or to accommodate your own preference for international flavors. On the other hand, the list includes some ingredients that should be incorporated into a well-stocked pantry, even though you won't need them to prepare the recipes in this book. Regardless, consider this a beginning, a reference point that you can build on, and you will find yourself and your pantry in good stead.

Beans. Beans have been nourishing us for as long as we have been an agricultural people. They have an earthiness and a vitality that is especially sustaining, and since they make themselves at home in soups, salads, spreads, and more, they deserve a place of honor in our pantries. It's best to shop for beans in stores that have a good turnover, as old beans take longer to cook and are, well, old. It's fine to keep your beans in the cupboard where it's somewhat cool and dry; I keep mine in large mason jars, and they are a pleasure to look at. If you're fortunate enough to be able to buy local, just-dried beans, you may want to make room for them in the refrigerator during the summer months. Also, keep in mind that these fresh treasures take less time to cook than dried beans.

Butter. Butter is much maligned, but it has been a staple in the diets of many long-lived people and can surely be used in an intelligent way. Butter contains antioxidants that prevent damage to our cells and strengthen immunity. And butter, quite simply, tastes good. If you don't make it yourself, your butter should come from cows that eat grass, and it will be labeled this way. It should also be made from cream that's free of pesticides, antibiotics, and hormones. It's best to buy unsalted butter for two reasons. First, unsalted butter allows you to control the quantity of salt in recipes for baked goods. Second, salt is a preservative and is added to butter to extend its shelf life. This means unsalted butter in stores is often fresher than salted butter.

Coconut oil. Coconut oil has received bad press for being a saturated fat. Yet, if you do some research, you will find praise from reputable sources. "Virgin, organic coconut oil" is what you want in your pantry. It has become a treasured ingredient in my own kitchen, stepping in for butter in baking on occasions when dairy is unwelcome, and performing over high heat without breaking down. It has a longstanding tradition of use, and though it is saturated, the populations that rely on it as their main fat are reported to have low rates of disease. Coconut oil is naturally sweet, retains a subtle coconut flavor even after cooking, and keeps well on a shelf in the pantry. It will become hard in cool months, melted in warm months, and either is fine. Simply scoop it in the winter and pour it in the summer; its melting point is 76 degrees.

Condiments. The adage that your cooking can be only as good as your least good ingredient is most relevant with condiments like ketchup, mayonnaise, and mustard. If you purchase these or other condiments, be sure to read their ingredients lists. Try to choose brands that contain short, recognizable items and no refined sugar, corn syrup, or additives.

Cookbooks. I love cookbooks, and I read most of them cover to cover, as if they're novels; I also have a large variety that I rely on for both inspiration and instruction. While today's cookbook industry is driven more by celebrity than by scholarship, and while there are countless free recipes available online, I still appreciate being able to pull favorite cookbooks off the shelf, especially those that are embellished with my notes and that reflect my own hard-won wisdom. It's ideal if you can find a place for cookbooks within easy reach in your kitchen, especially those you use most often. Until recently, I kept many of mine on an infrequently used countertop, though I now have bookshelves in the kitchen, which is a handy improvement. Either way, it's uplifting to have warm support and good advice near at hand.

Cookware. Whenever possible and where your budget allows, strive to work with stainless steel, cast iron, or heavy, enameled cast iron cookware. Aluminum reacts to foods that are acidic or salty, and its toxic metal can be absorbed into the foods you eat. In my own kitchen, I rely on All-Clad pots and pans, and find that I can use extra-virgin olive oil much more liberally than I once did because it rarely smokes or breaks down in these pots. I also use Le Creuset and inexpensive Lodge cast iron cookware. My favorite pan, in fact, is a skillet I purchased for a paltry sum from Lodge years ago, and it will last me a lifetime. I would not recommend inexpensive enameled pots because they chip easily, and when they do, the surface underneath is exposed to food. As for baking sheets, stainless steel surpasses aluminum, although if you have aluminum sheet pans you want to keep using, you can line them with parchment paper before baking. Teflon and other synthetic, nonstick surfaces currently contain two controversial chemicals: PFOA and PTFE, which can contaminate your food if the pan is scratched or chipped. PTFE can also break down over high heat and emit fumes that can be bad for our health. There are new "green" skillets that have eliminated one or both of these chemicals—I'm currently experimenting with one made by Kyocera—but the technology is, as of this writing, still young. In my own kitchen, I continue to rely on one All-Clad Teflon skillet that, because I am concerned about fumes, I take care to use over a low heat when making omelets, scrambled eggs, or potatoes rösti. It is a high-quality pan that I treat with care and use as a tool when no other pan will do the job as well.

Dairy. When you buy dairy products, whether to eat directly or to use as the foundation for handcrafting other foods, they should ideally come from cows that eat grass. They should also be free of antibiotics and hormones, even if they are not certified organic. More and more, these products are available at grocery and health-food stores. If you prefer to get your milk straight from the cow, sheep, or goat, there are many states that allow the legal purchase of raw milk directly from farmers. If yours does not, try looking for milk that is lightly pasteurized but not homogenized. Homogenization is a method of processing that disperses fat molecules throughout milk and prevents a layer of cream from forming on top. This unnecessary process breaks up delicate fats, affects the flavor of the milk, and may work against our good health. Milk that is not homogenized is legal and readily available—you know you've found it when the label says "creamline" or "cream on top."

> None of the recipes in this book call for using a microwave oven because it has no role in the handcrafting of real food; further, the effect of microwaves on our food and our bodies is not yet fully understood. There are those who may say the microwave oven is perfectly safe, but I'm not convinced, and to be honest, I manage nicely without it in my kitchen. Traditional cooking methods—a soup pot, a sauté pan, and a real oven—do an admirable job of helping me handcraft the dishes I most enjoy. While it's true that a microwave might save me a few minutes and the washing of a pot, what's the potential trade-off? Since I don't know, and since there's no need for a microwave in the sort of home cooking I do, I choose not to use one.

Eggs and poultry. Happy hens wake up in the morning, lay their eggs, spend their days in the sunshine eating insects and grass, and come back to their protected space for dinner and rest. These are the hens whose eggs you want, and chicken, if you eat it, should come from the roosters that live alongside them. These products are from "pastured" poultry and they will be labeled this way. Keep in mind that eggs are thought to be one of the most nourishing and digestible foods available; they are a wonderful source of inexpensive protein and a powerhouse in the home kitchen. Eggs from pastured hens are the most nutritious, with rich orange yolks and an ideal balance of essential fats. Once you eat eggs like these, you will never turn back. If you do most of your food gathering at grocery stores rather than farmers' markets, you might look for eggs labeled "high omega." These come from hens that have flax or alfalfa added to their feed to increase the omega-3 fat content; they can be an option if you don't have access to eggs from pastured hens. What you want to avoid are powdered eggs, liquid eggs, factory-farmed eggs, egg substitutes, or any other egg-like product. No imitation can replace the real thing. *("The List" continues on page 12.)*

.... *FOOD THOUGHTS* ....
RAISING HENS FOR EGGS

It feels natural—if you have committed yourself to food gathering, cooking, and spending time putting meals on the table—to fantasize about raising some portion of the food you consume. For years this was my own wish until, finally, I took the leap into raising hens for eggs. If you are anything like I am, I cannot tell you what a joy you would find tending hens to be. They are smart (who knew?); they are wonderfully hardy and athletic; they run free on pasture, eating bugs and stirring up the compost pile; and here is the kicker: They turn grass and bugs and kitchen scraps into really superior eggs.

Although I didn't know it until I had them, raising hens can be a lot like cultivating fertile soil. In order to grow the healthiest plants, supremely rich in nutrients and able to hold their own against pests, one must nurture the soil with zeal. If you devote your energy to the soil, if you keep your focus there, where it belongs, the plants will mostly take care of themselves. So, too, the egg. For an egg to reach its zenith—to have a sturdy shell, a deep orange yolk that rises round and tall, and a white that's firm and holds together—you must throw yourself into nurturing the hen, the egg's own fertile soil.

Key to nurturance is the hen's diet, which should center on grass and bugs and include grain as a daily addition. I used to purchase grain from a local farmer who grows and mills his own replica of the mix devised by Joel Salatin, the mind and heart behind some of our most inventive methods of modern chicken tending; if you ask around, which is what I did, you might find such an arrangement for yourself. More recently, I've been offering my own mix of

grains: primarily wheat and oats in warm weather, with barley and corn added to warm the hens as the temperatures drop. There are also grain mixes available at feed stores, some soy-free and others not, so you can choose which you prefer. Because my hens are raised on grass, I've found that they are not especially interested in the leafy greens I offer. But they do relish all kinds of leftover summer fruits, tomatoes, and grated summer squash. They also eat seeds from melons and peppers. And most days I give my hens a little homemade yogurt or buttermilk, which provides them with some of the calcium they need to make a nice hard shell.

In the winter, my hens appreciate the vast array of sprouts I grow in a jar on the kitchen counter. I got that idea from Salatin, too, and came to rely on it because it made so much sense. Sprouts are exceedingly nutritious, and they give the hens the chlorophyll and living energy they miss during months when grass is buried under snow. When I have a few extra minutes, I warm soured raw milk or buttermilk and combine it with the hens' grain to make a winter mash. Since hens don't eat after dark, I take care to offer these riches when there's still light left in the day.

This careful cultivation of health in my hens consistently rewards me. Their eggs are incomparable, with deep orange yolks and a level of richness that makes it hard to eat more than one, which is a sorrow because they are especially good.

The only other basic requirement hens have is for protection: a well-ventilated space that's buffered from strong winds and fully enclosed to keep predators away. This space can be moveable across pasture (a chicken "tractor") or stationary (a "coop" with a door that remains open during the day, giving hens access to grass). In my own home setting, my preference for laying hens has, so far, been a stationary coop that I leave open to pasture in the daytime. With an arrangement like this, it's possible to contain roaming hens—if that is your wish—by permanently fencing a large area around your coop, or using less expensive but equally effective electric netting.

Anyone can do this. Anyone can lovingly and carefully tend hens with the goal of cultivating eggs that have reached their full potential—artisanal eggs, if you will—just as anyone can garden with the goal of creating deep brown, mineral-rich, life-giving soil. Nature does most of the work. Your role is mainly to move things along.

FOR THE LINGUIST IN YOU

There is an especially fun aspect to raising hens: There are so many figures of speech that come from chicken tending. They will come to mind daily and you will say, "Oh, that's where that turn of phrase originated!" Here are some examples to help you understand what I mean:

COMING HOME TO ROOST: At the end of the day, hens run to the coop and fly up to a horizontal bar (or a tree branch, if they live in the wild) to roost for the night.

ROOSTER: The male of the species sits high on a tree branch, where he "roosts" to watch over his hens.

HENPECK: When hens are irritated with each other, which doesn't happen often if they have ample space, they peck at each other with their sharp beaks.

DON'T PUT ALL YOUR EGGS IN ONE BASKET: If, when you go out to gather eggs, you put all of them into one basket, you might lose the whole bunch by dropping or knocking it. If you put half your eggs in one basket and the rest in another, there is a greater likelihood you will have eggs for breakfast.

RUNNING CHICKEN: When young hens are threatened, they don't run toward the aggressor to defend themselves; they turn and run away.

SCRATCHING OUT A LIVING: Chickens scratch the soil to find bugs to fill their bellies.

PECKING ORDER: Within a group of hens, there exists a hierarchy, and pecking is the means to put an up-and-comer in her place.

FLYING THE COOP: A hen will occasionally take flight and leave the coop, which brings us to a related figure of speech . . .

THE GRASS IS ALWAYS GREENER ON THE OTHER SIDE OF THE FENCE: Hens might roam on a pasture full of grass, weeds, bugs, and all that makes a chicken happy. But they will still stick their heads through the fence, or go over the fence, in search of some imagined improvement in circumstances.

Here are a few more examples to give you some idea of what an agricultural people we once were, with an entire lexicon established around the shared experience of chicken tending: nest egg, hatch an idea, cockeyed, feather your nest, hen house, mother hen, rule the roost, bad egg, walking on eggshells . . . and there are more. If you someday get your own hens, you will have the fun of conjuring up the rest yourself.

HOW TO MAKE SPROUTS FOR YOUR HENS OR YOURSELF

Sprouting seeds is easy. Almost any bean, grain, seed, or nut, when kept warm and moist, will sprout (see "Gathering Ingredients and Supplies" on page 315).

Here is a simple method I like to use for growing sprouts. Rinse a small handful of sprouting seeds in several changes of cool water, then immerse the seeds in a fresh batch of cool water in a half-gallon glass canning jar. Cover the jar with a purchased straining lid or with a small square of butter muslin, mosquito netting, or nylon held in place with a rubber band or a metal canning ring. Soak the seeds for 8 to 12 hours. *(Continued on next page.)*

Different seeds have different soaking requirements, and seeds that are mucilaginous should not be soaked, but this is a good general guideline for getting started.

At the end of the soak, turn the jar over and strain out the water. Shake the jar a few times to drain any remaining water that has collected among the seeds. Rinse, strain, and shake once more. Then set the jar upside down at an angle (a dish-drying rack works well) and out of direct sunlight.

Twice each day, rinse the seeds: Fill the jar with water, swish the seeds, and turn the jar over to shake and drain. Maintain this routine until the seeds have sprouted and the first small leaves have shed their hulls. When the sprouts are to your liking, rinse them one last time and air dry them on a paper towel for a couple of hours. Then store the sprouts in a sealed container and eat them yourself or serve them to your very appreciative hens.

Fish. If you eat fish and are concerned about quality, look for varieties that are wild instead of farmed because wild fish have a healthier balance of essential fats, which makes them better for you. The wild fish you choose should also ideally be small because small fish generally have fewer contaminants. Fish you may want to consider include anchovies, sardines, herring, sablefish, mackerel, and wild salmon; you may find other varieties of wild fish at farmers' markets or fine fish shops. For meals in a pinch, you might want to consider canned sardines, wild salmon, and mackerel. Keep in mind that for reasons of good health, oil-packed sardines should be packed in olive oil rather than vegetable oil. It's also good to know that all sockeye salmon is currently wild, whether labeled that way or not, and is readily available frozen, smoked, or canned.

Flours. White flour is suitable to a variety of purposes, and it's what many of us are used to using, but whole-grain flours can add complexity and interest to the foods you bake. It's good to remember, however, that whole-grain flours are perishable, and their nutritious oils can quickly go rancid at room temperature. I try to buy whole-grain flours from artisan producers or small businesses committed to first-rate quality and milling-to-order. Once I get them home, I keep them in glass jars or in resealable bags that I store in the freezer. You can use flour directly from the freezer, but it's better if you can bring it to room temperature before baking. Whole-wheat pastry flour is relatively low-protein flour that's good for making waffles, pancakes, cookies, cakes, and muffins. Whole-wheat bread flour is higher in protein and works well for bread, pizza dough, and some pancakes and quick breads. Keep in mind that flour, as a fundamental ingredient, matters. The variety of flour you choose, and the freshness of that flour—especially if it is whole grain—help create the texture, flavor, and fragrance of your finished baked goods.

Herbs. If you have the time and space to grow them, fresh herbs from your own backyard are ideal. The challenge of buying fresh herbs is that the packages sold in stores give you far more than you can typically use. I find that thyme is an exception because I can almost always find ways to finish it up. When you do opt for store-bought herbs, try keeping larger stems the same way you keep flowers: upright in a glass full of water, with fresh water every few days. Basil, however, seems to keep best if you place a plastic bag loosely over the herb-filled glass and store it in the refrigerator. In either case, trim the stems before placing them in water. If you have an abundance of sturdy herbs like rosemary, thyme, and oregano, you can preserve them by spreading them on a cooling rack, sushi mat, or even a rattan place mat—anything that allows for good air circulation around the herbs—and letting them dry in a cool, dark place. You can also tie them in bundles and hang them upside down out of direct sunlight. When the leaves become brittle, crumble them and store them in a jar in a darkened cupboard. If you buy dried herbs at the store, look for those labeled "nonirradiated."

Honey. As a onetime beekeeper, I have strong opinions about honey. So much of it today comes from bees that are treated with highly toxic medications to control mites and other parasites. When I shop for honey, I talk to the beekeeper about how he or she controls mites in the hive. There are many gentle approaches that were not available when I kept bees, and so I opt for nontoxic and natural. In lieu of talking to the beekeeper, look for certified organic honey.

Lemons. I know these are not local for most of us, but here I make an exception because I cannot imagine a well-stocked kitchen without plenty of whole lemons—*whole* being key. Bottled lemon juice is not the same. It lacks flavor and aroma and so will the foods you add it to. Though you should keep fresh lemons in the refrigerator for longer storage, it's easier, when you can plan ahead, to use lemons at room temperature because they release their juices more readily. If you want flavorful and aromatic lemon zest, it's a good idea to buy organic lemons and remove the zest using a microplane, which you can find at any good kitchen store.

Mirin, tamari, and shoyu. Mirin is a sweet Japanese rice wine that can generally be used as a one-to-one substitute for sherry in recipes. Mirin balances flavors in acidic foods like tomato sauce; it also mellows the saltiness of dishes cooked with shoyu or tamari, which is why they are often paired. Mirin keeps well, but its aroma lasts longer if you refrigerate the bottle after opening. Shoyu is to soy sauce what sea salt is to salt: the same in many people's minds, but worlds apart in every other way. Unlike commercial soy sauce, which is artificially fermented and petroleum-based, shoyu is a combination of wheat and soy fermented in a long, slow process using traditional methods. It is unpasteurized, has a mellow flavor, and should be refrigerated after opening. Like shoyu, tamari is also fermented slowly, but it is most often made from soy alone and does not include wheat. Tamari is smoother and more complex than shoyu is. It also adds its own flavor to foods, while shoyu tends to harmonize and enhance the other flavors in a dish. Even so, the two can sometimes be substituted for each other. Tamari does not need to be refrigerated after opening, though I usually keep mine in the refrigerator—a habit, I suppose.

Miso. Miso is a fermented soybean paste with an abundance of health benefits. It's used in Japanese dishes like miso soup or to add flavor to foods. Because unpasteurized miso, which is what you want, is "alive," it should be stored in the refrigerator. Dark and rich-flavored miso made from barley or red rice tends to be saltier than the sweeter, mellow white or chickpea misos. Be aware that to retain its health benefits, you'll need to avoid cooking miso. Instead, add it to dishes after the cooking is finished by dissolving it in stock or water and then adding the mixture to the finished dish.

Oils from seeds and nuts. If you use oils made from seeds and nuts, you'll want to store them in the refrigerator, as they easily go rancid. Darkness and cool temperatures are keys to preserving them. It's also a good practice to buy them in small quantities from a store with rapid turnover so you can be assured of freshness. If oil becomes rancid, you will know by its "off" odor. Keep in mind that nut oils and flaxseed oil are best used to dress a salad or to drizzle over hot foods; these oils are not stable enough to be used for cooking. Although we should all avoid high omega-6 oils like corn, safflower, sunflower, and soybean for reasons of good health, there may be room for small amounts of toasted sesame oil (used for finishing, not cooking) or sesame oil when your taste buds cry out for it. Again, store these perishable oils in the refrigerator.

Olive oil. If it isn't already, extra-virgin olive oil should become a staple in your kitchen because of its healthfulness and versatility. Many fine-quality olive oils are readily available, and all should be stored in a cool, dark cupboard once you get them home. There's no need to refrigerate olive oil because you will use it before it becomes rancid; it also solidifies in the refrigerator, which would require you to plan your cooking well in advance for it to be used in a liquid state. I use a less expensive extra-virgin olive oil for stove-top cooking and where its particular flavor is less important. But I rely on a high-quality oil with exceptional flavor for dressings and sauces, and for applying a finishing touch. Don't be afraid to taste olive oil by the spoonful to get a sense of how it compares to other oils and to develop your own preferences.

Parchment paper. While I try to avoid creating waste, I often use parchment paper to prevent the sticking of cakes, roasted vegetables, and much that would be otherwise crusted to the bottom of a pan. I also find it to be an indispensable barrier, ensuring that aluminum foil doesn't come into contact with the foods I cook. Parchment paper is made from plant fibers that are treated with silicone and sulfuric acid to be water and heat resistant. It's sold in rolls as well as flat sheets, and both work well. I've recently experimented with reusable parchment paper; although it works well, it is currently made with PTFE (see "Cookware," page 5), and so, like Teflon, it has not become a mainstay in my kitchen.

Produce in season. One centerpiece of an active and vibrant home kitchen is produce so fresh that it bursts with flavor and is as nutrient-rich as it can be. Most fresh vegetables keep best in high humidity in your refrigerator drawers; I often store them in resealable plastic bags that I wash and reuse. Mushrooms and cucumbers belong in paper bags in the refrigerator. Onions, garlic, and shallots keep best in dark, dry storage outside the refrigerator or in a closed paper bag. The same is true of potatoes, though they should be stored apart from onions. Tomatoes should always be stored on the countertop and never in the refrigerator because cold temperatures ruin both their flavor and texture. I also find that summer's stone fruits taste best when stored on the countertop, so it's ideal if you can buy them in a quantity that will last for a few days and no longer. Of course, the refrigerator keeps fruit going when this isn't possible. Be sure to store it in the low-humidity refrigerator drawer.

In mid-fall, I like to store large quantities of apples, pears, and root vegetables, and I find that, until the temperature drops to well below freezing outside, I can keep them in the garage and they don't freeze. This saves refrigerator space and allows me to stock up on local produce for the winter. I have also kept produce under the bulkhead doors in my basement. You may find secret spaces like these in your own home—nooks and crannies that will keep you eating well right into the cold season.

One note: If your produce is not organic, it is said that you can remove much of the pesticide residue by washing it in one part white vinegar to three parts water. This may be easiest to do if you keep the mixture in a spray bottle next to your kitchen sink.

Sea salt. Nearly all traditional cultures use salt, though not the highly refined and iodized salt many of us grew up on and continue to use. The healthiest and most flavorful salt is unrefined and created by the action of sun on seawater in clay vats, and this natural salt is what you want on your pantry shelf. I would not be alone in suggesting that it's the most important seasoning in your kitchen, enhancing the unique flavors of the foods you cook in an almost indescribable way. Sea salt is absent of fillers and anticaking agents and contains important magnesium salts and eighty or so trace minerals. Celtic Sea Salt is my favorite all-purpose brand. I use the less costly coarse variety for making pickles and adding imprecise quantities of salt to beans and grains before cooking. I add it to soups as they begin cooking and to sautéed onions as well. I use the fine variety for all other purposes. I call on less expensive kosher salt for adding to pasta water and for scrubbing my cast iron skillet clean. And I especially like fleur de sel, or "flower of salt," for finishing solid dishes like eggs, fish, and vegetables. When you start experimenting with different salts, you will see how much fun it can be. They will improve the taste of your food in noticeable ways, and I can almost guarantee that you will never turn back to manufactured iodized salt.

Sea vegetables. Seaweeds are used by many traditional cultures. Kombu, agar, nori, arame, and other sea vegetables are packed with minerals—including calcium, iron, and iodine—that are difficult to find in our modern diet. This is partly because so much of our topsoil, which was once mineral-rich, has washed into the sea, making sea life rich with concentrations of minerals we need for good health. Sea vegetables are said to bind with heavy metals and carry them out of our bodies, and their antioxidants are thought to strengthen the immune system. The four I listed above are mild and versatile and provide a good introduction to sea vegetables. As you gain experience, there are others you might want to try. Some people like to wash the faint white powder off of sea vegetables like kombu; I'm a fervent nonwasher because the white powder is a source of umami, or "fifth taste." It occurs naturally in certain savory foods, rounding out their flavors and helping to make them delicious. Sea vegetables are readily available at most health-food stores and keep indefinitely on the pantry shelf.

Seeds and nuts. Seeds and shelled nuts are indispensable in the kitchen. They are both highly perishable and can become rancid, so I store them in the refrigerator. To ensure their freshness, it's best to buy seeds and nuts raw and then toast them in the oven or on top of the stove as you need them. It also helps you avoid store-bought nuts that are roasted in vegetable oil, an inflammatory fat that, for reasons of good health, is best to minimize. You can roast seeds and nuts dry, in a skillet or a 325-degree oven, or coat them lightly in olive oil for added richness.

> Rest secure in the knowledge that, in the kitchen, we get back in exact proportion to what we give. If we spend time gathering ingredients for cooking, we'll benefit from having them on hand when we need them. If we make an effort to be inventive when we shop, seeking out seasonal farmers' markets, for example, we'll have inspiration when it's time to cook because the ingredients will excite us. If we commit to using fresh foods whenever possible, the more nutritious, delicious, and beautiful our meals will be, and the less we'll wonder what to make for dinner because fresh foods simply beg to be used. The more we smile and pour love into the gathering and cooking of food, the better it will taste, really!

Soy. Soy products can be confusing. They're promoted as being health-supportive by the food industry, while being considered unhealthful by food traditionalists. My own decision, in cooking artfully and for optimum health, has been to avoid refined products like soy milk, soy yogurt, soy cheese, soy crisps, and soy imitation meats. On occasion, I consume tofu as a condiment, although it is unfermented and so not a mainstay in my diet. I do use fermented soy products, which have a long tradition of use in Asian countries. Fermented soy is thought to be superior to unfermented because it is more digestible, has less phytic acid (which means it does not get in the way of mineral absorption), and has more available protein. The fermented soy products I consume include tamari, shoyu, miso, and, now and then, tempeh. If you purchase tempeh, you should refrigerate it until you use it. You may notice black mold on its exterior, which is said to be harmless, and I have found this to be true in the packaged tempeh sold in stores.

Spices. We're all familiar with using store-bought spices in cooking. Where it makes sense, you can improve the flavor of your foods by purchasing spices whole and grinding them with a mortar and pestle, or in a small spice grinder or coffee mill that you keep for this purpose. To maximize their flavor, you can toast whole spices in a skillet on the stove top before grinding; this releases their delicate oils and makes them easier to grind. It's best if the spices in your cupboard are labeled "nonirradiated." As for pepper, it should ideally be freshly ground, which is easy to manage with a small pepper mill.

Storage containers. In my kitchen, I have shelves filled with different sized wide-mouth glass canning jars, especially the quart and half-gallon sizes. I also have a wide-mouth funnel, which makes filling them easy. Canning jars are wonderful storage and freezer containers and have helped me do away with plastic. This is important because certain kinds of plastic leach an estrogen-like chemical, bisphenol A (BPA), into food. These environmental estrogens are thought to work with the body's own estrogen to increase the risk of certain cancers.

I also have an assortment of smaller glass containers with reusable lids, which means I almost never use plastic wrap in my kitchen—better for the planet and for me. When I have a bowl to cover that will sit on the counter, I top it with a plate. This works well and does away with the plastic wrap.

Sweeteners. Of all the industrial foods we've welcomed into our homes, refined white sugar has likely been the most calamitous. It can cause vitamin loss, bone loss, blood sugar spikes, and inflammation, and this is the short list. While all sweeteners should be used in moderation, when you find the need, you might want to rely on honey, maple syrup, and brown rice syrup, which handle many jobs respectably. Honey and maple syrup are relatively local for some of us. They are practically unrefined and, when used with a light touch, provide a gentle sweetness. While honey and maple syrup do raise blood sugar levels, they pair well with brown rice syrup, which is metabolized more slowly. Barley malt, a mild sweetener that steps in when I bake bread, is absorbed slowly and thus without blood sugar spikes. Maple crystals also work as a substitute for white and brown sugar in baking. These are more costly, but less refined, than white or brown sugar.

You may wonder about sweeteners with a low glycemic index. These are touted to be better for us and include agave nectar, coconut sugar, and stevia, all of which happen to be highly refined. Further, their low glycemic index tips us off to a hidden truth: These sweeteners contain high levels of fructose, often even more than is contained in high-fructose corn syrup. Why does this matter? Because when we eat, our bodies release hormones to signal that we have had enough food, but fructose fails to stimulate the release of these hormones, and this may lead to overeating. Too much fructose also triggers fat storage and increases the levels of circulating triglycerides.

In spite of these considerations, I wonder if the occasional use of low-glycemic sweeteners by people with blood sugar issues might be all right. More specifically, I wonder if these health issues have less to do with fructose itself and more to do with the amount consumed. After all, every concentrated sweetener should be used in moderation, even those that are less refined and natural to our region.

Vanilla. You will want to keep vanilla on hand, both as a pure extract and a whole bean. Madagascar (or Bourbon) vanilla is the most common variety on our store shelves, but you may want to experiment with the more floral Tahitian extract, which lends a clear vanilla note to baked goods, or with the fruity Mexican extract that rests subtly in the background. These extracts will last for months, or even years, on your pantry shelf.

Whole vanilla beans are worth splurging on when making yogurt or ice cream, or any time you want to infuse a liquid with the flavor of vanilla. Store whole beans in a tightly sealed container, and they'll last for months.

Vinegars. Although you may want to try making vinegars of your own, it's also useful to have store-bought versions in your pantry to brighten flavors in cooking and give foods an acidic boost. Sherry, red and white wine, apple cider, brown rice, and balsamic are some of the vinegars you might want to consider. All can be kept safely unrefrigerated.

Whole grains. In my mind, you cannot have too great a variety of whole grains in your kitchen, though it's best if you can store them in a cool, dry place because the oils in whole grains are perishable. In my own kitchen, I store whole grains in glass jars (which also prevent grain moths) on the countertop during the winter. In the spring and summer, I move as many jars to the refrigerator as will fit. For the rest, I throw caution to the wind and try to use them up quickly. I've never had them go rancid.

DOES ORGANIC MATTER?

"I arise in the morning torn between a desire to save the world and a desire to savor the world. This makes it hard to plan the day." —E. B. White

In our wide realm of experience, we apply labels—to ourselves, others, and the things around us—as a shortcut to help us make sense of our world. But labels can change in meaning over time and often become more or less important.

Consider this short history of the "organic" label. When our grandparents were young, food was grown on traditional family farms. No chemicals were used and so food was inherently organic, but without the label. In the middle of the last century, with young people moving away from family farms and with the introduction of pesticides, antibiotics, and hormones, farming became more industrialized. As a response, in the 1960s and 1970s, an "old-fashioned" organic movement took root. Its focus was practical—growing food without chemicals—but it was also philosophical; farmers were committed, above all, to permanence and sustainability. This was farming with integrity, a way of meeting current needs without compromising the ability of future generations to meet their own needs. Thus, the first "organic" label was created.

In the last decade, this label has grown in breadth and popularity as it has been shaped, in part, by large corporations that value profits over sustainability. "Organic" has developed a magical connotation and has been used to bestow a halo of good health, for us and the planet, which may not always be deserved. "Organic" has also been reduced to a marketing gimmick, a name to attract us that often offers no guarantee of goodness. There is nothing healthful about organic pop tarts, organic soda, or organic evaporated cane juice; this is simply organic junk food.

Sometimes labels can make it easier to understand our options, but I wonder about the value of an organic label that can increase our food costs without adding the meaning it once did, or the meaning we imagine it does. Under the law, "organic" currently refers to any food that is mostly free of synthetic substances, has no antibiotics or hormones, has not been radiated or fertilized with sewage sludge, was raised without pesticides, and contains no genetically modified ingredients. There is no question that this is all good. But is it enough? Does it tell us everything we need to know?

It can be hard for any of us to figure out the best choices to make, and difficult to measure the lengths to which we should go to acquire high-quality food. The answer, I think, is to care less about a "certified organic" label, which costs farmers both money and time, and more about a deeper set of ideals. Put another way, an organic attitude may matter more than an organic label.

So, where do we begin? First, we can use our food choices to invest in a way of life rather than a label, and we can think small instead of big, developing a more direct connection to the land where our food is grown and to local farmers who use sustainable growing practices. These are farmers who treat their animals as if they matter, and who care for their land as if they are stewards for future generations: working on a small scale, feeding animals grass instead of grain, distributing food nearby, and using no pesticides, antibiotics, or hormones. Their foods often cost less than those with a "certified organic" label, and you will know their quality because you will know the farmer. Second, regarding packaged organic food, we can look at ingredients lists and make every effort to avoid white flour, sugar—including evaporated cane juice and corn syrup—vegetable oil, and additives, even if they are labeled organic.

The bottom line is this: Regardless of the label, foods that are good for the planet and good for us come from farmers who pay attention to detail and define their work in the positive. These farmers not only care about producing food with an absence of chemicals, they also care about upholding old-fashioned organic goals and they maintain a genuine, forward-looking, and active approach to growing food in the same way that it has been farmed throughout time. To these farmers, "organic" is not a production method; it is a connected and protective attitude toward both the wider world and all of us who eat.

NOTES ON INGREDIENTS

- Salt, unless otherwise noted, is Celtic Sea Salt, fine or coarse (but always use finely ground for baking). If you rely on a different sea salt, you may need less than the amounts listed in these recipes because the Celtic brand is denser than many other varieties.
- Water is filtered and, for reasons of healthfulness, chlorine- and fluoride-free.
- Maple syrup is Grade B.
- Maple crystals are finely ground.
- Eggs are large.
- Butter is unsalted.
- Milk and yogurt are whole (full-fat).
- For baking, ingredients are at room temperature unless otherwise noted.
- Baking powder is double-acting and aluminum-free.
- Dry ingredients are measured with a kitchen scale or with dry measuring cups; these are cups that are meant to be filled to the top and leveled with a straight edge. Liquid ingredients are measured with a liquid measuring cup that has a pouring spout and is meant to be filled to the lines on its side.
- Where it matters—that is, where it serves the end result or makes preparing a recipe easier—I have listed ingredients in ounces as well as cups. Either way of measuring will work.

• •

The recipes that follow are full of ordinary goodness and comprised of ingredients that will nourish you well. They were inspired by generations of cooks and transformed by me, and I offer them to you for rediscovery. Your willingness to apply your hands and heart, and to experiment with your own ideas, will make these recipes your own. You will give them new life and they, in turn, will feed your imagination and satisfy your hunger.

• •

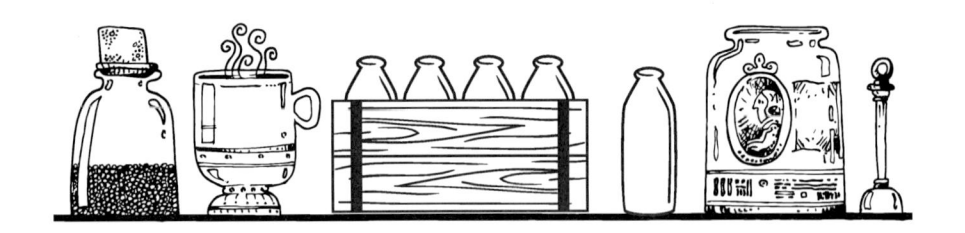

MILK AND CREAM

"What does unpasteurized milk taste like? Well, like pasteurized milk, only more so. There is no question that it has more flavor, just as fresh tomatoes have more flavor than stewed ones. Or fresh lettuce than boiled lettuce. These are fair comparisons, which is why I don't think 'raw' milk is the right name. Raw is what uncooked meat is—with the strong implication that it ought to be cooked. And so it should. But milk is a finished product as it comes from the cow. One might as well speak of raw orange juice, or a breast-fed baby guzzling raw mother's milk." —Noel Perrin

....

In a book devoted to handcrafting food, I begin with milk, as it forms the basis of our own human beginning. Milk itself is a wonder, and I feel this way as well about the dairy animals from which it comes: cows, sheep, and goats. These animals eat grass and hay, which are plentiful though inedible to us, and generously and efficiently turn it into gallons of nutritious milk and cream. In your own kitchen, you can use milk and cream to craft butter, buttermilk, cheese, and ice cream, in addition to an array of other dishes that contain these as ingredients. The textures and flavors, not to mention the healthfulness, of these foods will be far superior to those you can buy in any store.

The recipes that begin this section are relatively simple and meant to help you handcraft dairy staples that take basics you have always known, like butter and yogurt, and bring them to a higher level of goodness. You can use these staples as food on the table. Or you can rely on them as ingredients in cooking—rich yogurt, homemade butter, and pure fresh cheese are complex and delicious and will lift even old favorite recipes to new heights. The recipes in the second part of this section will give you a way to experiment with using these basics in cooking.

As you will see, the basis for all of these recipes is milk, and almost any variety will do, whether from cows, goats, or sheep. But because modern farming and processing methods have left us with adulterated dairy products, we need to pay close attention to quality; this, perhaps even more than technique, will impact the flavor and texture of your end result. Quality will also help determine whether the foods you create support your health or interfere with it in ways that matter.

MILK QUALITY

When it comes to milk quality, there are several aspects to consider: what dairy animals eat, whether the animals are given antibiotics or hormones, and how the milk is processed as it's turned into food.

WHAT THE ANIMALS EAT

Dairy animals, no matter what kind, should eat grass, hay, and little else. They can manage with small quantities of grain, but they need to get the bulk of their nutrients from pasture. A diet of grass during the spring, summer, and fall, and hay in the winter, ensures that the milk the animals provide is optimally nutritious. It also keeps the animals well, which is good for us since those animals are our food source. Any label should say "grass-fed."

WHETHER THE ANIMALS ARE GIVEN ANTIBIOTICS OR HORMONES
This issue is a simple one: No dairy product that comes from an animal that receives antibiotics and hormones can be good for us. Dairy products need not be certified organic; they should simply say "antibiotic and hormone free" on the label. The hormones that are given to animals are growth hormones, and their purpose is to stimulate animals to produce far more milk than they would naturally. These hormones make animals sick and they're no better for us. Since, as adults, we have completed our physical development, if we ingest growth hormones, the only two things we can continue to grow are fat and tumors.

HOW THE MILK IS PROCESSED
Most of the dairy products that we find on grocery-store shelves come from milk that is pasteurized and homogenized. Pasteurization is a form of processing that heats milk to kill bacteria, both good and bad, and also extends its shelf life. Farm-fresh raw milk, which is unpasteurized, lasts about one week. Standard pasteurized milk lasts two or three weeks. Ultra-pasteurized milk, which is processed at even higher temperatures that kill more bacteria, lasts eight weeks, and milk packed in aseptic packages lasts for ten months on a shelf. The more milk is processed, the less alive it becomes and so the longer it keeps, even without refrigeration. This means it has less flavor and is less able to nourish us in any meaningful way. To be clear, foods that sustain us on a deep level and that perform well in the kitchen are as unprocessed as they can be; these are the foods we want to rely on and consume.

Beyond pasteurization, we've grown used to seeing homogenized milk on our store shelves. Homogenization uses extreme pressure to super-mix milk, doing serious damage to its structure. It breaks up large fat molecules into smaller ones that blend with the milk and stay suspended, which prevents cream from rising. Instead of fats being digested slowly as they pass through the digestive system, they can be absorbed directly into the blood stream, which is why homogenized milk may not be good for us. It is also why homogenization affects both the flavor and texture of milk in a negative way. Fortunately, unhomogenized milk is perfectly legal and readily available. You'll find it labeled "creamline" or "cream on top."

There is another aspect to processing that we should consider: removing fat to create low-fat and fat-free milk. Reduced-fat milk lacks flavor, which impacts what it can do for us in the realm of handcrafting foods. Removing fat also diminishes milk's healthfulness. The butterfat that is removed is what helps us digest the protein in milk and absorb calcium to develop and strengthen our bones. It is also the source of fat-soluble vitamins B and D, and without vitamin D, most of the calcium in milk is unavailable to us. It's true that some milk is enriched with synthetic vitamins, but there are questions about whether these matter to us in any meaningful way. Finally, because reduced-fat milk lacks body and texture, processors add dry milk powder to it, though they don't list it as an ingredient. This powder is produced under high pressure and at high temperatures and contains oxidized cholesterol, which is thought to be a carcinogen. This is another good reason to stick with whole milk. If you're worried about weight, keep in mind that whole milk generally won't cause weight gain because we naturally consume smaller quantities; due to its fat content, we are satisfied with less. Like real butter, we are surely capable of consuming whole milk wisely, and in handcrafting food it lends itself to far superior results.

MILK FRESH FROM THE COW

It's worth taking a moment to consider milk in its purest form: fresh, raw, and whole. For most of time and all around the world, this is the milk people have sworn by for sustaining good health and crafting delicious foods. It is milk from healthy cows, goats, or sheep that eat grass. So why, in some states, is it illegal today?

As I understand it, the raw milk story began in the middle of the 1800s when Americans had their way with a time-honored process and decided to feed dairy cows leftover waste grains and mash from beer and whisky making, housing cows in cellars and feeding them "swill." These were the industrial confinement farms of an earlier century.

Naturally, these new methods didn't work out well for cows, and the "slop milk" that resulted was deadly and passed off to the poor for pennies. The advent of transportation made a bad situation worse because those drinking milk generally lived far from its source without a way to verify its cleanliness. By the early 1890s, tainted milk caused diphtheria, typhoid fever, scarlet fever, tuberculosis, and cholera. Infants were dying; so were cows. And by the turn of the century, the demand for clean milk became a national cause.

Some argued for a return to "country milk," believing that its healthful properties were deserving of special protection. But others worried that it could be contaminated during transport. One group suggested imposing strict rules to ensure careful handling as a remedy. But an opposing group argued for dairy inspections, as well as for pasteurization to kill dangerous microbes. Pasteurized milk was given away free and people stopped dying, and so for nearly a century, raw and pasteurized milk existed side by side. But certified raw milk was more costly, and in the end, pasteurized milk dominated the marketplace.

In the U.S. today, most cows, organically fed or not, live on industrial farms eating corn and soy. They never feel sunshine on their backs and they're pushed to produce gallons more milk than any cow safely can. This leads to disease and, eventually, death, with a life expectancy for industrial cows that's a decade shorter than for cows living on pasture.

In many states raw milk is legal, and the movement to legalize it further is growing in strength. The debate seems almost provincial when all over Europe and in parts of the U.S. raw milk is safely consumed and sold in every corner store, and for good reason: It has countless beneficial microorganisms and superior flavor. If you're going to drink milk or use it as the basis for handcrafting foods, this is the gold standard and so may be worth looking into. Raw milk, like all milk, should come from small, well-managed, grass-based dairies, and the cows that provide it should have sunlight, space, and fresh air.

THE BASICS

YOGURT

Makes 1 quart

Exceptional yogurt should taste of sweet, fresh milk, and it should be rich, with a pleasing tang. It's not hard to achieve this result as long as you begin with the best quality milk and cream available to you.

Making yogurt requires two simple steps. The first is to heat the milk, or a mixture of milk and cream, and then partly cool it. The second is to add a culture and ferment it for a period of hours. All varieties of milk—sheep, cow, and goat—work for making yogurt, with each providing a slightly different result.

Managing Your Time

Making yogurt takes a minimum of 8½ hours from start to finish, although very little of this is active time on your part. Breaking it down, you will need 10 to 15 minutes to measure ingredients and bring the milk mixture up to heat. The mixture will take about 1 hour to cool; you can, however, reduce this to 15 to 20 minutes by cooling the mixture in an ice bath. Fermentation takes at least 7 hours; for a thick, lactose-free yogurt, you may want to ferment it for up to 24 hours (see "Notes").

1 quart whole milk—or, for a richer, creamier yogurt, use up to 1 cup heavy cream and 3 cups whole milk

⅛ teaspoon yogurt culture or 2 tablespoons store-bought plain yogurt with live cultures (see "Gathering Ingredients and Supplies" on page 315)

1. In a heavy saucepan, heat the milk (or milk and cream) to 180 degrees, watching carefully to be sure it doesn't boil. Elevating the temperature in this way thickens the final yogurt by altering the structure of the milk protein (casein).

2. When the milk reaches 180 degrees, remove it from the heat and cover the saucepan to hold the temperature for 30 minutes. Then remove the cover and let the milk cool gradually. Or, to speed the cooling process, immerse the saucepan in a bowl of cold water.

3. Check the temperature of the milk every 5 to 10 minutes (or every 20 minutes if you're cooling it gradually) until it reaches 107 degrees, the optimum fermentation temperature.

4. Add the culture or store-bought yogurt, mixing well. Keep the mixture at 107 degrees for 7 to 24 hours (see "Notes").

5. Refrigerate the finished yogurt and use within a few weeks.

Notes

- I rely on two different approaches for holding the temperature of warm milk. With the first approach, I transfer the heated milk to a glass canning jar and place the jar into a one-quart yogurt maker. (Because of the potential for leaching chemicals, I prefer not to hold warm milk in the plastic container that came with the yogurt maker.) With the second approach, I put the jar into a small, sturdy cooler (not a lunch bag, but a real cooler) and surround it with warm, wet towels. With this second approach, you'll need to rewarm the towels every couple of hours. There are other ways to hold the temperature as yogurt ferments. If your oven has a reliable 107-degree setting, put the jar into a pot of 107-degree water and place the pot into the oven for the desired amount of time. Or you can use a countertop bread proofer or a food dehydrator. Excalibur brand dehydrator, for one, is large enough to hold several glass jars of yogurt and will maintain a steady 107-degree temperature.

- The culture you use to make yogurt will affect both the flavor and texture of the finished product. You might say that, other than the milk you begin with, it is the culture that will give your yogurt its defining characteristics. This makes it especially important to sample several cultures, either by purchasing them from a supplier (see "Gathering Ingredients and Supplies" on page 315) or by trying various varieties of store-bought yogurt as a starting point. Experimentation will lead you to the culture you like best.

- Purchased culture should always be stored in the freezer until the moment you are ready to use it. Shake the jar well, pour the amount of culture needed onto your measuring spoon, and then put the culture back into the freezer immediately, even before you stir the measured portion in. I have learned the hard way not to dip a spoon into the culture or leave the jar of culture sitting at room temperature, as either could contaminate the entire batch.

- To make Greek-style yogurt, place a sieve over a large bowl and line the sieve with butter muslin or cheesecloth. Pour the yogurt into the lined sieve, then gather up the sides of the cloth to make a pouch. Tie the pouch closed and suspend it over the bowl. (Hang it from a hook, a cupboard knob that sits over a counter, or the faucet of the kitchen sink.) Drain for 2 hours or to your liking. Reserve the whey that drains out of the yogurt for another use.

- If you want to scale this recipe up to make more than 1 quart of yogurt, start with this rule of thumb: For more than 1 quart but less than 1 gallon (4 quarts) of milk, use ⅛ to a scant ¼ teaspoon culture. For 1 to 4 gallons of milk (4 to 16 quarts), use ¼ teaspoon culture. Starting with these measures and making yogurt regularly, your own trial and error will help you fine-tune your quantities.

- Finished yogurt will thicken as it cools in the refrigerator, so don't worry if your yogurt is thinner than you would like it to be when it has just finished culturing.

- If you are fortunate enough to have milk from your own cow as a starting point for making yogurt, simply leave it at full-fat (do not remove any of the cream, or remove only a portion), and you will have a rich and delicious end result.

- If you are starting with raw milk, keep in mind that heating the milk to 180 degrees pasteurizes it, though you will still taste a noticeable difference between this and homemade yogurt that uses pasteurized milk as a starting point. To keep it "raw" and preserve both enzymes and nutrients, heat the milk to 107 degrees and then follow this recipe from step 4. The resulting yogurt will be thinner than pasteurized yogurt and pourable, but delicious still.

- There are many ways to adapt plain yogurt to your liking. To make vanilla yogurt, add ½ vanilla bean when you heat the milk mixture: Slice the half-pod lengthwise through the middle, and using the back edge of a small knife, scrape the tiny inner seeds into the milk mixture. Add the half-pod as well, leaving it in the mixture until just before you add the culture. Although you'll remove the pod before fermentation begins, you will probably find small black vanilla seeds in the finished yogurt. To sweeten plain yogurt, use honey or maple syrup to taste, or flavor it the way professionals do: with jam. Start with your favorite artisanal jam or make one of your own, and place a small spoonful of jam on the bottom of a serving bowl. Then pour a quantity of yogurt over it, stir, and serve.

- Yogurt fermented for 24 hours is said to be lactose-free. I have no way to gauge this myself since I am not lactose intolerant, but if you want to use this approach for making yogurt, add the culture of your choice and hold the milk mixture at 107 degrees for a full 24 hours before cooling and refrigerating it. This long fermentation produces an especially thick yogurt, so it's a method you might appreciate whether or not you are lactose-intolerant.

> These recipes are my attempt to pick up the dropped thread of a generational "passing on." Traditional cultures learned through experience and shared their wisdom from grandparent to parent to child. While our own lack of know-how might be attributed to, and is the lifeblood of, our modern food industry, we all have the power to step around it and, in our own homes and without much difficulty, understand and reclaim decades of loss.

CULTURED BUTTER AND TRADITIONAL BUTTERMILK

Makes 1½ to 2 pounds butter and 3 to 5 cups buttermilk

Years ago, when I set out to make whipped cream, I let the process go a little too far. The cream turned into butter, though I didn't realize at the time that butter is what I had, and this "mistake" offered me a new ability and a wonderful gift. You will love making homemade butter and, as a bonus, the traditional thick buttermilk that is its by-product. These are foods you cannot find in any store. Once made, you can either refrigerate the butter or keep it on the countertop where, because it is cultured, it will remain spreadable and keep for several months. Buttermilk, when refrigerated, keeps for about 1½ weeks.

Managing Your Time

The first step to making butter is culturing the cream. You can culture it for as little as 8 hours, but 24 hours will give you a finer end result. So, if you can, start the culturing process at a time when you can predictably be home about 24 hours later to put the cream in the refrigerator, where it will need to stay for at least 3 to 4 hours (though I have successfully pushed this step for up to 1 week).

The second step is making the butter, but before you do, you will need to warm the cream to about 65 degrees by leaving it on the countertop; this will take 1 hour in warm months and 2 to 4 hours in cold months. Butter making itself takes no longer than 30 minutes, including cleanup. I often complete steps 1 and 2 in the morning on day 1, and then finish the butter in the afternoon on day 2.

2 quarts heavy cream

⅛ teaspoon mesophilic culture (see "Gathering Ingredients and Supplies" on page 315)

1½ to 2 teaspoons flaked, non-iodized salt, optional (see "Notes")

1. Pour the cream into a heavy pot—I use enameled cast iron because it's heavy and nonreactive—and gently warm it to 80 degrees. This is the temperature most conducive to encouraging the growth of bacterial cultures that add flavor to butter. Cream heats quickly, so keep a close eye on the thermometer.

2. Remove the pot from the heat, and then remove the culture from the freezer. Pour the quantity of culture needed onto your measuring spoon. (Do not dip the spoon into the culture, as this may contaminate the entire package.) Sprinkle the culture over the cream and immediately return the package of culture to the freezer. Let the culture sit on top of the cream for about 2 minutes, then stir it in until it's well mixed.

3. Cover the cultured cream and let it sit for about 24 hours, ideally at as close to 80 degrees as possible. Then move the cream to the refrigerator and let it cool for several hours.

4. Before making butter, remove the cream from the refrigerator and let it return to 65 degrees. In cool weather, it works to remove the cream in the morning and make butter in the afternoon; in warm months it works better to remove the cream about 1 hour before butter making. Cream that is much colder than 65 degrees will not efficiently turn to butter when you mix it, and cream that is too warm is hard to handle after it turns into butter.

5. Pour the cream into the bowl of a stand mixer and, using a paddle attachment (the whisk beats in too much air), start mixing

the cream on low. If you have a splatter shield, you will be glad for using it. As the cream starts to thicken, continue increasing the speed until you are mixing the cream on high. (Do not walk away during this step; I have spent many hours scraping butter off the ceiling when a batch has turned to butter more quickly than I expected it to.)

6. Within 5 to 10 minutes, the cream will begin its transformation into butter. At this point, gradually lower the speed of the mixer and watch carefully. As soon as you begin to see buttermilk in the bowl, along with newly created butter, turn the mixer as low as it will go to avoid serious splattering. Stop the mixer 2 to 3 times to strain the buttermilk into a jar, and continue this process of mixing and straining until most of the buttermilk is released and your bowl is filled with fresh butter. Refrigerate the buttermilk.

7. Leaving the butter in the bowl, add about 2 cups cold water. In the warm season, you may want to refrigerate or add ice to the water you use for this step. Using your hands or a wooden spoon, press the butter to release any remaining buttermilk into the water. Pour off the water and discard it, repeating this process several times until the water pours off mostly clear.

8. If you want salted butter, this is the time to knead in 1½ to 2 teaspoons of salt, or to taste. If not, simply press the butter into a bowl or molds and store it in or out of the refrigerator. When storing butter outside the refrigerator, protecting it from light preserves its flavor and keeps it fresher longer.

Notes

- It is not necessary to add a culture to cream before turning it into butter, but doing so imparts depth and complexity by adding bacteria that promote thickness as well as acid development; the latter creates a buttery flavor and lowers the pH. This, in turn, thickens and stabilizes the butter and extends its shelf life. Sweet cream, or uncultured butter, has a simpler flavor and lasts only as long as the cream would have before "churning." The sweet buttermilk that is its by-product is nonacidic. So, unlike cultured buttermilk, it cannot be paired with baking soda to leaven baked goods. Like cultured buttermilk, however, it does improve the texture and slow the staling of baked goods. To use sweet cream buttermilk in baking, substitute ¾ to 1 teaspoon baking powder for every ¼ teaspoon of baking soda called for in the recipe.

- As with yogurt, the culture you use to make your butter will affect the flavor and personality of the finished product and, other than the cream you begin with, it is what will give your butter its defining characteristics. This makes it especially important to sample several cultures from a supplier (see "Gathering Ingredients and Supplies" on page 315) before settling on one. Experimentation is how you will impart the qualities you like best.

- Purchased culture should always be stored in the freezer, where it should stay until the moment you are ready to use it. Shake the packet well, pour the amount of culture needed onto your measuring spoon, and then immediately put the culture back into the freezer. I have learned the hard way not to dip the spoon into the culture or leave the packet sitting at room temperature, as either could contaminate it.

- At the end of step 3, what you have is crème fraîche. This is cream that is thickened and given a tart, buttery flavor by the cultures added for butter making. Less sour than sour cream, you can use it as the French do as a substitute. Crème fraîche also works as a base for sauce because it doesn't curdle; or you can serve it over fresh fruit or add it to soup or mashed potatoes.

- If you want to scale this recipe up to make more butter and buttermilk, continue to use ⅛ teaspoon culture for quantities of cream under 2 gallons (8 quarts). For 2 to 5 gallons of cream (8 to 20 quarts), increase the quantity of culture to ¼ teaspoon.

- If you are starting with raw cream (see page 44), the butter-making process will be very quick. Raw cream at 65 degrees will whip into butter in less than 5 minutes. Pasteurized cream takes longer and tends to splatter more because it's thinner than raw cream is.

- It is possible to make butter without a stand mixer, though it will take more time and muscle. Start with a glass jar about one-third filled with cream that is at churning temperature: about 65 degrees. Shake the jar, watching for butter to form and buttermilk to separate. You may need to shake for quite some time before this happens. When you are sure you have butter, stop shaking, drain off the buttermilk, and rinse the butter as in step 7.

- If you begin making butter with more or less cream than is called for in this recipe and you want to make salted butter, use a quantity of salt that equals 1 to 2 percent of the finished butter weight, measured in grams (my own preference is for 1 percent). It's best to use a flaked, non-iodized salt (or cheese salt) since granular salt crystals can get "caught" in the butter and fail to dissolve. Sea salt may work, although organisms in the salt can have a negative impact on flavor. Experimentation will be your best guide.

···· **MAKING BUTTER FROM RAW (UNPASTEURIZED) CREAM** ····

Culturing raw cream for butter making is easy to do, with or without using a commercial culture, because raw cream is active, biologically speaking, and full of beneficial bacteria that ferment and sour cream naturally if you leave it at room temperature.

To culture raw cream without using a commercial culture, remove it from the refrigerator, pour it into a bowl or jar (I use a half-gallon glass canning jar), and cover it with a double layer of cheesecloth. If your kitchen is especially cool, you might want to heat the cream to 80 degrees. If not, you can let it warm naturally.

Allow the cream to rest at room temperature for at least 6 to 8 hours, depending on how ripe you want the cream to be. If your kitchen is very warm, you may want to place the bowl or jar of cream in a container full of cool water to keep it from getting much warmer than 80 degrees.

You can use the cream for butter making at any stage of fermentation. When you are pleased with its flavor, cover the cream with an airtight lid and move it to the refrigerator, where you can let it ferment longer, for days or up to a week. As it ripens, the smell and taste should continue to be pleasing and become more interesting. The longer you ripen the cream before "churning," the more intensely flavored your butter will be. Although I have never had this happen, if your cream curdles or smells or tastes "off," discard it and begin again.

What's nice about relying on the wild cultures in your own environment is that it's easy and economical. The results, however, can be unpredictable. When you use wild cultures, you cannot be sure what qualities your butter will possess because the bacteria within your environment change all the time. So you might like the results one week, and not like them as well the next. I have also found that the buttermilk I get when I rely on wild cultures is thin and watery compared to the thick, rich buttermilk that commercial cultures give me. One is not necessarily better than the other, but my own preference is for a full-bodied buttermilk, and in my kitchen, I have needed commercial cultures to create it.

You may want to think of it this way: Within your home environment, you have everything you need to culture raw cream before churning it into butter, just as people have had for all time. What purchased commercial cultures do for you is help you control the ripening process, allowing you to choose the qualities you want to impart and ensuring which beneficial microorganisms dominate.

Handcrafting any food is art as much as science; there is no precise formula. So the best approach may be to experiment in order to find the method you like best.

······ FOOD THOUGHTS ······

KEEPING A FAMILY COW

"Cows are amongst the gentlest of breathing creatures; none show more passionate tenderness to their young when deprived of them; and, in short, I am not ashamed to profess a deep love for these quiet creatures."

—*Thomas De Quincey*

Not long ago, a family cow could be found on nearly every farm, as well as in the backyards of homes across America. These cows, smaller than the commercial dairy cows of today, were the most useful and generous of farm animals, turning grass into fresh milk and cream for the family, which could then be turned into yogurt, butter, buttermilk, cheese, and ice cream. Cows were so valuable that they were directly linked to the worth of a farm and to the well-being and wealth of the farm's owner.

No one thinks much about cows anymore, and most are kept indoors from birth, which means they enjoy neither grass nor sunshine. Our most reliable source of vitamin D is the sun, and if a cow lives outdoors eating grass, its milk naturally will have vitamin D; if it doesn't, it won't. Cows fed fresh grass also give richer, more flavorful, and far more nutritious milk. This milk is lower in cholesterol and higher in the quality fats that help safeguard the health of those who drink it.

It's hard to imagine that anyone could use as much milk as a typical modern dairy cow gives: from 2 to 8 gallons a day, depending on the size and breed of the cow and on what and how much she is fed. But within a household and for the passionate home cook, it has many uses. There is milk for drinking or using to craft yogurt and cheese; and cream for thickening and enriching soups, whipping, or using to make butter, buttermilk, and ice cream. And for every quart of cream used, the lucky cow owner has skim milk left over to feed any chickens or other animals on the farm (or to feed people who prefer their milk skimmed of cream).

Hobby farms most often rely on the Jersey, which has always been the queen of family cows. Both intelligent and gentle, she grazes efficiently on even less than ideal pasture and produces milk rich in butterfat, with more protein, minerals, and vitamins than milk from any other breed. For the home artisan, more butterfat means more cream for making butter; it also means flavors that are well-balanced, subtly sweet, and beyond compare.

There are those who will tell you that cows must be milked twice a day and at firm times, that they must eat grain, and that you must breed them yearly. There are reasons for these rules on a commercial farm, but not when farming on a home scale. Based on my own experience, I've learned that cows don't need to eat grain, nor do they require twice-a-day milking. You will get a drop in production, but the family cow can exist quite nicely and give a good portion of milk and cream if you milk her once a day, feed her grass and hay with a mineral supplement, and breed her as infrequently as every couple of years.

Your store of equipment can be equally simple. Visits to commercial dairies will lead you to believe you need a small milking machine, a cream separator, and a full-scale barn with a stanchion and milk house. One visit to a family farm, however, will teach you otherwise. Your hands can serve as a most effective milking machine. Your cream separator can be a refrigerator and spoon. Your stanchion can be a thick leash nailed to the wall of a barn, which may be as simple as a three-sided shed opened to the east. Your milk house can be one half of that shed. As for equipment, you can manage nicely with two buckets, a milking stool, a funnel with a strainer insert, and a stack of cloth hand towels for washing the cow's udder and teats.

It is a comfort to be self-sufficient, to know that there will always be milk, cream, butter, yogurt, and cheese on the table, and to be close to the source of your food. These are riches beyond measure, and there is beauty in the chain of caring and giving that a family cow helps to create. You tend your cow lovingly, while growing and improving the pasture from which she eats. She generously offers milk and cream daily, which you use to feed your family and to craft the foods you most enjoy. In all of this, your hands become a cherished tool: From seeding and tending the pasture, to grooming and milking your cow, to making the foods you consume each day, your hands give shape to a circle that begins and ends with love.

QUARK CHEESE

Makes 2½ cups or 1½ pounds of cheese

Quark cheese, which resembles farmer cheese, is a versatile and traditional European soft cheese—the oldest in Europe, in fact—and it's served as often for breakfast as it is for dessert. There are enough interesting ways to use quark as an ingredient in cooking and baking, as you will see in the recipes that follow, that it is worth getting to know. To make quark cheese, you can use a combination of heavy cream and whole milk, or whole milk alone. Either way, you'll enjoy its tangy flavor and, especially, the many ways you can use it to handcraft exceptional baked goods.

Managing Your Time

It works well to begin this recipe with steps 1 and 2 in the evening, which take no more than 15 minutes, and the cheese is then ready 36 hours later, in the morning. Alternatively, you can begin the recipe in the morning, and the cheese will be ready 36 hours later, in the evening. Either way, after 18 to 24 hours for ripening, you will need to spend 20 minutes on step 4 and then drain the curds for about 8 hours.

2 quarts whole milk, or up to 1½ cups heavy cream and 6½ cups whole milk
⅛ teaspoon buttermilk culture (see "Gathering Ingredients and Supplies" on page 315), or 2 tablespoons really fresh buttermilk

Special equipment: **Butter muslin** (see "Gathering Ingredients and Supplies" on page 315)

1. In a heavy pot—I use enameled cast iron because it is both heavy and nonreactive—heat the milk, or milk and cream, to 80 degrees,

MILK AND CREAM • 49

then remove it from the heat. This is the temperature that best encourages the growth of bacterial cultures that add flavor to cheese.

2. If you are using purchased buttermilk culture, remove the culture from the freezer and pour the quantity needed onto your measuring spoon. (Do not dip the spoon into the culture as this may contaminate the entire package.) Sprinkle the culture over the mixture and immediately return the package of culture to the freezer. Stir the mixture well. If you are using fresh buttermilk to culture the cheese, add it to the warmed mixture and stir well.

3. Cover the pot, and let the mixture ripen at room temperature for 18 to 24 hours. When it's finished ripening, the mixture should look like a firm, well-set yogurt.

4. Line a sieve with a single layer of butter muslin and place it over a large, deep bowl. Pour or ladle the mixture into the butter muslin. Then use a piece of cooking twine or other sturdy string to tie the muslin closed. Hang the muslin-wrapped curds from a cupboard knob, allowing the whey to drain into a bowl on the counter below. Or leave the muslin-wrapped curds resting in the sieve and drape any excess muslin over the top of the curds. Place a small plate over the curds. Then put a plastic bag filled with water, or another weight, on top of the plate and drain the whey from the curds like this.

Allow the curds to drain overnight, or for about 8 hours. You can drain the curds at room temperature, but in a hot kitchen it may be best to drain them, covered, in the refrigerator.

5. After draining, remove the curds from the muslin. Don't worry if the curds seem loose and runny; they will thicken as they cool.

6. Store quark cheese in the refrigerator for up to 2 weeks. Set the drained whey aside in a separate container and reserve it for another use (see "Notes").

Notes

- If you use fresh buttermilk to culture the cheese, it's a risky gambit to rely on anything but the freshest. Even with week-old buttermilk, I have found the culture isn't active enough to turn milk and cream into cheese.

- Store purchased culture in the freezer until the moment you are ready to use it. When you are ready, shake the packet well and pour the amount of culture needed onto your measuring spoon; then put the culture back into the freezer right away. Dipping the spoon into the culture or letting the culture sit at room temperature may contaminate it.

- I have found that quark made from a combination of milk and cream is especially rich and good for spreading on toast, but for making baked goods, quark made from milk alone gives a better result.

- Butter muslin has a tighter weave than cheesecloth does, which makes it superior for draining soft cheese. After using it, you can rinse butter muslin by hand in the sink, hang it to dry, and then boil it before reusing. After boiling, pour the piece of muslin, along with the boiling water, over your sieve and both will be sterile and ready for draining cheese.

- At the end of the cheese-making process, you will be left with whey, a milky-yellow liquid that's said to be packed with protein, vitamins, minerals, and enzymes. When you find ways to consume it, you turn cheese into a whole food by taking in all the edible parts—both curds and whey. You can use whey as a substitute for up to one-third of the water in bread baking; it adds sweetness to a loaf and can improve the rise. Likewise, you can add a portion of whey to soaking water for beans or grains before cooking; you can also replace some of their cooking water with whey, though in this case you may need to extend the cooking time. Whey can be used to make delicious fermented vegetables; for recipes and instructions on how to do this, I can refer you to *Nourishing Traditions*, by Sally Fallon. And any animals you have, including many farm critters, will enjoy whey as a special treat. Finally, because quark whey is acidic, you can use it outside the kitchen to water acid-loving plants like blueberries or azaleas.

MAPLE VANILLA ICE CREAM

Makes 1 quart

Making your own ice cream expands the possibilities for what you can craft out of milk, cream, and eggs in a most delicious way. And if ice cream is to be an occasional flourish, rather than an everyday indulgence, this rich, custard-style recipe is one you can enjoy without remorse. What I most appreciate is that, in its simplicity, it lets the essence of really first-rate ingredients shine.

Managing Your Time

Making the milk and cream mixture that will become ice cream, steps 1 through 6, takes no more than 30 minutes. You will then need to refrigerate the mixture for 2 to 24 hours. Plan to spend 30 minutes turning the mixture into ice cream in your ice-cream maker and, unless you want to serve it soft like custard, allow several more hours for it to harden fully in the freezer.

2 cups heavy cream
1 cup milk
½ cup maple crystals
⅛ teaspoon fine sea salt
2 whole vanilla beans

4 egg yolks, whites discarded or reserved for another use

Special equipment: Ice-cream maker

1. Place the heavy cream, milk, maple crystals, and salt into a heavy saucepan.

2. With the tip of a knife, slice each vanilla bean in half lengthwise. Use the back edge of the knife to scrape the tiny vanilla seeds into the cream mixture; then add the pod halves as well. Bring the

mixture just to a boil, turn off the heat, and move the saucepan off the burner.

3. Meanwhile, whisk the egg yolks in a medium-sized bowl.

4. Using a ladle or measuring cup, add the hot cream mixture to the egg yolks in a slow, steady stream, whisking constantly. The idea is to add the hot cream without cooking the eggs, so adding it slowly is essential.

5. When most of the cream mixture is incorporated into the eggs, add the egg mixture to any remaining cream in the pot. Using an instant-read thermometer, measure the temperature of the mixture. If it is less than 170 to 175 degrees, reheat it gently until it reaches this temperature.

6. Strain the mixture back into the bowl you used for the eggs, discarding the pods and any pieces of cooked egg. Then let the mixture cool on the countertop.

7. Once cool, cover the mixture and transfer it to the refrigerator, where it should cool for at least 4 hours, or as long as 24 hours.

8. Follow the instructions on your ice-cream maker for turning the refrigerated mixture into ice cream. Then cover and freeze.

9. Before serving, it's ideal if you can bring the frozen ice cream to 10 to 20 degrees in the refrigerator; refreeze leftovers right away, covering the surface with waxed paper to inhibit the formation of ice crystals.

Notes

- If, when you are adding the cream mixture to the eggs in step 4, a small portion of the eggs scramble, do not toss the mixture. The cooked eggs will come out when you strain the mixture in step 6. To prevent this from happening in the future, add the cream mixture to the eggs very slowly and whisk constantly.

- There are many ways to vary this recipe. If you don't want a maple flavor, for example, substitute refined white sugar for the maple crystals. For reasons of good health, I try to avoid refined white sugar, but the adaptation will work. If you don't want a vanilla flavor, omit the vanilla beans. To infuse the ice cream with herbal flavors, experiment with adding fresh herbs. You might start with ¼ cup loosely packed basil leaves, 1 cup lemon verbena sprigs, or ¾ cup loosely packed mint leaves in step 1—increasing or decreasing the quantity of herbs depending on how intensely flavored you want the ice cream to be. You can discard the leaves when you strain the custard in step 6. If you want to include fudge or nuts, add them in step 8 just before putting the finished ice cream into the freezer. In whatever way you adapt this recipe, take care to flavor the custard with some level of boldness, because assertive seasoning becomes muted once the custard is frozen.

- The berry sauce on page 66 makes a delicious ice cream topping, and that itself can be adapted by substituting other berries.

USING THE BASICS

YOGURT CHEESE

Makes approximately 1½ cups cheese and 2 cups whey

Making yogurt cheese is as easy as separating curds from whey—and if you like making yogurt as much as I do, you will find yourself looking for ways to use it. Consider this as an option. It's good spread on a thick slice of sourdough bread and warmed under the broiler; it works as a tangy dip or vegetable cream cheese; or you can turn it into savory *labneh* (salted yogurt cheese), as is done in the Middle East.

Managing Your Time

Plan to spend 5 to 10 minutes setting the yogurt up to drain. The longer you allow it to drain, the firmer and thicker your cheese will be, but there is no right or wrong: from 4 to 24 hours works. Most often, I set the yogurt up to drain in the evening, and in the morning I consider it ready.

1 quart plain yogurt
Special equipment: **Butter muslin** (see "Gathering Ingredients and Supplies" on page 315)

1. An easy and effective way to strain a quart of yogurt—to separate curds from whey—is to loosely drape a square of butter muslin over the opening of a half-gallon glass canning jar. Then, supporting the muslin, spoon the yogurt into the jar so that the muslin eases gently down inside. Take care to leave plenty of open space at the bottom of the jar for whey to collect.

2. Once a full muslin-wrapped sack of yogurt is hanging into the jar

and the top layer of yogurt is even with the jar's opening, screw on the cap. The yogurt should hang above the whey that has collected in the bottom of the jar for it to adequately drain. Transfer the jar to the refrigerator.

3. From 4 to 24 hours later, depending on how loose or firm you want the yogurt cheese to be, remove the jar from the refrigerator and carefully lift the cheese through the opening. You may have to maneuver to get it out. Spoon the cheese into a bowl and serve it at once, or store it covered in the refrigerator for up to 1 month.

> Living foods are crafted out of the microorganisms—the living forces—within and around your home. So your yogurt, your bread, and your pickles are your own: intrinsically local, intensely personal. This is significant because when you handcraft living foods, you connect with the energy in your own environment, using it for nourishment and to develop your body's inner ecology.

Notes

- Alternative methods for separating curds from whey in step 1 include using twine or string to hang muslin-wrapped yogurt from a cupboard knob, allowing the whey to drain into a bowl below. Or rest muslin-wrapped yogurt in a sieve over a large bowl, draping any excess muslin over the top of the yogurt. Place a small plate over the muslin-wrapped yogurt. Then, if needed, put a weight or a plastic bag filled with water on top of the plate and drain the whey like this.

- There are many ways to embellish yogurt cheese. One favorite is to use it as the base for veggie cream cheese. To 8 ounces of yogurt cheese, add 1 tablespoon each sliced scallions (both white and green parts), finely chopped carrot, and finely chopped celery. Season to taste with sea salt and freshly ground pepper. Another favorite is to turn it into *labneh*. Start by salting the yogurt cheese to taste and mixing well. Then use the cheese to fill a shallow bowl and make a slight depression in the middle of the cheese. Fill the depression with good-quality extra-virgin olive oil. Place whole kalamata olives (or, if you prefer, olives that are halved and pitted) around the edge of the bowl and sprinkle the top with chopped mint leaves. Serve with toasted pita triangles.

COMPOUND BUTTER

MAKES 4 OUNCES FLAVORED BUTTER

Compound butter is butter with flavorings mixed into it, and when you use homemade butter as a starting point, it really shines. Below is the recipe I use most often, and it's probably the most common compound butter: a classic. The ways you can adapt this recipe are almost endless, so improvise and come up with combinations you enjoy. You can improvise on how you use it, too. Add compound butter to mashed potatoes, cooked pasta, or steamed vegetables; melt it over cooked fish; spread it on bread; use it as the base for cooking scrambled eggs; or rub it on corn on the cob.

Managing Your Time

It takes 10 to 15 minutes to make compound butter.

---

1 stick butter, or 4 ounces homemade butter, at room temperature
1 clove garlic, minced
2 to 3 tablespoons fresh herbs, finely chopped—for example, basil, thyme, dill, rosemary, chives
Zest of ½ organic lemon and a squeeze of juice to taste, optional
¼ teaspoon fine sea salt
Freshly ground pepper

---

1. Place the butter into a small bowl.

2. Add garlic, fresh herbs, lemon zest, and juice (if using), salt, and pepper. Mix to combine.

3. Spoon the flavored butter onto a rectangle of waxed paper; roll it into a log, overwrap it in foil, and chill it for several hours before serving. Or, if you want the butter to be spreadable, place it in a pretty bowl and serve it at room temperature. Store compound butter in the refrigerator, covered, for up to 2 days.

HERBED BUTTERMILK SALAD DRESSING

Makes ½ cup

This dressing takes little time to make and tastes fresh and light served over tender salad greens like butterhead or young red leaf lettuce. Using homemade buttermilk as a starting point makes a noticeable difference.

Managing Your Time

Ideally, the ingredients for this dressing should be at room temperature (see "Notes"). Once they are, allow 5 to 10 minutes to make the dressing, which keeps for 2 days in the refrigerator.

Scant ¼ teaspoon Dijon mustard
1 tablespoon fresh lemon juice
¼ cup buttermilk (if homemade, strain out any butter pieces)
¼ teaspoon fine sea salt
1 tablespoon fresh herbs, coarsely chopped—for example, tarragon, chives, parsley, basil
1 egg yolk
¼ cup extra-virgin olive oil

---

1. Into a blender, place the mustard, lemon juice, buttermilk, salt, and herbs. Mix until the herbs are finely chopped and the ingredients are well combined.

2. Add the egg yolk to the blender. With the blender running on low, slowly drizzle the olive oil into the mixture, blending until smooth.

3. Taste and adjust the flavor by adding sea salt or lemon juice as needed. The flavor should be bright and fresh. Use it at once to dress a salad, or refrigerate, covered, for up to 2 days.

Notes

- Egg yolk is an ideal emulsifier for salad dressing because the yolk itself is an emulsion of fat and water. For it to do its job, however, the yolk is best used at room temperature, which means bringing the other ingredients to room temperature as well. (A cold yolk has difficulty coating fat droplets as oil is drizzled into the dressing.)

- Refrigerating the dressing before using it will thicken it and help it better cling to washed lettuce leaves. If your salad greens are very delicate, however, you might prefer a thinner, lighter dressing. In this case, use the dressing at room temperature.

AMARANTH-BUTTERMILK CORN BREAD

Serves 6 to 8

This tender, golden corn bread puts fresh cultured buttermilk to good use. It not only adds a welcome tang to the corn bread, but because it's acidic, it also tenderizes the gluten in the recipe, which, in turn, softens the texture and improves the rise. Stone-ground cornmeal, if you have it, makes a noticeable difference, and amaranth—not technically a grain, but generally referred to as one—distinguishes this bread visually and adds a sort of nuttiness.

Managing Your Time

This recipe is made from first-rate ingredients, yet it comes together easily. You will need 20 minutes to make the batter and 30 minutes more for baking. You can combine the dry and wet ingredients ahead of time (steps 2 and 3) and hold them separately; likewise, you can bake the corn bread early in the day and serve it later on.

1½ cups cornmeal
1 cup whole-wheat pastry flour
½ cup unbleached all-purpose flour
½ teaspoon baking soda
1 teaspoon baking powder
¾ teaspoon fine sea salt
¼ cup amaranth, toasted in a dry skillet over low heat for 4 to 5 minutes

3 large eggs
1⅓ cups fresh buttermilk
¼ cup maple syrup
2 tablespoons butter, melted, plus more for buttering dish

---

1. Preheat the oven to 350 degrees. Butter a 9 x 11-inch baking dish and set it aside.

2. Into a large bowl, sift the cornmeal, flours, baking soda, baking powder, and salt. Return anything left in the sifter back to the ingredients in the bowl. Then add the toasted amaranth and stir to combine.

3. In a small bowl, whisk the eggs, buttermilk, maple syrup, and melted butter.

4. Add the wet ingredients to the dry ingredients and stir just until the lumps are gone.

5. Transfer the batter to the prepared baking dish and bake for 30 minutes, or until the top is golden and the edges are lightly browned. Place the baking dish on a rack and cool somewhat before slicing.

Notes

- If you have a 9- or 10-inch cast-iron skillet, you can use it to bake the corn bread. Butter it as you would a baking dish, add the batter, and put it in the oven. The edges of the corn bread crisp nicely when cooked this way, and you get pretty pie-shaped wedges instead of squares.

- My favorite way to serve corn bread is to cut the wedges or pieces in half through the middle (not top to bottom, but side to side) and then pan-fry the halves in butter until they're golden brown.

DELICATE WHOLE-WHEAT PANCAKES

SERVES 4

This recipe is a good example of the way replacing milk with buttermilk or yogurt makes pancakes delicate, tender, and especially tasty. These pancakes work best when cooked on a griddle and flipped with a metal spatula, but if you're without one or the other, or both, forge ahead anyway. They are worth the bit of special handling they require.

Managing Your Time

You will need 15 to 20 minutes to make the pancake batter. You can cook the pancakes right away or, if you plan ahead, you can make the batter, refrigerate it overnight, and then cook the pancakes in the morning.

---

1 cup whole-wheat pastry flour
2 tablespoons cornmeal
½ teaspoon sea salt
1 teaspoon baking soda
1 cup buttermilk

1 cup whole milk yogurt
1 large egg
2 tablespoons maple syrup
1½ tablespoons unsalted butter, melted, plus extra for griddle

---

1. In a medium bowl, stir together the flour, cornmeal, salt, and baking soda (wait to add the baking soda if you plan to rest the batter overnight).

2. In a small bowl, combine the buttermilk, yogurt, egg, and maple syrup.

3. Add the wet ingredients to the dry ingredients and stir until just combined. (If you plan to rest the batter overnight, you will enjoy

the improvement it gives. In this case, cover and refrigerate the batter. In the morning, add the baking soda and proceed with step 4.)

4. Gently mix the melted butter into the batter. Then let the batter sit on the countertop for at least 15 minutes while you preheat the griddle.

5. Lightly coat the griddle with butter, gently wiping off any excess. Drop the batter by ¼-cupfuls onto the griddle and cook until the pancakes are light brown on their bottoms and the tops are slightly bubbly and set around the edges, 3 to 4 minutes. Carefully flip the pancakes. Cook the other side for about 2 minutes, and serve at once with maple syrup or your favorite toppings. Alternatively, hold the pancakes in a 200-degree oven until all are made and ready to serve.

Notes

- One of life's small but enduring mysteries is why the first batch of pancakes never cooks up quite as well—as brown and crisp and just so—as later batches do. One remedy I rely on is to preheat the griddle or skillet without any fat added for at least 30 minutes before cooking. Another remedy is to wipe any excess butter off the griddle or skillet before cooking the first batch. There should be no visible layer of fat between the pancakes and the cooking surface—just a slight sheen.

- If you like, try substituting an equal quantity of quark cheese (see page 49) for the yogurt, which makes these pancakes more substantial than they would otherwise be.

> Remember this: Food is fun; it's delicious; it nourishes and satisfies and brings people together. It's a pleasure we can afford. Strive to fill your kitchen with wonder. Laugh a lot. Think joyful thoughts. Believe you can create beautiful and nourishing food out of your own imaginings.

MILK AND CREAM • 65

CHEESE SOUFFLÉS WITH MAPLE-SWEETENED BERRIES

Serves 6

These soufflés are based on a recipe by Alice Medrich and offer an impressive close to a summer meal. In the winter, when berries are not in season, you can serve the soufflés plain or use frozen berries to make the fruit sauce and it will still be very good. As with any soufflé, you'll want to serve these immediately, though you can prepare the ramekins a little bit ahead of time and wait to bake the soufflés until just before serving.

Managing Your Time

Start to finish, the soufflés and berries take 20 to 25 minutes to prepare, with another 15 minutes for baking. You do, however, have options for preparing the soufflés and berries in stages throughout the day on which you plan to serve them.

My own preference is to make the cheese mixture in step 2 and the fruit sauce in step 6 early on serving day, refrigerating both and bringing them to room temperature before proceeding. I usually resume with steps 3, 4, and 5 just before sitting down to dinner, which means I can put the soufflés into the oven 15 minutes before I want to serve them.

Another option, if dinner is to be long and you don't mind being away from the table for a short while, is to bring the cheese mixture and fruit sauce to room temperature while dinner is being served, and then proceed with steps 3, 4, and 5 between dinner and dessert.

FOR THE SOUFFLÉ
1 cup quark cheese
3 large eggs, separated
3 tablespoons whole-wheat pastry flour
⅛ teaspoon sea salt
1 teaspoon vanilla
⅛ teaspoon cream of tartar
¼ cup plus 1 tablespoon maple crystals, divided, plus more for sprinkling ramekins

FOR THE MAPLE-SWEETENED BERRIES
1½ cups fresh blackberries, raspberries, or strawberries (halved or quartered)
1 tablespoon maple syrup
1 tablespoon water
Up to 1 tablespoon fresh lemon juice to taste

1. Preheat the oven to 375 degrees, butter 6 ramekins, and sprinkle the bottoms with maple crystals. Place the ramekins on a baking sheet and set aside.

2. In a medium bowl, stir the quark cheese, egg yolks, flour, salt, and vanilla until combined.

3. In the bowl of a stand mixer or in a large mixing bowl, combine the egg whites with cream of tartar and beat until soft peaks form when the beaters are lifted. Slowly add ¼ cup maple crystals and continue beating until the whites are stiff but not dry.

4. Using a rubber spatula, gently fold the egg whites into the cheese mixture.

5. Divide the batter among the ramekins and sprinkle the top of the soufflés with the remaining tablespoon maple crystals. Bake at once, as described in step 7, or let the soufflés sit on the counter in a cool kitchen for up to 1 hour until you are ready to bake.

6. To make the berry sauce, place half the berries into a small saucepan. Add the maple syrup and water and cook, covered, over medium-low heat until the berries release their juices, about 3 minutes. Uncover the saucepan, add extra water if needed, and

cook the mixture until the berries collapse and the juices are rich and syrupy. Fold in the remaining berries and warm until heated through. Taste and adjust the flavor with fresh lemon juice. Serve warm or at room temperature.

7. Bake the soufflés until puffed and slightly browned, about 15 minutes. Top each soufflé with a spoonful of fruit sauce and serve at once.

FOOD THOUGHTS

A PATH TO GRATITUDE

Expressing thanks for our many blessings, chief among them good and ample food, should come naturally. But in our American world of plenty, it can be hard to feel honest-to-goodness gratitude when we sit down to eat. Few of us are wondering *whether* there will be food on our plates tomorrow; the only real issue is *what* we'll choose to eat.

In spite of this, I've observed that when I take personal responsibility for my food—either by growing, raising, or cooking it myself—gratitude comes easily. Watching a sourdough starter bubble and then power the rise in a loaf of bread puts me in touch with a mysterious force, and this, I think, may be a missing link, a necessary starting point for gratitude.

One obstacle to feeling thankful, then, may be the striking disconnect around food within our culture. What we eat appears to many of us to originate at the grocery store, and so what is there to be grateful for? And there is an exchange that may also interfere: I offer money and receive food in return. It's an even exchange. Everyone gets something, and so, again, is there anything more to be grateful for than the dollar that enabled the deal?

In the artisanal home kitchen, there is a different energy exchange, one I can't fully explain. I mix flour and water, and together these turn into bread. I put cucumbers and salt into a crock and get pickles 10 days later. I raise a cow on grass, and that grass becomes milk and cream. I agitate the cream and get butter. These are wonders, all of them, and I am amazed by transformations that I can never fully understand. I'm grateful, too, because they are powered by a force beyond my grasp, one I cannot touch or see but have learned to rely on as I work to put food on my table.

You could say, then, that instead of engaging in commerce, I am working in collaboration with a mysterious force, and it's my connection to this force that stokes the fires of gratitude. Crafting food by hand is, for me, a flame that lights the path to this connection.

QUARK PUFF PASTRY DOUGH

Makes one 24-ounce dough

Here is a recipe for a light puff pastry dough that you can put to imaginative use in baking. The characteristic flakiness of this dough is achieved by folding and refolding layers of fat—in this case, quark cheese and butter—while keeping them as cold as you can. You will be amazed that you can make a dough like this yourself, and without much trouble once you familiarize yourself with the steps involved. It's recipes like this one that remind us why handcrafting food is so liberating and so much fun.

Managing Your Time

Rolled quark dough, which takes under 1 hour spread over a day or two, keeps in the refrigerator for about 10 days, so you can make it ahead of time. With regard to pacing, steps 1 and 2 (making the dough) take 15 minutes. You will need to rest the dough for at least 1 to 2 hours or as long as 24 hours before beginning steps 3 through 6 (rolling the dough). These remaining steps take under 30 minutes.

1½ cups whole-wheat pastry flour
½ cup plus 2 tablespoons all-purpose flour, plus extra for flouring the countertop and dough

2 sticks butter, or 8 ounces homemade butter, at room temperature or slightly chilled
¾ cup (6 ounces) quark cheese
1 teaspoon fine sea salt

---

1. Place all of the ingredients into the bowl of a stand mixer and, using the paddle attachment, mix at the lowest speed until they are well blended and there is no loose flour left on the bottom of the bowl.

2. Using your hands, form the mixture into a disk about 6 inches in diameter and wrap the disk in waxed paper. Overwrap the disk in foil, or place the wrapped disk in a resealable plastic bag and refrigerate until the dough is cold enough to roll, 1 to 2 hours or as long as overnight.

3. Remove the dough from the refrigerator. In a cold kitchen or after a long refrigeration, allow up to 30 minutes for the dough to warm slightly. Then lightly flour the countertop and pound on the dough with the side of a rolling pin to flatten and soften it.

4. Sprinkle the top of the dough with a light coating of flour and roll it into a large rectangle. Continue rolling, flipping the dough once or twice and keeping it lightly floured, until it is about ¼-inch thick. Using the palm of your hand or a dry pastry brush, remove any excess flour. (If, while rolling, the dough sticks to the rolling pin, refrigerate the dough for a few minutes before proceeding.)

5. Take one short end of the rectangle in your hands and fold it in toward the center. Then fold the other short end in toward the center and lay it over the first side. You should have a 3-layered rectangle. It may not look especially neat; don't worry about appearance for now.

6. With the dough rectangle in front of you, once again flour and roll it as you did in step 4 until you have another large rectangle, this time about ⅛-inch thick. (Again, if the dough sticks to the rolling pin, refrigerate it for a few minutes before proceeding.) Brush off any excess flour. Then take one short end of the rectangle in your hands and fold it until its edge meets the center of the rectangle. Fold the other side in until its edge also meets the center. This is slightly different from the way you handled the fold in step 5. This

time, the two short ends will be touching. Then fold the two halves of the dough over each other to form a long, thin rectangle. The finished rectangle should be long and thin, look neat in appearance, and be comprised of 4 layers.

7. Wrap the dough in parchment or waxed paper. Then overwrap it in foil and refrigerate it for at least 1 hour or up to 10 days before using it in a recipe.

Handcrafting foods out of fresh, seasonal ingredients is one of the few opportunities we have left for preserving cultural memory. The traditional kitchen arts that were once our birthright have been nearly lost as our definition of "food" has broadened. While real food can still be found here and there and in the kitchens of committed home cooks, most of what is gathered and consumed on a daily basis is its modern industrial counterpart. This nearly necessitates, then, the classification of handcrafting foods using old-fashioned methods as a food revolution.

QUARK TWISTS

Makes 15 to 16 twists

This special recipe was demonstrated for me by Hermann Spindler, a most generous chef and head of the kitchen at the Lukas Klinik, a cancer hospital in Arlesheim, Switzerland (now part of the Klinik Arlesheim). I returned to the United States and busied myself in the kitchen until I figured out how to make these quark twists myself. Their texture and taste are fleeting, so they must be eaten within about 2 hours, but they are worth the effort for a celebratory meal. All of the work can be done in advance, with baking left until just before serving.

Managing Your Time

This recipe begins with Quark Puff Pastry Dough (see page 71). Once that's made and stored in the refrigerator, you can prepare the twists in under 1 hour. They'll need to rest for at least 30 minutes before going into the oven, and baking takes less than 15 minutes. What I appreciate about this recipe is that, even though the twists are best eaten within 2 hours of baking, you can roll and refrigerate the unbaked twists ahead of time, resting them in the refrigerator for up to 24 hours. Then you can bake them just before serving.

2 tablespoons butter
1 recipe (24 ounces) Quark Puff Pastry Dough (see page 71)

2 teaspoons fleur de sel for sprinkling

1. In a small saucepan, melt the butter and set it aside to cool slightly. Line a baking sheet with parchment paper.

2. Remove the Quark Puff Pastry Dough from the refrigerator and cut it in half widthwise (through the long sides of the rectangle), handling it as little as possible to keep it cold. Lightly flour the countertop and roll half the dough into a ⅓-inch thick rectangle, about 8 x 10 inches. Brush the rectangle with a thin layer of melted butter and, over that, sprinkle ½ teaspoon of fleur de sel. Lightly roll over the salt to keep it in place.

3. Flip the dough over, brush the second side with a thin layer of melted butter, and gently roll it to ¼-inch thick. Sprinkle with ½ teaspoon of fleur de sel, and roll it lightly to keep the salt in place.

4. Using a pizza or pastry cutter, slice the dough into strips about 4 inches long and 1 inch wide. Twist each strip into a corkscrew, using 2 to 3 twists. Then place the strips onto the baking sheet, about 1 inch apart.

5. Repeat the process with the second half of dough. When all of the twists are transferred to the baking sheet, cover and refrigerate for at least 30 minutes or up to 24 hours. Chilling the dough helps it relax and prevents the twists from shrinking in the oven. It also keeps the layers of butter from melting prematurely.

6. About ½ hour before you are ready to bake, preheat the oven to 425 degrees. Bake the twists for 12 to 14 minutes or until lightly browned. Cool on a rack and enjoy within 2 hours.

QUARK RUGELACH

Makes 32 cookies

My heritage gave me, among other gifts, a childhood filled with Eastern European Jewish cuisine. So whether I should attribute it to genes or experience I cannot say, but I have a particular fondness for rugelach—rich rolled cookies filled with fruits and nuts. Here's my own take on rugelach, with quark filling in for cream cheese and providing a good, rich result.

These cookies typify what often happens in artisanal home cooking: loving making something and then needing to find ways to use it so you can make it again. Look at these as one example, then, of how you can have fun with quark, using it in place of cream cheese, ricotta cheese, sour cream, or yogurt in a substitution that often works well.

Managing Your Time

You can organize the making of these cookies into separate steps. Preparing the cookie dough takes 15 minutes; the dough then needs to rest for 2 to 12 hours. Combining ingredients for the filling takes another 15 minutes. And rolling the dough, filling the cookies, and baking takes 1 hour, with only about half of that as active time. This recipe is especially fun to make with children, as there are many kid-friendly jobs like rolling dough and using a pastry brush.

FOR THE DOUGH:
2 sticks cold butter, or 8 ounces cold homemade butter, cut into chunks
1 cup cold quark cheese
2 tablespoons maple crystals
½ teaspoon fine sea salt
1 cup all-purpose flour, plus extra for flouring countertop and dough
1 cup whole-wheat pastry flour

FOR THE FILLING:
½ cup walnuts
½ cup pitted dates, thinly sliced
⅓ cup maple crystals
½ teaspoon cocoa powder
½ teaspoon cinnamon
¼ teaspoon vanilla extract
¼ cup apricot jam, gently warmed

1. Make the dough. In the bowl of a food processor, combine all of the dough ingredients and pulse just until they come together and form small pieces.

2. Transfer the loose dough pieces to the countertop and pat them into a large ball. Then divide the ball into 4 relatively even sections. Taking one section at a time, use the heel of your hand to push and smear the dough across the countertop, spreading and evenly distributing the fat. Then form each section into a round, and flatten it into a small disk, about 1 inch high. Wrap each of the 4 sections in waxed paper, overwrap in foil, and refrigerate for at least 2 hours or as long as 12 hours.

3. Make the filling. Coarsely chop the nuts on a cutting board and arrange them in a rough circle. Slice the dates, discarding any pit pieces, and place the date slices on top of the circle of nuts. Then chop the two together; the walnuts will keep the dates from sticking to the cutting board and facilitate chopping them finely. Transfer the mixture to a medium bowl. Add the maple crystals, cocoa powder, cinnamon, and vanilla and stir to combine.

4. Line a large cookie sheet with parchment paper and preheat the oven to 350 degrees. Remove the dough disks from the refrigerator. (In hot weather, you may want to remove the disks one at a time.)

5. Unwrap 1 dough disk and place it on a lightly floured countertop. Sprinkle the top of the dough with flour and, using a rolling pin,

> If you have ever, in a discreet or barely conscious way, used artisanal cooking as a way to earn love and approval and to receive the admiration of those around you, you may have felt more disappointed than gratified at the end of many meals. I have found that it helps to turn things around: to handcraft foods as a way of giving love, offering approval, and expressing admiration for those at the table. It takes the jitters out of cooking for company and enlivens the task of preparing everyday meals. And you may find that you no longer feel underappreciated because receiving isn't the point. Using cooking as a means of self-expression, of giving love and showing appreciation, is an approach that can work better and invites thankfulness to the table in tangible ways that you're sure to notice.

roll it into an 8- to 9-inch round. Use a dough scraper or similar tool to cut the dough into 8 equal pie-shaped wedges, but keep the round together instead of pulling the sections apart. Repeat with the remaining rounds or, if the kitchen is warm, complete steps 6 and 7 below for each round before taking another from the refrigerator.

6. Using a pastry brush, spread 1 tablespoon jam in a thin layer over each round (try not to let any jam drip over the sides as it will burn in the oven). Then sprinkle a quarter of the filling over each round, leaving a 2-inch diameter space in the center of the round and a 1-inch border around the edge. Lightly press the filling into the dough.

7. Starting at the wide outer edge of each dough section, fold the corners in a quarter inch and then roll the outer edge inward to form a rolled cookie. Turn the ends of the roll in to form a crescent, and place each cookie, pointed seam down, on the cookie sheet. The cookies should be about 1 inch apart.

8. Bake the cookies for 25 to 30 minutes, or until they are golden brown. Cool on a rack and serve warm or at room temperature. You can store the cookies covered at room temperature for several days or frozen for up to 3 months.

BREAD AND PLENTY

"It seems to me that our three basic needs, for food and security and love, are so mixed and mingled and entwined that we cannot straightly think of one without the others. So it happens that when I write of hunger, I am really writing about love and the hunger for it, and warmth and the love of it and the hunger for it . . . and then the warmth and richness and fine reality of hunger satisfied . . . and it is all one." —M. F. K. Fisher

Bread is love. This is, for me, a truth that has endured since childhood. I attribute my passion for bread to the fact that, for most of my school years, my grandfather brought a fresh loaf of rye bread to our house every afternoon. It was an offering left warm and beckoning on our Formica countertop, steaming in its paper wrapper and welcoming us—my brother, my sister, and me—home from school.

My grandfather was "Poppy Leo" to us kids. He lived about fifteen minutes away by car, but close enough to the bread bakery to walk there each day before driving to our house. We always hoped he would wait for us to return from school, and no matter how often we heard his voice welcome us home, we remained captivated by his thick Eastern European accent and the way he always had a surprise in his pocket. A stick of gum or a dollar; the choice was ours.

Poppy Leo's particular joy was feeding us, but he found more pleasure than most in feeding all living creatures, especially our pet canaries. Once, when we went to Florida and left him in charge, we came home to find two stiff dead birds on the bottom of the cage and more food beside them, especially small pieces of bread, than you can imagine. Poppy took the task of feeding one step further than most people did.

Poppy Leo was born in 1900 and grew up in a small village in the shadow of the Carpathian mountains. His childhood afforded no riches other than the small pleasures that may have filled his days. In winter, Poppy's family got by on little more than potatoes and cabbage, with an occasional chicken on the Sabbath and noodles and cheese the rest of the week. Summer was only a little better. So to Poppy, bread must have represented plenty. When he was ten or eleven, he was sent to learn in a nearby town, where he lived with an aunt who couldn't afford to feed him. He slept on a wooden bench in the kitchen, with only a thin blanket to cover him, and he ate "days." This meant that he was forced to go to various houses in the village and ask permission to eat at each one on a given day of the week. How Poppy hated this ritual. Some of the women were mean, others were bad cooks, and many were stingy with the portions for a growing boy who had an enormous appetite. So to him, a young man with little to hang on to, the vision of a life with fresh bread on the countertop must have been the picture of a life in which everything would be all right.

When Poppy Leo was seventeen, he was drafted into the Hungarian army and was shot in the war; I know this because I saw the scar on his leg. No one ever explained the details, and I couldn't imagine my Poppy as a young man having someone point a gun at him and shoot, but he was at least able to finish out the war as a radio operator in the safety of northern Italy. When the war ended, Poppy Leo went home and found a Communist revolution brewing. Knowing there would be no meaningful future for him, he forged a passport and, without a penny, left all he had known to cross the world. A kind lady gave him an orange, which was all he had with him when he arrived in America.

In the special way that genes and experience weave their magic, I inherited Poppy's pleasure in feeding people and, even more, his passionate appreciation of bread. For years of my adult life, I stockpiled it in the freezer:

bagels, sandwich loaves, rolls. It made no sense, really. But on some deep level, I needed the reassurance that I would always have food on my table. After many years, I learned to bake my own bread, and today I enjoy it fresh and warm whenever I want it, just as Poppy Leo would have wished.

My Grandma Ernie, Poppy's wife, was not to be outdone. She was a wonderful cook and taught me to bake challah when I was in high school. We used her KitchenAid mixer to help with the job, and I was transfixed by the process: the kneading, the braiding, and, finally, the baking. When I got married, I wanted a KitchenAid mixer of my own and asked for it as a wedding gift. A lot of people joked about that. It was so expensive, I was so young, and I knew how to cook next to nothing. But I was sure of where I was going even if they weren't. I was headed toward a world filled with fresh food, and homemade bread would be the centerpiece. It would be a world in which my primary concrete goal after giving birth to each of my children would be to get back to baking bread within weeks. I did, and I haven't stopped since, because bread is love. And I have children to feed. And I want them to receive it fresh and warm, waiting on the countertop when they return home from school.

SOURDOUGH

"Food reveals our connection with the earth. Each bite contains the life of the sun and the earth. The extent to which our food reveals itself depends on us. We can see and taste the whole universe in a piece of bread!"

—Thich Nhat Hanh

In our move-fast, modern world, baking sourdough bread appeals to my own need for that which is intrinsically slow; it may for you as well. Sourdough synchronizes its pace to an ancient rhythm, taking time to develop flavors and textures that are reminiscent of simpler times. While yeasted breads go from mixer to oven in a few hours, sourdough takes a full 24 hours or longer. But what we get for this time is a completely different loaf of bread, because the process changes its nature, making it more digestible and nourishing. It affects the flavor, too, making it complex and delicious and nothing like the flavor of ordinary yeasted bread—even good yeasted bread.

When you're ready for a challenge that may ask more of you in the kitchen than you have given in the past, yet one that will reap huge dividends, baking sourdough bread belongs at the top of your list. Leavening sourdough loaves with the power of wild yeast creates a burnished brown crust; it also imparts complex flavors that can't be achieved in breads made from commercial yeast, which offer in their place the lure of predictability and standard form.

There is also our good health to consider: I don't know of any breads that do a better job of keeping us well than those I describe in this chapter. Using sourdough for leavening, even when white flour is on the ingredients list, lowers bread's glycemic index. Put another way, sourdough limits both how high our blood sugar goes and how quickly it falls. In addition, fermenting flour with an acid and at warm temperatures for even 8 hours (and every recipe in this chapter requires a longer fermentation) virtually eliminates the phytic acid. This means minerals like iron, zinc, and magnesium are not bound up but are instead available for our bodies to absorb. Sourdough also contains lactic acid, which preserves bread and makes it easier to digest.

What's especially nice is that, once you get used to working with sourdough, you can craft baked goods other than bread—muffins, quick breads, and pizza dough, to name just a few—and there are good reasons for doing so. The addition of sourdough to everyday baked goods, when combined with a rest for the batter or dough, confers upon them all the same benefits of healthfulness and flavor that it offers to bread.

If you're wondering how to transition to this way of baking, and if that wondering leaves you feeling confused or overwhelmed, take heart. The real recipe for baking with sourdough is to practice and practice more. It's the doing, the development of a knowing touch and a connection with the dough that matters; it's not merely a precise measure of ingredients that turns a loaf into a loaf.

For those who might argue that using sourdough is too complicated an approach to baking bread, I would counter with this: It becomes easy—much easier than baking with commercial yeast—because the process is flexible and ultimately controlled by you. It also offers the bonus of engaging your intellect because it asks that you learn to understand this bread as you create loaves with a flavor so indescribable that, once you come to expect it, nothing else will do. Baking with sourdough is, without a doubt, the most satisfying and enjoyable time I spend in the kitchen. When the starter bubbles and the bread begins to rise, when the mood is as it should be in my kitchen and those around me are well-fed, I am certain I've spent my time well.

SOURDOUGH STARTER

"It is nearly impossible for a society to acquire a naturally healthy diet without guidance from traditions. We need, therefore, to carefully examine our traditions and keep the best of them in practice." —William Coperthwaite

Sourdough bread begins with sourdough starter, a combination of flour, water, and wild yeast that causes bread to rise. While making your own sourdough starter can be a fascinating way to spend time, it is not a requirement; you can purchase starter from many sources (see "Gathering Ingredients and Supplies" on page 315).

For a decade, I made bread with a starter I received at a class before ever attempting to make it on my own. If you do decide to take the leap, you can make starter with nothing more than flour and water and, a crucial addition, mild outdoor temperatures (see page 91).

I used to make my starter with whole-wheat flour. I had known that whole wheat has the potential to be unstable in starter, but I felt this was "the real thing"—starter in its most traditional form. I found, however, that the frustration of maintaining and reclaiming an unstable starter was not worth the heartache. So I have returned to a white-flour starter, which doesn't elevate blood sugar to the same degree that ordinary white flour does when it's used for baking bread. What's more, I can easily convert it to whole-wheat or rye for the baking of a particular loaf.

Keeping Sourdough Starter Alive and Well
Once you have a vibrant sourdough starter, you will need to keep it well nourished. This is an easy task to work into your weekly routine. It is referred

to as "feeding the starter," and its purpose is to keep your wild yeast alive. You will need to do this before baking or about every 10 days, whichever comes first.

Feeding Before Baking Bread

A day or 2 days before you bake bread, you will need to feed your sourdough starter in order to give it a strong, well-fed population of microorganisms. I find it best to feed and store my starter in a container that I can see through. I use a wide-mouth glass canning jar, which allows me to see the starter and measure its growth, or height, using the lines on the jar. Glass is better than plastic because this will be the jar you use to store your starter over time, and its nonporous surface will prevent the release of toxins into the starter.

As you begin to work with your starter, keep in mind that you will want to cultivate an intimate relationship with it; your starter is, after all, the foundation of the breads you will bake. So, now and then, taste your starter when you feed it. Smell it and touch it, too. Learn how to characterize its good health. This connection, along with astute observation, will help you maintain your starter in vibrant good form.

These feeding instructions will give you enough to bake one loaf of bread, with starter left over for making other sourdough baked goods. *For the surest results, the water you use to feed your starter should be filtered or bottled.*

1. Stir in or pour off any gray liquid floating on top of your stored starter. Then discard all but ¼ cup of starter, which you can leave in your jar.
2. Add ⅛ cup (2 tablespoons) white all-purpose flour and ⅛ cup (2 tablespoons) water to the starter. What you are making is referred

to as a "100% hydration starter," because the quantity of water is 100% the quantity of flour. Mix the starter well and let it sit in a warm spot, covered, for about 4 hours. Your aim is to have the starter resemble a thick milkshake or pancake batter, and to have it approximately double in volume before you feed it again. So 4 hours is a general guide—the process is flexible. A little more time or a little less is not going to hinder the process.

3. Add ¼ cup white all-purpose flour and ¼ cup water to the starter. Again, mix the starter well and let it sit in a warm spot, covered, for 1 to 2 hours more. If you will use the starter for baking Sourdough Wheat and Rye Bread (page 97), this is the last step to feeding your starter. You can return it, covered, to the refrigerator for up to 2 days until you are ready to make your levain.

4. If you are feeding starter to make baked goods other than Sourdough Wheat and Rye Bread, allow the starter to finish rising until it has approximately doubled in height from the last feeding. Then add ½ cup white all-purpose flour and ½ cup water to the starter. Let the starter sit in a warm spot, covered, for 1 to 2 hours before returning it to the refrigerator.

Some bread bakers leave starter on the countertop overnight, but refrigerating it and then bringing it back to room temperature has always worked better for me. In the ideal, you want to bake with starter that is at its maximum height and full of gas. In other words, you don't want it to collapse back onto itself before baking.

Feeding When You Are Not Baking Bread

If you are taking time off from baking bread or other sourdough baked goods, you should ideally still feed your starter every 10 to 14 days. In this case, stir in or pour off any gray liquid floating on top of the starter. Then discard all but ¼ cup of sourdough starter. Add ⅛ cup (2 tablespoons) white all-purpose flour and ⅛ cup (2 tablespoons) water to the starter. Mix it well, let it sit on the countertop for 1 to 2 hours to allow the reactions to develop, and then return it to the refrigerator.

Storing Starter for the Long Term

I have left my starter for two weeks when I have had to be away and have had no problems. Longer storage can also work, but you may need to spend a few days feeding and discarding starter to adequately revive it. There are those who say fresh starter can be successfully frozen, but many strains of wild yeast will not survive the cold.

If you need to store your starter for a longer period of time, it's best to dry it before freezing. You can do this by taking a few ounces of fresh starter and smearing a thin layer across a piece of waxed paper or parchment paper. Let the starter dry where it won't be disturbed; a cupboard, for example, can be a good storage spot. Check the starter after a few days to see if it is fully dry. It may take up to a week, depending on the humidity and on how thick and wet your smear of starter was. When the starter is dry, peel it up and crumble it into a freezer bag or a glass jar. Stored in the freezer, it should remain viable almost indefinitely.

In order to reactivate dried starter, add water and flour in equal amounts to make a small quantity of thin batter. Then feed the starter in gradually increasing amounts of equal parts flour and water every 12 hours. Within a few days, the revived starter should begin to bubble and display signs of life.

Reinvigorating or Reclaiming Sourdough Starter

From time to time, your starter may begin to perform in a less energetic way. I find that this can happen in the spring, after a long, cold winter. Or it may be that you have a ruined starter that needs to be reclaimed.

How do you know when your starter has gone bad? Your bread will not rise well, your crumb will be dense, your bread will taste unpleasantly sour, and your starter will taste and smell "off." These are all clear indications that your starter has been contaminated by organisms that are making it difficult for wild yeast to flourish. This rarely happens to my white-flour starter, but it happened many times when I was maintaining a whole-wheat starter.

If you need to reinvigorate your starter or reclaim it entirely, don't panic. There is a way to do this, and the process is referred to as "washing the curds." It is most effective in temperatures between 70 and 80 degrees, though if you have a ruined starter, you will have to try it no matter the weather.

1. Discard all but 1 cup of starter. Set the reserved cup of starter aside in a small bowl. Clean your jar with soap and water and then rinse it with baking soda and water to remove any residue from the dishwashing liquid. Return the cup of starter to the jar.

2. Wash the curds. Add 1 cup room temperature filtered water to the jar of starter and stir vigorously. Then discard all but 1 cup of this mixture. You may feel nervous doing this, as if you are watering down your starter, making it less potent, and throwing half of it away. But this step is crucial, as it dilutes the organisms that are inhibiting your wild yeast.

3. Feed the starter. Add 1 cup white all-purpose flour and ¾ cup filtered water to the starter. Stir the mixture well and let it sit, loosely covered, on the countertop for 24 hours. Room temperature should ideally be between 70 and 80 degrees.

4. Repeat the process. Each day, you will need to repeat this process until your starter seems vibrant and smells good. It can take 3 or 4 days to fully reclaim the starter. Once it is as it should be, return the starter to the refrigerator and maintain it as you usually do.

The Wisdom of Discarding Starter

It took me many years of baking with sourdough to believe that I really needed to discard starter before feeding it. I couldn't bear to throw any away, and couldn't understand why I needed to. The whole process seemed wasteful, but if you are going to keep extra starter on hand, it really is important to discard a portion before feeding it.

Starter, to be ideally nourished, needs a precise ratio of new flour to existing starter. If you begin the feeding with too much starter, you will waste huge volumes of flour in an effort to preserve this ratio. Or, you will not preserve the ratio, and over time, you will have a weakened starter. So, in an ironic twist, throwing starter away actually saves you flour.

When I discard starter, I like to transfer the portion I'm tossing into another jar, rather than into the sink or compost bucket, for two reasons. First, it eliminates the possibility of mistakenly pouring out all of the starter. Second, it leaves me with a backup jar of starter in case anything happens to the first. (I'm always afraid my jar of starter will drop and break, leaving me with nothing to show for my years of devotion.) I ultimately discard the backup starter when I have more starter to add to the backup jar, but by then it is less vital and easier to part with.

Making Your Own Sourdough Starter

There are many recipes for making sourdough starter, and some work better than others. What follows is a simplified version of a well-considered

> **THE NO-DISCARD METHOD**
> **(IF YOU DO NOT WANT TO KEEP EXTRA SOURDOUGH STARTER ON HAND)**
>
> Like many bakers, I keep extra sourdough starter in the refrigerator for making baked goods other than bread. If you prefer not to maintain extra starter, simply change the quantities you use when feeding your starter for baking bread. Start with whatever quantity of starter you like, and feed it with half as much flour and water. For example, feed 2 tablespoons of starter with 1 tablespoon each of flour and water. Make the second feeding with twice the amount of flour and water you used in the first feeding, and for the final feeding use twice the previous measure of flour and water. In this case, you would make the final feeding with 4 tablespoons, or ¼ cup, flour and water. With this approach, you can get just the quantity of starter you need, with a little left over to save for the next feeding.

method for making starter that Emily Buehler describes in her book *Bread Science*. It begins with rye flour, which starts the process, but ends with white flour. Making starter can take a week or more, so be sure to attempt it when you will be consistently available to nurture new life.

Points to Keep in Mind

• When making starter, your goal is to harness the power of wild yeast in your environment. As there are abundant populations of yeast on the skins of some organic fruits and vegetables—grapes, for example—many recipes for making starter include them in the process. But microbes that come from "outside" sources are less able to thrive in the presence of only flour and water, which are the ingredients we use to bake bread. So we'll rely on the microbes present in the bran of whole-grain flours because they are all we need.

• A warm kitchen is bliss for a developing starter. *The optimal room temperature for cultivating starter is 70 to 75 degrees,* so begin your starter at a time of year when this temperature will be easy and economical for you to maintain, both day and night. Winter is not ideal; neither are the very hot days of summer, those over 85 degrees.

• During the initial creation phase, you will feed your starter once each day, at approximately 24-hour intervals. Be sure to pick a time that will allow you to be relatively consistent in your feedings. For example, feed your starter every day before breakfast.

• Use filtered water at room temperature for making starter. Bottled water also works, but tap water may fail to give consistently good results.

• Use a container that provides room for your starter to double in volume; it should ideally be a container you can see through. I use a half-gallon glass canning jar, which allows me to see the starter and to measure its growth (height) using the lines on the jar.

• Dishwashing soap may leave a residue that can harm your starter's growing microorganisms. You can avoid this by rinsing the jar and utensils with baking soda and water after washing to remove any soapy residue.

• Be sure the lid fits loosely. You will need to cover the developing starter to get good results, but gas will form, and with a tight-fitting lid the container could burst open. Plastic wrap and a rubber band work. I use either a metal or plastic canning lid, which I screw on somewhat loosely to prevent the jar from becoming airtight.

• Every day you will discard half your starter. It feels wasteful, but you must get used to doing this because the health and vitality of your starter will forever depend upon your willingness to take this step.

Steps to Making Starter

Day 1: Add 1 cup rye flour to ½ cup filtered water. Mix it into a thick, sticky paste, taking care to incorporate all the flour. Let it sit, loosely covered, on the countertop.

Day 2: Notice air bubbles within the starter as you look through the side of the jar. Relax and enjoy observing your starter, but do nothing.

Day 3: Your starter should have increased in volume, which you will be able to see by looking through the side of the jar; don't worry if the starter collapses before feeding time. Before feeding, discard approximately half the starter. To the remaining starter, add ¼ cup rye flour, ¼ cup white flour, and ¼ cup filtered water. Mix well to incorporate oxygen and let it sit, loosely covered, on the countertop.

Day 4: Your starter should again have increased in volume, and it might again collapse before feeding time. As you did yesterday, discard half the starter. To the remaining starter, add ⅛ cup rye flour, ⅜ cup white flour, and ¼ cup filtered water. Mix well and let it sit, loosely covered, on the countertop.

Day 5: Repeat yesterday's feeding. Since you added less rye flour, your starter may have trouble rising; look for bubbles to confirm that there is life. Whether or not you see bubbles, mix well and let it sit, loosely covered, on the countertop.

Day 6: Repeat the day 4 feeding. Again, you will want to check your starter to see if it has increased in volume. Check it regularly because it can rise and then collapse back onto itself within several hours. Keep feeding it as you did on day 4 until it increases in volume. This may take several days or longer. Bubbles are a good sign; so is starter that resembles a milkshake. Liquid may separate at the top, and this is all right. Smell the starter—it should smell slightly sweet, as well as sour and a bit fruity. If it smells sharp or putrid, it is not developing as it should and you may need to start again.

After your starter begins rising to almost double in height: Stop using rye flour and feed your starter with only white flour. Discard half the starter. To the remaining starter, add ½ cup white flour and ¼ cup filtered water. Mix it well and let it sit, loosely covered, on the countertop.

Next day: Check to see if your starter has increased in volume. It may be unhappy with its diet of only white flour. Repeat yesterday's feeding recipe. Discard half the starter. To the remaining starter, add ½ cup white flour and ¼ cup filtered water. Mix it well and let it sit, loosely covered, on the countertop. Do this each day until you see bubbles and your starter is rising well.

After your starter is stable: Once your starter reliably increases in volume about 4 to 6 hours after you feed it, you have a viable sourdough starter. If you like, you can keep up your daily feeding schedule to watch the starter and be sure. Or you can move the starter to the refrigerator and then transition to a regular feeding schedule (see page 85).

······················· *FOOD THOUGHTS* ·······················

BROTFORM

A brotform is a willow proofing basket that provides a beautiful and effective way to keep hand-shaped artisan loaves from spreading sideways as they proof. Dusted with rye flour, which best prevents sticking, the brotform keeps loaves rising upward, maintaining their shape and integrity and creating a circular pattern of flour that contrasts nicely with the scoring.

To prepare a brotform for use, pour 2 to 3 tablespoons rye flour into the bottom and, using your hands, dust the inside until it's thoroughly coated. The first few times you do this it may be challenging to coat the brotform well, but over time this gets easier. Some people suggest oiling the brotform before flouring it for the first time, but I have had better results using flour alone.

A brotform requires no regular washing, and in fact, water can work against good results; I suspect it may wash away the microorganisms that help fermentation along. To remove bread dough from a brotform, use your hands to loosen the dough around the edges and gently tip it into the baking pot. Then shake out the brotform, discarding any excess flour. Finally, store the brotform in a drawer or cupboard for the next time you make bread.

Now and then, you may want to use a chopstick or the end of a spoon to gently scrape off any hardened flour. If the brotform develops mold, you can wash it in warm water and air-dry it thoroughly before beginning anew.

For the round loaves in this book, an 8- or 9-inch brotform works best.

SOURDOUGH WHEAT AND RYE BREAD

"Bread makes itself, by your kindness, with your help, with imagination streaming through you, with dough under hand, you are bread making itself, which is why bread making is so fulfilling and rewarding."

—*Edward Espe Brown*

MAKES ONE 2-POUND LOAF

People have been baking sourdough bread for as long as they've been baking bread at all. If it was really that complex and difficult, it would never have found its way into our modern, convenient times. This loaf is the one I bake most often; you might call it my signature loaf. It is beautiful and aromatic, and has a flavor I still crave and enjoy after years of baking and eating it. It's also a perfect loaf to begin with, to make and make again until you have your technique down.

Managing Your Time

Over months and years, as you work the making and baking of this loaf into your routine, you will find that it hardly imposes on your schedule because the timeframe is both flexible and forgiving. In the large scheme, you will feed the starter on day 1 (you can even feed it 1 to 2 days before that if it works better for you). You'll make the levain on day 1 also. Then you'll make the dough on day 2, and bake bread on day 3.

More specifically, you will need to allow 30 to 90 minutes for making the dough (steps 2 through 5); about 20 minutes of that will be active time. The dough will then rise on the countertop, and this can take anywhere from 3 to 7 hours, depending on factors explained in the recipe. During this time, you can be home or not, in the kitchen or not; you will have no active involvement with the dough. Shaping the boule and moving the dough to the refrigerator takes about 30 minutes, and baking the next day takes just under 2 hours—but, again, you will do little other than move the dough from refrigerator to counter, counter to oven, and oven to cooling rack.

The most important piece of information I can give you is this: Sourdough bread will work itself around your life and schedule. Feeding the starter will happen over the course of a day, as you can get to it. Feeding every time the starter doubles in volume is ideal, but even less-than-ideal works. Making the levain takes moments, and the dough will happen over the course of a day, but the process is flexible, and other than in the first hour, you will have little direct involvement with the dough. And baking happens on day 3 during whatever 2-hour block you happen to have available.

FOR THE LEVAIN:
1 tablespoon sourdough starter, fed on baking day or on the day before
1¼ cups (7 ounces) whole-wheat bread flour
Scant 1 cup (7 ounces) room-temperature filtered water

FOR THE DOUGH:
1⅛ cups to 1¼ cups (9.5 to 10 ounces) room-temperature filtered water
1½ tablespoons barley malt
2½ cups (12 ounces) whole-wheat bread flour

½ cup rye flour (2.2 ounces), plus additional for dusting brotform
½ cup (2.2 ounces) white bread flour
4 teaspoons sea salt
Rolled oats or cornmeal for dusting loaf

Special equipment: Heavy lidded pot, ideally cast iron, and at least 4 quarts; single-edged razor blade; spray bottle

---

1. Make the levain. About 12 hours before making bread dough, add the ingredients for the levain to a medium bowl and mix well. Cover and let sit at 65 to 70 degrees for 12 hours (see "Notes").

2. Make the dough. Once the levain is bubbly and well risen, combine it with the water and barley malt in a large bowl or the bowl of a stand mixer. Stir until the ingredients are combined and the levain is dispersed throughout.

3. Add the flours and, with your hands, mix the dough into a ragged mass, rubbing the newly formed dough against the side of the bowl to pick up any stray bits of flour. The dough should be wet enough that you can do this, and the bowl should be fairly clean when you are through. If it is not, add a spoonful of water or two and pick up any remaining flour. Strive for dough that is on the wet side and tacky to the touch, but not soggy.

4. Cover the bowl and let it sit in a warm spot (ideally 80 degrees) for at least 20 minutes or up to 1 hour. For holding the temperature of bread dough in a cool kitchen, I can recommend using a countertop bread proofer. As an alternative, you can use an oven with a "proof" function or one with the interior light left on. With either option, take care the dough doesn't get too warm.

5. Add salt and knead the dough for 10 minutes. If you use your hands to knead the dough, it should be as wet as it can be, yet still dry enough for you to handle. If you use a stand mixer, the dough should be wet enough that it only just clears the bottom and sides of the mixing bowl. Using enough water will ensure a good rise and an open, airy crumb.

6. When you are finished kneading, form the dough into a ball, put it into a lightly oiled bowl, and let the dough rise, covered, for 4 to 4½ hours at about 80 degrees. If your room is warmer, let it rise for less time, about 3 hours. If your room is cooler or your starter less vibrant, compensate by giving the dough

SOURDOUGH • 99

a longer rise; in the winter, this rise might take up to 6 hours.

7. Meanwhile, dust a smooth cotton or linen dish towel—one with no texture or pill that will "catch" the dough—with a generous helping of rye flour. Place the towel inside a medium-sized bowl, floured side up. (For a simpler approach and a beautiful finished look, you can use a floured brotform. See page 95.)

8. Remove the dough from the bowl and gently shape it into a boule (see page 109). Invert it so the seam is faceup, and place the loaf on top of the towel in the bowl or into the brotfrom. Pinch closed any bottom creases that remain opened. Cover the bowl or brotform and transfer the covered dough to the refrigerator. The dough should rise in the refrigerator for 8 to 36 hours.

9. One or two hours before you're ready to bake, remove the dough from the refrigerator and let it come to room temperature on the countertop. One hour before you are ready to bake, place a heavy, lidded pot inside the oven and preheat it to 450 degrees.

10. When the oven is adequately preheated, dust the surface of the dough with rolled oats or cornmeal and gently invert the dough onto a piece of parchment paper. (The side with the oats or cornmeal should rest on the parchment, and the floured side will now be the top.) Using a single-edged razor blade, slash the top in a tic-tac-toe pattern with a wide center square.

11. Remove the pot from the oven and ease the bread, still on the parchment paper, into the pot. Then, using a spray bottle filled with warm water, spritz the inside of the pot lid, cover the pot quickly, and place it into the oven for 5 minutes. It's okay if the top of the loaf gets damp when spritzing.

12. Using thick pot holders, carefully remove and uncover the pot

and spray the inside once more. Cover it again and put the pot and dough back into the oven for 30 to 35 minutes more. When the bread is ready, it will have a deep brown crust and an internal temperature of 207 degrees (checking the temperature with a thermometer will not harm the bread in any way).

13. Remove the bread from the pot and let it cool on a rack for at least 1½ hours before slicing. While it's tempting to slice the bread sooner, the steam contained within the loaf extends the baking. So cutting it before it cools will make the crumb gummy and negatively affect the quality of the loaf.

Notes

- The amount of liquid you need will vary based on the protein content of your flour, the hardness of your water, and the humidity in the air. When you are new to baking sourdough bread, start with 1⅛ cup liquid. After mixing the dough, and again before kneading, add the remaining liquid by the spoonful until you achieve the desired texture. To create bread with an open crumb, light texture, and good flavor, the dough should be tacky when you touch it but not sticky and wet. Over time, the amount of liquid you need to hydrate *your* flour, with *your* water, in *your* home will be relatively predictable.

- You can use whey as a substitute for up to ⅓ of the water in baking this loaf; it adds sweetness and can improve the rise. My own experience using whey to replace more than ⅓ of the water, however, is that it results in bread with a tough crumb and poor keeping quality.

- There is an adaptation to this recipe that you might find useful in warm weather. It works best on hot days when the dough is proofing quickly on the countertop. The purpose of this adaptation is to slow the rise, allowing for a longer fermentation and stronger dough. Here is how you work the adaptation into step 6. After kneading and transferring the dough to an oiled bowl, let the dough proof, covered, for 2 to 3 hours. Then take it out of the bowl and place it on the countertop. Flatten the dough into a disk, and then pat it with your open palms until you have a rectangle about 1 inch thick. Take care to gently press or slap out any large air bubbles or they will appear in your final loaf just under the crust. Now fold the left half of the rectangle into the middle, and fold the right half over the left half. Fold the top down and the bottom up so that you have a ball. Place the ball back into the oiled bowl, seam side down, cover it, and let it rise for 1 to 2 hours more. Again, in a cooler room the bread will need more time to rise and in a warmer room it will need less time. Then proceed with step 7. The purpose of this step is to expel some of the gas in the bread and allow for a longer fermentation by exposing still-active yeast to new nutrients.

- The ratio of flours within a recipe will directly impact the quality of the crumb; it will also determine how high a loaf rises, and as you might expect, it will affect flavor. In this loaf, you might use 1 cup of rye flour with 2½ cups of whole-wheat bread flour. The loaf will be very good, with a somewhat dense crumb and a low, less-rounded appearance. If you modify this slightly, using 1 cup rye flour, ½ cup white bread flour, and 2 cups whole-wheat bread flour (replacing ½ cup of whole-wheat flour from the variation above with the same quantity of white flour), the crumb will be lighter and more open and the loaf will be more rounded, but it will still retain a distinct rye flavor. Finally, if you reduce the rye flour to

½ cup, and use ½ cup white bread flour with 2½ cups whole-wheat bread flour, just as the original recipe is written, the crumb will be more open, the loaf will be lighter, and it will have less rye flavor but still be distinctly whole-grain.

- If you're not used to a primarily whole-grain bread, you may want to start with a version of this recipe that is closer to what you usually enjoy. In this case, try using 1½ cups white bread flour, 1½ cups whole-wheat bread flour, and ½ cup rye flour. You will likely need to decrease the salt to about 3 teaspoons to make the recipe work.

> **Crust and Crumb**
>
> The crust is the hardened exterior portion of a bread loaf, and it is one of the defining characteristics of an artisanal approach. The crumb is a term bakers use to define the fluffy interior. By looking at the way the cells within the crumb are formed—at their shape and size, their color and lack of uniformity—a baker can analyze much about a loaf. With ample water and a long fermentation, artisanal sourdough bread will have a crumb with irregular holes, some larger and some smaller, and a thick brown crust. This crust reveals that there was both steam in the oven and a long, slow rising time. These are visual clues that the bread will be full of complex flavors.

Troubleshooting

I have made this exact loaf more than one thousand times, which is another way of saying that I have probably made every mistake there is to make. Here, then, are answers to questions that may come to mind as you gain experience using sourdough starter and making this bread:

Can I use white bread flour to feed sourdough starter?

Yes, this will work. But keep in mind that bread flour has a higher gluten content than all-purpose flour does, which means a starter fed with bread flour will also have a higher gluten content. This won't matter if you use your starter only for artisanal breads like this one. But if you want to add starter to everyday baked goods like pancakes, quick breads, and cakes, feeding it with bread flour will cause the starter to impart chewiness where you would prefer tenderness. To maintain an all-purpose starter you will need to feed it with all-purpose flour.

My refrigerated starter has a layer of gray liquid on top; did I ruin it?
No, the layer of gray liquid, called "hooch," is perfectly normal. Either stir the liquid in or pour it off before feeding the starter. I do it both ways and have observed no discernible difference in the starter, though stirring it in is said by some to make the starter more acidic.

What happens if I forget to refrigerate my starter and leave it out overnight?
This is one mistake I haven't made because I'm somewhat obsessive about my starter. My hunch, though, is that it depends on the temperature in your kitchen. If it's warm, the starter and, hence, your bread may become overly sour. If it's cool, the starter may be fine, though it will reach its full height and fall and might need to be fed again before baking. Remember, the goal is to work with a starter that is full of gas and at its maximum height. Regardless, your starter will not be ruined. If in doubt about its current liveliness, toss out all but ½ cup and begin the feeding process again. Your starter will be fine.

What happens if I forget to refrigerate rising dough and leave it out overnight?
When I made this mistake, it was the one and only time I completely ruined a loaf. It looked fine, but it was far too sour to eat. It was even too sour to turn into bread crumbs. If your experience is like mine, you may have to toss the loaf or feed it to any critters you may have.

How do I keep a crust from forming while the dough is rising?
Unlike yeasted doughs, which can be covered with a damp towel while

rising, sourdough bread seems to need an airtight cover. A plate works well as a covering, as does plastic wrap. Keep in mind that when a crust forms on the surface of rising dough, it hinders the rise in a noticeable way.

I use two sheets of parchment paper under my loaf for baking and still the bottom gets too dark. Should I shorten the baking time?
It may be that your oven is too hot. I suggest buying an inexpensive oven thermometer and checking to be sure you're not overheating the bread. Similarly, you can use an instant-read digital thermometer to check the temperature of your bread when it comes out of the oven. If it is higher than 207 degrees, shorten the cooking time, lower the oven temperature, or have your oven temperature recalibrated.

What's the most efficient way to feed starter if I want to bake every day?
In this case, my preference—rather than feed the starter daily, which can be time consuming—is to feed the starter 2 to 3 times during the week with enough flour and water that you'll have the starter you need plus ¼ cup or so left over to begin feeding again.

When I get into a rhythm of baking and feeding starter often, I find the glass jar awkward to use. Is there any reason why I can't use a bowl covered in plastic wrap for feeding and storing starter?
No reason at all. Any covered container that works for you is fine.

Does the shape of my loaf matter? Is there any reason not to use a standard loaf pan if I want a more familiar shaped loaf for making sandwiches?
I have not made this bread in a loaf pan for three reasons. First, loaf pans are more typically used for soft batters or for dough that spreads when it bakes. Second, I especially enjoy bread crust, and there would be less of it in

a standard-shaped loaf. Third, without a Dutch oven to contain steam, the crust that would form would not be as memorable. That said, if you want to bake this bread in a loaf pan, grease the sides and bottom of the pan and line the bottom with a layer of parchment paper to prevent sticking. Transfer the dough to the loaf pan before the refrigerated rest—you may need two pans to hold all the dough—and bake the loaf until the internal temperature is 207 degrees.

What is the best way to store sourdough bread?
Conventional wisdom suggests storing this bread in a paper bag, cut side down, on a wooden board, but this is not my preference. Although a paper bag preserves the crust longer than other storage methods do, it causes the cut edge of the crumb to stale. I wrap my bread in waxed paper and over-wrap it in foil, which works well for me. For same-day storage, a smooth dish towel also works.

TOPPINGS FOR A SLICE OF SOURDOUGH BREAD

Here are topping ideas for one slice of sourdough bread, toasted or not, as you prefer:

- A smear of goat cheese and a smear of pesto, with or without thinly sliced ripe tomato.
- A thin layer of butter or Dijon mustard, a sardine or two, and a forkful of traditional sauerkraut.
- A brushing of extra-virgin olive oil, a rub of a halved garlic clove, a layer of mashed avocado, and sea salt.

- A layer of butter or homemade mayonnaise, a sliced hard-boiled egg, and a sprinkling of sea salt.
- Grated and melted raw milk cheese, with or without caramelized red or yellow onions underneath.
- A layer of butter, a fried egg, and a sprinkling of sea salt.
- A layer of butter, thinly sliced radishes, and a sprinkling of sea salt.
- White bean spread and a leaf or two of baby arugula, with or without sundried tomatoes.
- A layer of butter, an anchovy or two, and, if you like, slices of tomato and/or hard-boiled egg.
- A layer of butter or homemade mayonnaise, a sprinkling of celery salt, and a perfectly ripe tomato.
- A layer of herb butter (mash in a couple teaspoons of fresh parsley, basil, thyme, or chives and a sprinkling of sea salt) with smoked salmon layered on top.
- A layer of chopped chicken liver with or without a sliced hard-boiled egg.
- A smear of marrow from roasted marrowbones topped with a salad of chopped parsley dressed in enough olive oil and lemon juice to coat. Finish with a sprinkling of sea salt.

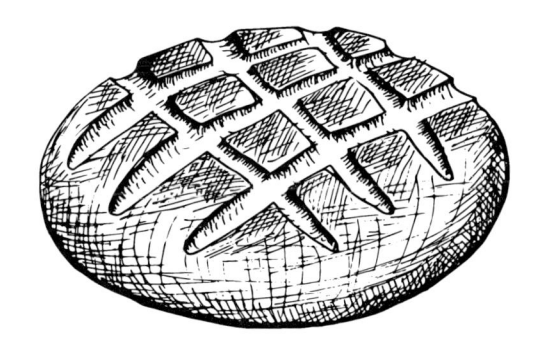

MAKING SOURDOUGH WHEAT AND RYE BREAD: AT A GLANCE

Day 1: Feed Starter and Make Levain

To ¼ cup starter, add ⅛ cup each flour and water; then ¼ cup each flour and water at roughly 4-hour intervals.

Return starter to refrigerator.

When ready to make levain, mix 1 tablespoon starter with 7 ounces each whole wheat flour and water. Stir well, cover, and rest at 65 to 70 degrees for about 12 hours.

Day 2: Make Dough

Combine levain, water, flours, and barley malt. Rest, covered, 20 minutes to 1 hour. Add salt and knead 10 minutes.

Put dough into lightly oiled bowl and rest, covered, 3 to 6 hours (depending on temperature).

Shape boule and transfer dough to refrigerator for 8 to 36 hours.

Day 3: Bake Bread

Remove dough from refrigerator and let it come to room temperature.

Preheat oven and pot to 450 degrees for 1 hour.

Sprinkle oats on bottom of loaf and score top. Spritz inside of pot twice in first 5 minutes of baking. Bake 30 to 35 minutes more. Remove bread from oven and cool before slicing.

.... *FOOD THOUGHTS* ....

BOULE

After a sourdough loaf has risen on the countertop, you'll need to shape the dough and transfer it to a bowl or brotform for longer fermentation in the refrigerator. The shape artisans use for loaves like these is called a *boule* (pronounced "bool"). As you shape your boule, you will gently remove any gas bubbles that have formed on the surface of the dough, creating tension on its outer layer and helping your loaf hold it's round, domed shape as it ferments. This, in fact, is the purpose of the boule: to form tight surface tension that will maintain the integrity of your loaf, enabling it to rise upward rather than just outward.

To form a boule, begin by lifting your ball of dough and holding it in the palms of your cupped hands. Then shape the loaf by applying gentle pressure, from the top of the dough downward, stretching the surface and, in effect, bringing the thin top "layer" of dough to the bottom of the boule and into your hands. Do this gently several times, rotating the dough as you work, until you have a tight, smooth surface to the dough. Your goal is to remove air bubbles from the outer layer, while avoiding overworking the dough and pressing gas out of the interior of the loaf. It took me years of practice to get this right, but rest assured that "good enough" also works.

Gently transfer the boule to the countertop, cover it with an inverted bowl, and let it sit for 20 to 30 minutes until the bottom seams close. Turn the dough over so it is seam side up, pinch together any bottom creases that remain opened, and transfer the boule into a floured brotform or a bowl lined with a smooth, floured cloth.

······················· *FOOD THOUGHTS* ·······················

Crispy Eggs

MAKES 2 EGGS

This is my favorite way to use sourdough bread that has begun to stale. The recipe is especially nice when made with chopped fresh herbs, but using nothing more than eggs and stale bread, it will still be memorable.

1 cup coarsely chopped bread crumbs, from 2 to 3 slices stale Sourdough Wheat and Rye Bread or any country-style loaf
1 tablespoon finely chopped fresh chives, parsley, or thyme, optional
¼ teaspoon fine sea salt
2 tablespoons extra-virgin olive oil
2 eggs
Fleur de sel for finishing

1. In a heavy skillet—a 10-inch cast-iron skillet works well—combine the bread crumbs with fresh herbs (if you're using them), salt, and olive oil. Spread the mixture across the bottom of the skillet so it forms a thin layer, and cook it over a low heat until it begins to sizzle.

2. Crack 2 eggs over the bread crumbs and continue cooking over a low heat. If you like, partly cover the skillet with a lid to finish the tops of the eggs.

3. When the eggs are cooked to your liking, transfer them to a plate and sprinkle any extra toasted bread crumbs over them.

4. Finish with fleur de sel.

SOURDOUGH FRUIT AND NUT BREAD

Makes one 3-pound loaf

This bread is wonderfully aromatic and its flavor is beyond compare. Even better, it keeps on giving for a week as a most magnificent toast. Crucial to your success with this loaf, because it's filled with so many fruits and nuts, is that the dough not be too wet. If it is, the weight of the ingredients will leave you with a dense dough that doesn't fully rise. There are two ways to avoid this. First, mix a slightly drier dough than you would for Sourdough Wheat and Rye Bread to allow for the added water that comes with the soaked fruits in step 6. Second, press the soaked fruits to remove excess water before adding them to the dough.

Managing Your Time

There are similarities and differences between the making of this loaf and Sourdough Wheat and Rye Bread. With this recipe, I feed the starter during the day and make a preferment in the evening, which is something like a levain, though with different ratios of starter, flour, and water. Then I make the dough in the morning and bake the bread in the early afternoon.

When measuring ingredients to bake bread, there are guidelines and starting points worth relying on, but these are not perfect because there are so many variables: flour variety, level of hydration, humidity, and room temperature, to name just a few. The most trustworthy guide will be your hands. Use them to determine if your dough is too sticky and wet, or too dry. Rely on them as you decide whether your dough has proofed long enough or too long. In the beginning, you will have no way to gauge, so the best way is to touch every dough and learn. Then touch and learn some more. Over time, you will be able to draw conclusions, and this is how you will come to bake the bread you most desire. I can promise you this: there are rarely grave mistakes with this bread. Regardless of the result, you will eat and learn, and then use what you learn to bake again.

More specifically, steps 2 and 3, making the dough, take 45 minutes. The dough then sits on the countertop to rise for 2½ hours, with no involvement from you. Steps 4 and 5, soaking the fruits and toasting and chopping the nuts, take 30 minutes. You can complete these steps while you're making the dough or toward the end of the 2½-hour rest. Adding the fruits and nuts to the dough and shaping the boule, steps 6 and 7, take 10 minutes. And you will need 2 hours and 45 minutes more to rest the dough and bake, with little active time on your part.

One other note about timing: If you reach the end of step 7 and your schedule changes—you need to leave the house and bake the bread later in the day—this can work. Cover the dough and put it in the refrigerator. Then remove it later in the day when you preheat the baking pot and proceed with the recipe as written.

FOR THE PRE-FERMENT:
½ cup (4 ounces) sourdough starter
½ cup (4 ounces) room-temperature filtered water
1 cup (5 ounces) whole-wheat bread flour

FOR THE DOUGH:
¾ cup (6 ounces) room-temperature filtered water
¼ cup (2 ounces) sourdough starter
¼ cup (2 ounces) maple syrup
2 tablespoons unsalted butter, melted
1 teaspoon vanilla extract
1½ cups (9 ounces) unbleached bread flour
1 cup (5 ounces) whole-wheat bread flour

1 teaspoon ground cinnamon
3½ teaspoons fine sea salt
⅓ cup (1.4 ounces) raisins
½ cup (2 ounces) dates, pitted and roughly chopped
¼ cup (1 ounce) dried cranberries
½ cup (2 ounces) currants
1½ cups (6 ounces) pecans
Zest of 1 organic orange
Rolled oats or cornmeal for dusting loaf

Special equipment: **Heavy lidded pot**, ideally cast iron, and at least 4 quarts; **single-edged razor blade**; **spray bottle**

1. Make the pre-ferment. Mix together the starter, water, and flour and let the mixture sit at room temperature overnight or for 10 to 12 hours.

2. Make the dough. Combine the pre-ferment with the water, starter, maple syrup, melted butter, and vanilla in a large bowl or in the bowl of a stand mixer. Using a wooden spoon, stir to combine. Add the flours and cinnamon and knead the dough for 10 minutes. If you use your hands to knead the dough, it should be dry enough for you to handle but still on the moist side. If you use a stand mixer, the dough should just clear the bottom and sides of the mixing bowl. In either case, the dough should feel somewhat less tacky than the dough feels for Sourdough Wheat and Rye Bread. At the end of kneading, it should be smooth, shiny, and speckled with grains of wheat. Cover the dough and let it rest for 20 minutes.

3. Add salt and knead the dough for 5 minutes more. Form the dough into a ball, put it into a lightly oiled bowl, and let it rise on the countertop, covered, for 2½ hours or until doubled in volume.

4. About 30 minutes before the end of the rest, preheat the oven to 325 degrees. Combine the raisins, dates, cranberries, and currants in a small bowl. Add warm water to cover and soak for 15 minutes. Drain well and set aside.

5. Spread the pecans on a cookie sheet and toast them in the oven for 7 minutes. Cool and chop medium-fine.

6. Uncover the risen dough and gently spread it across a lightly floured surface, forming a round and taking care not to press out the gas (if your surface is stone, the flour is not necessary). Spread the drained fruits, toasted pecans, and orange zest across the dough. Fold the dough over itself to contain the fruits and nuts. If you are using a stand mixer, place the dough into the mixing bowl and knead it on the lowest speed until the fruits and nuts are

well mixed, about 1 minute. If you are kneading by hand, work the dough until the fruits and nuts are thoroughly incorporated.

7. Shape the dough into a boule, without worrying if it's loose and less than perfect. Place the boule on the countertop, seam side down, with the bowl inverted over it as a cover. Let it rest for 30 minutes. The goal is for the seam to disappear and the dough to be smooth enough on the bottom that the loaf holds together. Then transfer the boule, seam side up, into a floured brotform or a bowl lined with a smooth, floured cloth. Pinch closed any bottom creases that remain opened and let the dough proof, covered, for about 1½ hours more, which is when you will bake the loaf.

8. One hour before baking, place a heavy, lidded pot inside the oven and preheat it to 450 degrees.

9. When the pot and oven are adequately preheated, dust the surface of the bread dough with rolled oats or cornmeal and gently invert the dough onto a piece of parchment paper. (The side with the oats or cornmeal should rest on the bottom of the pot, and the floured side will now be the top.) Using a single-edged razor blade, slash the top in a tic-tac-toe pattern with a wide center square. Remove the pot from the oven and ease the bread, still on the parchment paper, into the pot. Then, using a spray bottle filled with warm water, spritz the inside of the pot lid, cover it quickly, and place the pot into the oven for 5 minutes. It's okay if the top of the loaf gets damp when spritzing.

10. Using thick pot holders, carefully remove and uncover the pot and spray the inside once more. Cover it again and put the pot back into the oven for 40 minutes more. When the bread is ready, it will have a deep brown crust and an internal temperature of 207

degrees (checking the temperature with a thermometer will not harm the bread in any way). Remove the bread from the pot and let it cool on a rack for at least 1½ hours before slicing.

Note

- Beginning this dough with a pre-ferment—a mixture of starter, water, and flour—helps unlock and improve the flavor of the loaf. It also encourages a better rise in what might otherwise be a dense loaf of bread.

·· *FOOD THOUGHTS* ··

A Memorable Loaf

Over years spent baking bread, I have discovered approaches that help me consistently turn out more memorable loaves:

• The time frame for creating a loaf of bread changes as the temperatures change throughout the year. Paying attention to temperature will help you create good loaves of bread *within a predictable time frame.* If you're less interested in monitoring temperature, you can still create delicious loaves of bread, but your time frame will vary depending on how warm or cold your room temperature and ingredients are. In general, if you are monitoring temperature, your kneaded dough should be about 72 degrees. You can determine its temperature by pushing an instant-read kitchen thermometer into the middle of the kneaded dough. If it's warmer, start with cooler ingredients the next time. If it's cooler, start with warmer ingredients. With a 72-degree dough in a room that is about 75 degrees, moving from mixing the dough to putting the dough in the refrigerator should take 4 to 6 hours (it depends, in part, on the liveliness of your starter). By monitoring the temperature in this way, you will be able to predict your time frame with some precision.

- Making sourdough bread is an art and not a science. As a result, I can't tell you exactly how long bread dough should rest on the countertop before you put it in into the refrigerator; you will ultimately do it often enough that you will be able to read each dough yourself. I can, however, offer some general guidelines. In cool weather and starting with room-temperature ingredients (without measuring precise temperatures), the time frame from mixing dough for Sourdough Wheat and Rye Bread through putting it in the refrigerator takes anywhere from 5 to 8 hours. In contrast, in warmer weather the same process may take a total of 3 to 4 hours.

- A long, slow rise gives bread better flavor and a longer shelf life. You might see and taste this difference during colder months; when bread is fermented slowly in cooler temperatures it can stay moist and good-tasting for up to a week.

- You will need to use filtered or bottled water for feeding your starter and making bread dough if you notice that the chemicals in your tap water are interfering with chemical reactions in the dough. Experimentation and observation will indicate whether this is an issue for you. When considering water, it's also good to know that the best artisan breads begin as relatively wet doughs. It is water, as much as the starter itself, that defines the character of sourdough bread. Although differences in the way you shape, proof, and bake your loaf can create variations in the crust, it is water—adequate hydration—that facilitates chemical reactions within the dough and creates and defines an open, airy crumb.

- Each time you make a loaf of bread, use your eyes to help you achieve the results you're after. The height and appearance of your ideal loaf won't change much from week to week, but the time it takes to achieve this ideal will change. So, if you like, worry less about time and more about the "look" of the loaf you desire. Consider how high each loaf rises in the bowl or brotform before you put it into the refrigerator. Take notes and correlate which rise matches the best loaves. This is the height you will consistently strive for, whether it takes you 4 hours or 8 hours to get there. Look also at the roundness of your loaf, which will help to tell you if you shaped your boule adequately; each loaf should rise high and round, and its shape should be sturdy rather than floppy.

> Each loaf of bread you bake reflects your level of skill at a particular moment in time, and so the "imperfections" you see have little or nothing to do with carelessness; rather, they testify to the best you had in you when you created the loaf and to your willingness to let go of a self-defeating notion of perfection. So press on and learn to read each loaf as one page in the ongoing story of your development as a baker.

• Early on, I assumed that scoring—making a pattern of cuts on the loaf just before baking—was mostly decorative; observation and experimentation have taught me otherwise. Those who have given birth to children might rightly consider scoring an episiotomy for the bread: It facilitates and controls the direction of the rise, and it also controls the tear. It works best to score your bread at a relatively shallow angle, perhaps 30 or 40 degrees. So rather than cut straight into the dough, cut just under the crust. For dough that is adequately proofed but still has some rise left in it—in other words, an ideal loaf—you might cut about ½ inch into the bread. For loaves that are slightly underproofed, cut a bit deeper to encourage the rise. And for loaves that are overproofed, make shallow cuts, otherwise the dough may collapse and not make a full recovery. How do you know whether your loaves are well proofed? Experience will be your guide. But if a dough is wobbly rather than firm, and if it begins to deflate when you score it, it is overproofed. When this happens, don't worry; just make a shallow score and the loaf will likely rise, just not as high as it might have otherwise. It will still taste good, and you will then know to give your next loaf less time on the countertop before refrigerating. On a related note, keep in mind that different loaves may benefit from different scoring patterns, which is something you may want to explore as you expand your repertoire.

- I've listed measurements first in "cups" and "teaspoons" in order to keep the process familiar and simple, and in "ounces" for precision. But if you're going to continue baking sourdough bread, you might eventually refer to the many artisan bread books that have been written. And this, in turn, may leave you feeling overwhelmed by unfamiliar terminology (like the "hydration" of your sourdough starter) and metric measurements for flour (like "grams"). Do not be deterred by language that is new to you. What you have is a 100% hydration starter, which means that you feed it with equal quantities of water and flour. As for the metric measurements, you can manage them by purchasing a kitchen scale; they currently sell for under $30 and are easy to use. Simply turn on the scale and put a bowl on top. Push "tare" to bring the weight to zero. Add the first ingredient until you measure the proper amount, and push "tare" again. Then keep doing this. You will appreciate having no more dirty measuring cups and spoons, and you will also appreciate the ease and precision a scale will bring to your baking.

ROSEMARY-PARMESAN FOCACCIA

Makes one 13 x 13-inch focaccia

Focaccia dough is referred to as "high-hydration" because it is made with a high percentage of water; and while the water makes the dough a challenge to handle, it's also what gives the finished bread its characteristic irregular open holes. It's what makes this bread "focaccia." The only real mistake you can make is to add more flour or less water, which will give you a dense loaf and a crumb that is less open and airy than it should be.

This recipe works best with a stand mixer. Without a mixer, hold the bowl in your lap and, with damp hands, pull the dough up and fold it back down on itself, and this form of kneading will be adequate.

As for shaping, focaccia is rustic enough to be somewhat free-form, so you can unleash your creative spirit. And with regard to flavor, it works to keep focaccia simple, limiting your topping to olive oil and coarse sea salt, for example. Or you can embellish it with an herb oil and Parmesan cheese, as this recipe has you do. Another option is to spread ingredients across the top, like caramelized onions or kalamata olives (see "Notes").

Managing Your Time

For the first 11 steps—that is, for making the dough—you will need a span of 5 to 6 hours, but the dough will mostly mind itself during this time and require only occasional involvement from you. The dough will then ferment in the refrigerator for 8 to 36 hours. On baking day, you'll need 1 to 3 hours to bring the dough to room temperature and preheat the oven, which again requires almost nothing in the way of active time. Baking takes about 15 minutes.

FOR THE DOUGH:

2 cups (14 ounces) sourdough starter

1⅓ cups (10.5 ounces) room-temperature filtered water

1 tablespoon barley malt

1¾ cups (10 ounces) white bread flour, plus extra for dusting

1¾ cups (10 ounces) whole-wheat bread flour

⅓ cup (2.5 ounces) extra-virgin olive oil

2 tablespoons fine sea salt

FOR THE HERB OIL AND TOPPING:

⅓ cup extra-virgin olive oil

1 tablespoon chopped fresh rosemary

2 cloves garlic, minced

1½ teaspoons coarse sea salt

¼ teaspoon freshly ground pepper

½ cup freshly grated Parmesan cheese

1. Make the dough. In the bowl of a stand mixer, combine the starter, water, and barley malt. Using a wooden spoon, stir until the ingredients are combined and the starter is dispersed throughout.

2. Add the flours and, using the same wooden spoon, mix the dough into a wet mass. Scrape any wet dough from the spoon into the mixing bowl. Then cover the bowl and let it sit on the countertop for at least 20 minutes or up to 1 hour.

3. Add olive oil and salt, and knead the dough for 10 minutes. The dough should be wet and will not clear the sides or bottom of the bowl. It will be more like a batter than a dough at this stage, and this is the effect you are after. This is the desired consistency of high-hydration doughs like focaccia, so resist the temptation to add more flour.

4. Once the dough is kneaded, remove the dough hook from the mixer, rinse it, and set it aside. Allow the dough to rest in the mixing bowl, covered, for 1 hour.

5. While the dough is resting, prepare the herb oil by combining

olive oil, rosemary, garlic, salt, and pepper in a small bowl. Cover the bowl and set it aside.

6. After the 1-hour rise, uncover the dough, reattach the dough hook, and knead for a moment, just long enough for the dough hook to make a few revolutions around the bowl. Turn the dough over as best you can and repeat once more. Then remove the dough hook from the mixer, rinse it, and set it aside. Allow the dough to rest in the mixing bowl, covered, for 1 hour more. Repeat this process two more times until you have re-kneaded the dough 3 times.

7. After the third knead, allow the dough to rest in the mixing bowl, covered, for 2 hours more.

8. Following the 2-hour rest, line a standard rimmed baking sheet (about 17 x 13 inches) with parchment paper. Using both hands, gently scoop the dough out of the bowl and transfer it to the baking sheet.

9. Pour the herb oil over the dough and, using only your fingertips (not the palms of your hands), "dimple" the dough as a way of encouraging it to spread. The dough will not spread enough to fill the pan; what you are after is a 13 x 13-inch square. If necessary, wait 10 minutes for the gluten to relax and dimple the dough until you can approximate this size. Remember again that a dough this wet will have a somewhat loose form. Perfection is not a goal.

10. Once the dough is the size you desire, cover it with a layer of waxed paper and slide the baking sheet into a clean plastic kitchen trash bag and tie it closed. If you prefer, substitute a layer of waxed paper and a layer of aluminum foil for the trash bag.

11. Transfer the dough to the refrigerator and allow it to rise for 8 to 36 hours.

12. At least 1 hour before baking (or as long as 2 to 3 hours in a cool kitchen or if the refrigerated rise was under 24 hours), remove the dough from the refrigerator and let it come to room temperature on the countertop. Preheat the oven to 500 degrees.

13. When the oven is adequately preheated, once again use your fingertips to "dimple" the dough, gently pressing out some, but not all, of the gas to prevent the focaccia from rising round and high in the oven. Then sprinkle the Parmesan cheese evenly over the top of the dough. Place it into the oven and, at the same time, lower the oven temperature to 475 degrees. Let the focaccia bake for 13 to 16 minutes, turning the pan halfway through baking.

14. Remove the focaccia from the baking sheet and let it cool on a rack for at least 1 hour before slicing. Leftovers are best stored wrapped in waxed paper.

Notes

- A wet dough like this one benefits from a gentle resumption of kneading during its initial rise on the countertop. This is traditionally accomplished by "folding," which strengthens the dough and degasses it to release carbon dioxide and encourage fermentation. I generally use the method described in step 6 of this recipe, which is to allow the dough to rise in the bowl of the stand mixer and hourly take it a few times around the bowl with the dough hook; then turn it over and do it again. The trick is to be gentle, keeping the gluten strands in tact, so that you get the benefit of an optimal rise. If you prefer to fold with your hands, it will help to wet them before working the dough. Then gently pull the dough up and over itself, turning the bowl as you do, so that the entire dough is folded.

- In step 9, you may prefer to spread the oil over the focaccia dough first, holding back the garlic and herbs until the dough is dimpled to its appropriate size. Then, carefully and evenly, spread the garlic and herbs over the dough.

- In step 13, before putting the focaccia into the oven, you can embellish it with almost anything: anchovies, sundried tomatoes, lightly precooked vegetables, fresh greens like arugula or frisée, pitted kalamata olives, caramelized onions, or fresh herbs. Sprinkling the dough with freshly grated Parmesan cheese, as the recipe suggests, slightly browns the finished focaccia.

SOURDOUGH CHALLAH

MAKES 2 MEDIUM LOAVES OR 16 ROLLS

Whether you make this challah as loaves or rolls, it's lovely on the table and deceptively easy to make—easier I think than yeasted loaves. Challah is traditionally made with white flour, but I prefer to use at least half whole-wheat flour when I bake, so that's how I've written this recipe. If you want a fully white challah, I've included an easy adaptation in the notes that follow the recipe.

Managing Your Time

Mixing the pre-ferment takes no more than 5 minutes, and it works well to prepare this the evening before baking day. In the morning, it takes 20 to 25 minutes to make the dough, followed by a 2-hour rise. Shaping the loaves or rolls takes 15 to 30 minutes, followed by another 2-hour rise and up to 35 minutes for baking.

FOR THE PRE-FERMENT:
½ cup (5 ounces) sourdough starter
2 cups (10 ounces) whole-wheat bread flour
½ to ¾ cup (4 to 6 ounces) room-temperature filtered water

FOR THE DOUGH:
½ cup (5 ounces) sourdough starter
2 cups (11 ounces) white bread flour
2 eggs
¼ cup plus 2 tablespoons (5.3 ounces) honey
3 teaspoons fine sea salt
¼ cup (2 ounces) extra-virgin olive oil, plus extra for bowl
1 egg for brushing
Poppy or sesame seeds for sprinkling

1. Make the pre-ferment. Combine the sourdough starter, flour, and water, and mix to combine the ingredients into a relatively firm ball of dough. Be sure to use enough water to bind the ingredients,

and pick up any stray bits of flour in the bowl. Once mixed, transfer the pre-ferment to an oiled bowl and let it sit on the countertop, covered, for about 12 hours.

2. Make the dough. Transfer the pre-ferment to a mixing bowl or to the bowl of a stand mixer. Add the full list of dough ingredients, except the egg for brushing and the seeds, and use a sturdy wooden spoon to mix and combine them. Then knead the dough for 10 minutes or until it's smooth and elastic. If you're using a stand mixer, the dough should just clear the sides of the mixing bowl. If needed, add flour or water by the spoonful until the consistency is correct. The same approach will work for hand kneading, with the ideal consistency being a dough that is wet, but not sticky. You should be able to handle it and, later, shape it.

3. Place the kneaded dough into a lightly oiled bowl and let it rest, covered, at room temperature for 2 hours or until doubled in size.

4. Line a baking sheet with two layers of parchment paper and remove the dough from the bowl. For 2 loaves, divide the dough into 6 equal portions, each weighing 7 to 7.5 ounces; for 16 rolls, divide the dough into equal portions, each weighing 2.8 to 3.2 ounces. Measuring the portions by weight ensures that they will be close to the same size and require the same baking time.

5. Using your hands, roll and stretch each dough portion into a strand: For 2 loaves, make 6 strands, each 12 inches long; for rolls, make 16 strands, each 7 inches long.

6. If you are making loaves, braid 3 strands per loaf, pinching the ends together and tucking them under; then transfer the loaves to the baking sheet. If you are making rolls, wrap each strand around

2 fingers and pull the "loose" end through the center hole to form a knot. Place each knot onto the baking sheet.

7. Dampen a smooth towel with warm water, squeeze it dry, and cover the loaves or rolls. Allow them to rest on the countertop for another 2 hours, or until they have doubled in size and are ready to bake.

8. One hour before baking—that is, one hour into the second rise—preheat the oven to 400 degrees. Make an egg wash by mixing the egg with 1 tablespoon water.

9. When you are ready to bake, brush each loaf or roll with egg wash. Take care to brush evenly, leaving no bare spots that will show after baking. If you like, sprinkle the loaves or rolls with poppy or sesame seeds.

10. If you are baking loaves, place them into the oven and reduce the heat to 350 degrees. Bake the loaves for 20 minutes; then rotate them in the oven and bake for 13 to 15 minutes more. If you are baking rolls, place them into the oven, keeping the heat set at 400 degrees. Rolls will take 14 to 15 minutes to bake. Each loaf or roll should be golden brown on the outside and the internal temperature should be 200 degrees. Remove the baking sheet from the oven and cool the challahs on a rack for at least 1 hour before serving.

Notes

- To make a more traditional challah using all white flour, substitute 2 cups of white bread flour for the whole-wheat flour in the preferment; you may need to decrease the salt in the recipe to about 2 teaspoons. The best method for adapting this recipe is to adjust the quantities of white flour and salt each time you bake until you have a result that pleases you.

- The instructions in steps 4 to 6 assume you will make simple 3-strand braided loaves. If you want to make more ambitious 4-, 5-, or 6-strand braided challah loaves, here is how you do it: Separate the dough into the number of strands you will need. Then line the dough strands vertically, one next to the other. Pinch the strands together at the top and, in your mind, number each strand according to its position in line—with the strand on the far left being 1 and the strand on the far right being the highest number you are using. It is important to note that the number refers to the position in line, rather than to the strand itself, so as the strand moves, it's number changes. With this in mind, here are braiding patterns to follow. For a 4-strand braid: 4 over 2, 1 over 3, 2 over 3, repeat. For a 5-strand braid: 1 over 3, 2 over 3, 5 over 2, repeat. For a 6-strand braid: 2 over 6, 1 over 3, 5 over 1, 6 over 4, repeat. If braiding many strands is new to you, it may help to practice with thick yarn before attempting to braid sticky bread dough. For a visually beautiful finish, tuck the ends under at the top and bottom of the braid.

SOURDOUGH PIZZA

MAKES 2 OVAL 12 X 14-INCH PIZZAS, OR 4 ROUND 9-INCH PERSONAL PIZZAS

No matter how many recipes I've experimented with over the years, I have always found homemade pizza to be time-consuming labor when hungry people need to be fed. Not so with sourdough; this crust is easy to make, easy to handle, and especially easy on the schedule. What you'll get for your efforts is a hearty, flavorful crust that can support many toppings—though it's equally nice with tomato sauce or pesto and fresh mozzarella.

Managing Your Time

You have a lot of options with this dough, which takes about 40 minutes of active time to pull together. (Since the dough needs 4 hours after kneading to rest on the countertop, be sure to make it when you will be home or awake 4 hours later to refrigerate the dough.) You can make the dough early in the morning and it will be ready to turn into pizza for dinner, which is my favorite way to do it. Or you can make the dough at any time of day to serve any time the next day. Rolling, topping, and baking the pizzas take about 45 minutes.

FOR THE DOUGH:
1½ cups (8 ounces) sourdough starter
1 tablespoon extra-virgin olive oil
1½ cups (8 ounces) white bread flour
1 cup (5 ounces) whole-wheat bread or pastry flour
¾ to 1 cup (6 to 8 ounces) room-temperature filtered water
2 teaspoons fine sea salt

FOR THE PIZZA:
2 cups tomato sauce (see "Notes")
1 pound fresh, or 6 to 8 ounces shredded, mozzarella cheese
Freshly grated Parmesan cheese, optional

Special equipment: Pizza stone

1. In a medium-sized bowl or in the bowl of a stand mixer, combine the sourdough starter, olive oil, and flours and, using a wooden spoon, mix into a ragged dough; there will still be plenty of loose flour in the bottom of the bowl. Add ¾ cup water and, using a wooden spoon followed by your hands, mix into a soft dough. You may need to add up to ¼ cup more water. The goal is to have a dough that is not soggy or sticky, but wet enough that you can use it to pick up any loose flour in the bowl. Let the dough rest, covered, for 20 minutes.

2. Add salt to the dough and knead it for 10 minutes, either by hand or in a stand mixer. If you are using a mixer, the dough should ideally adhere to the bottom of the mixing bowl, but clear the sides. If needed, add more water or flour by the spoonful to achieve this effect. At the end of kneading, put the dough into a lightly oiled bowl, roll it so that it's lightly coated with oil, and let it sit in a warm spot, covered, for about 4 hours. Then move the dough to the refrigerator to rest for 6 to 24 hours. If you opt for a longer rest, you may need to punch down the dough and deflate it if it's well risen and full of gas.

3. One hour before you are ready to bake pizza, place a pizza stone on the oven rack closest to your heating element. Then preheat the oven to 550 degrees and remove the pizza dough from the refrigerator.

4. While the oven is preheating, divide the dough as evenly as you can into the number of pizzas you want to make. Put each dough section onto an individual piece of parchment paper that is about the size you expect the finished pizza to be.

5. Using the palms of your hands, press and stretch each piece of dough into a round about ¼ inch thick, keeping it on the parchment

paper. If needed, you can lightly oil your hands to prevent the dough from sticking. For now, the dough doesn't need to look perfect. When it's "good enough," dampen a smooth dish towel with warm water, squeeze out any excess, and cover the dough rounds. Let them rest this way for 15 to 20 minutes to relax the gluten and make the dough easier to shape.

6. Using a lightly oiled rolling pin, gently shape each dough into a neat round. The finished dough should be ⅛ to ¼ inch thick. Top the pizzas with sauce and cheese, and transfer each pizza, still on parchment paper, to the oven. (If you will be baking the pizzas one at a time, top each one just before baking.) Bake on a pizza stone for 11 to 14 minutes, or until the cheese is lightly browned and the sauce is bubbling. If you like, sprinkle each pizza with freshly grated Parmesan cheese as it comes out of the oven.

7. Serve hot, or transfer to a cooling rack to keep the crust crisp until serving time.

Notes

• If you prefer a more whole-grain crust, increase the quantity of whole-wheat flour and decrease the white flour by the same amount. You may need to add extra salt or water to make the substitution work.

• To make 2 cups of tomato sauce: In a saucepan combine one 28-ounce can of

---

In the years that I have put into mastering sourdough, I can't say that I have succeeded. Mastery is not really an option, because baking with sourdough is an art form rather than a science. It requires patience, as well as a keen and observant eye. I can't, for example, tell you precisely how long to proof a dough before moving it to the refrigerator. You just have to do it until you are able to read the dough with your eyes, your hands—all your senses, really. And every time you begin a sourdough recipe, it is almost as if you are starting fresh. There are so many variables, and the process is, to some degree, new. That's what makes it so engaging and so much fun.

whole or diced tomatoes, 2 peeled garlic cloves, ½ teaspoon sea salt, 1 tablespoon olive oil, and a pinch of red pepper flakes. Simmer for 30 minutes; cool slightly, and puree in a blender or with an immersion blender.

- To make ½ cup of basil puree: In the bowl of a food processor combine the leaves from 1 bunch of basil, 2 to 3 peeled garlic cloves, ⅓ cup olive oil, and ¼ teaspoon sea salt. Puree until smooth.

- If you want to freeze crusts for future use, make the dough and roll it out as you normally would. Just before baking, prick each crust with the tines of a fork to keep it from rising as it cooks. Bake for 3 minutes. When you remove each crust from the oven, prick it again to release any trapped air. Once crusts are prebaked, cool on a rack and freeze to use as needed. Use straight from the freezer; after adding your toppings, bake for 10 minutes.

HERBED PARMESAN BREAD TWISTS

MAKES 18 TWISTS, PLUS AN EXTRA FEW KNOTS

This is a special recipe and a reminder of why handcrafting food is so rewarding: You simply can't buy food like this. You can use this recipe to make 18 bread twists, and the trimmings will give you a handful of additional small and large "knots." Both are best served shortly after you make them.

Managing Your Time

Assuming you have pizza dough in the refrigerator, these twists will take 60 to 70 minutes to make, including cooking time. While I haven't tried every permutation, it is possible to shape the twists early in the day and then bake them just before serving. In this case, cover and refrigerate the twists after shaping in steps 7 and 8. Then take the twists out of the refrigerator 1 hour before baking, preheat the oven, and proceed with step 9.

1 batch dough for sourdough pizza crust (follow recipe on page 130 through step 2, ideally using less water to make a slightly drier dough than you would for pizza)
1 tablespoon each finely chopped rosemary and thyme
⅓ cup plus 1 cup freshly grated Parmesan cheese
¾ teaspoon fine sea salt, divided

Freshly ground pepper
⅓ cup plus ¼ cup extra-virgin olive oil
1 to 2 large cloves garlic, minced
¼ cup finely chopped parsley leaves

1. Preheat the oven to 400 degrees. Put the oven racks in the lower and upper third of the oven and line each of 2 baking sheets with 2 layers of parchment paper.

134 • FOOD & SOUL

2. Remove the pizza dough from the refrigerator, divide it in half, and let each half rest, covered, on the countertop.

3. Make an herb mixture. In a small bowl, stir together the chopped rosemary and thyme, ⅓ cup Parmesan cheese, ½ teaspoon of the salt, and a grind or two of pepper. Set aside.

4. Make an oil mixture. In another small bowl, combine ⅓ cup of the olive oil, minced garlic, the remaining ¼ teaspoon salt, and a grind or two of pepper. Set aside.

5. Uncover one dough round and place it on a lightly floured or oiled countertop. Using your hands, shape the dough into a rectangle. Then, with a lightly oiled rolling pin, roll the dough into a 12 x 10-inch rectangle. If the dough springs back, cover it and let it rest for 5 to 10 minutes more before trying again.

6. With the long ends of the rectangle on the top and bottom, sprinkle either the right or left half of the dough with *half* the herb mixture. Then fold the half without herbs over the half with herbs. Again, roll the dough, this time into an 8 x 10-inch rectangle. As before, if the dough springs back, cover it and let it rest for 5 to 10 minutes before trying again.

7. With the long ends of the dough on the top and bottom, trim any uneven edges and set them aside. Then make vertical cuts, slicing the dough into 9 strips, each about 1 inch wide and 8 inches long. Twist each strip 3 to 4 times, but avoid pulling or stretching as you do. After twisting, compress the twists by pushing each end toward the center; twists with an even thickness are ideal. Place the twists on a baking sheet, 1 inch apart. Then, using a pastry brush, coat each twist with the oil mixture. Repeat this process with the second dough round.

8. Take any trimmings and shape them into round knots. Coat each knot with the oil mixture and place them on the baking sheets along with the bread sticks.

9. Bake the twists and knots for 25 to 30 minutes, switching the trays on the oven racks halfway through baking. Both are ready when they are lightly browned.

10. While the twists are baking, stir together the remaining 1 cup Parmesan cheese and chopped parsley. Spread the mixture over a tray or a large plate long enough to accommodate the twists. Add the remaining ¼ cup olive oil to the bowl containing leftover minced garlic from the oil mixture.

11. When the bread twists come out of the oven, brush them with the oil mixture. Then roll them in the Parmesan-parsley mixture. Do the same for any knots. Place the finished twists and knots on a wire rack and serve warm or at room temperature.

Note

- These bread twists are easy to adapt to your liking. For example, I prefer thick twists, so I roll and twist them with this goal in mind. Others like thin twists and roll and twist them more assertively. Likewise, you might like more or less herb mixture on your finished twists. You can work with the subtleties of this recipe to create the twists you most enjoy.

SOURDOUGH BISCUITS

Makes 8 biscuits

Sourdough biscuits pair equally well with a plate of eggs or a bowl of soup. Either way, a smear of homemade butter makes a nice addition. Keep in mind that the extent to which sourdough adds personality to these biscuits depends on how much you add: More sourdough means more sour tang. While the recipe calls for ¼ cup, you can safely incorporate from ⅛ cup to ½ cup of sourdough starter. You may need to adjust the quantity of flour up or down to accommodate the change.

Managing Your Time

It takes less than 30 minutes to make this dough, and you can bake the biscuits from 6 to 24 hours later, so you have some flexibility with this recipe. If you want to serve the biscuits warm for dinner, consider cutting them after the refrigerated rest and then refrigerating the cut biscuits until shortly before dinner when you bake them. Brushing with buttermilk and baking take no more than 20 minutes.

1¼ cups whole-wheat pastry flour
1¼ cups all-purpose flour
1½ teaspoons fine sea salt
1 teaspoon maple crystals
1 stick butter, or 4 ounces homemade butter, chilled and cut into chunks
1 cup buttermilk, plus more for brushing

¼ cup sourdough starter
2 tablespoons cornmeal
½ teaspoon baking soda
1 teaspoon baking powder

---

1. Up to 24 hours before you want to bake the biscuits, place the flours, salt, and maple crystals into the bowl of a food processor. Pulse 5 to 7 times to combine.

SOURDOUGH • 137

2. Add the butter, and pulse several times until well mixed, ideally retaining some small chunks of butter.

3. Transfer the mixture to a large bowl, and add the buttermilk and sourdough starter. Using a spatula, fold the ingredients from the edge of the bowl into the middle. Rotate the bowl with each fold until the mixture is evenly moist and sticky. There may be some remaining dry patches, but aim for as few as possible.

4. Cover the dough and let it rest in the refrigerator until you are ready to bake, for at least 6 hours or up to 24 hours.

5. Before baking, preheat the oven to 450 degrees and butter an 8 x 10-inch baking dish. Sprinkle cornmeal over the bottom of the dish.

6. Remove the dough from the refrigerator and add the baking powder and baking soda to the bowl, using your hands to work them into the dough. The idea is to fully integrate the baking powder and baking soda.

7. Place the dough onto a lightly floured countertop. Dust your hands with flour and gently ease the dough into a rectangle. With a bench scraper or a sharp knife, cut the dough in half and stack one half on top of the other. Repeat 3 more times: flattening the dough into a rectangle, cutting, and stacking.

8. Transfer the dough to the baking dish, and using your fingertips, gently press it to fill the dish completely. Because the dough will be cold, it may spring back as you try to shape it. It can help to rest the dough for 5 to 10 minutes and then resume shaping until the dough is evenly thick in all places. Using a bench scraper or a sharp knife, cut the dough into 8 evenly sized rectangles.

9. Lightly brush the biscuit tops with buttermilk, and bake for 17 to 20 minutes, or until the biscuits are golden brown.

10. Cool on a rack until gently warm and serve.

Notes

- Although the white flour in this recipe imparts a noticeable lightness and tenderness to the finished biscuits, you can use all whole-wheat pastry flour if you like. In this case, you may want to increase the quantity of salt just slightly.
- If you like biscuits with a lighter brown bottom, bake them on a double layer of parchment paper (placed under the cornmeal).
- Consider adding up to ¼ cup chopped chives, ¼ cup freshly grated Parmesan cheese, or ¼ cup grated sharp cheddar cheese to the dough with the baking powder and baking soda in step 6.

A SCIENTIFIC INTERLUDE:

USING SOURDOUGH TO LOWER THE GLYCEMIC INDEX OF EVERYDAY BAKED GOODS

Both sweet and savory baked goods can pose health concerns for a variety of reasons:

• When we eat baked goods made with *white* flour, blood sugar can spike upward after eating (the glycemic index, or carbohydrate component, is too high).

• When we eat baked goods made with *whole-grain* flour, blood sugar remains relatively stable, but phytic acid stored in the bran may prevent us from absorbing minerals like iron, calcium, magnesium, and zinc. Over time, this can lead to mineral depletion and bone loss.

• When we bake with white or whole-grain flour and allow the batter to rest for a period of hours before baking, phytic acid is reduced, but grains become super-digestible and the result is a dramatic spike in blood sugar (the glycemic index is again too high).

The problem, then, is circular in nature, with each solution creating a new problem. As a sourdough bread baker, I know that sourdough creates an ideal carbohydrate: bread with a low glycemic index and almost no phytic acid due to the dough's long rest before baking. So I wondered if I could use sourdough to improve the healthfulness of everyday baked goods by adding it to a batter and then allowing it to rest for a period of hours, just as when making sourdough bread. I believed this approach would lower the glycemic index of baked goods and reduce their phytic acid, a simple and elegant solution to the challenges listed above.

This approach might be useful to those with insulin resistance, diabetes, or mineral deficiencies (like low calcium or iron), or to those who simply wish to lower the blood-sugar impact of the baked goods they consume.

The paragraphs that follow describe my tests (using a home blood-sugar monitor) and their promising results.

TEST RESULTS

I conducted four series of tests, each centered around two recipes using sourdough, one savory (buttermilk biscuits) and one sweet (banana muffins). In each case, I prepared the recipes using stone-ground whole-wheat flour, which may be important. The results of these tests were consistent and clear.

The savory biscuit dough that I rested for 24 hours caused only a modest rise in blood sugar and gave the most impressive result. These biscuits had the lowest blood-sugar impact after 30 minutes, which is when blood sugar typically spikes upward, and provided the most substantial satiety and blood sugar stability. I could see this in a low arc and a slow, steady blood sugar decline. This last factor illustrates why lessening the impact of blood sugar can also prevent hunger and overeating. In contrast, resting a whole-wheat batter with only buttermilk, and without the addition of sourdough, caused blood sugar to spike and then plummet.

The sweetened banana muffin dough that I rested for 12 hours gave the best result. These muffins caused a moderate increase in blood sugar, coupled with sustained blood-sugar levels over a full 2 hours and a slow, steady decline. Interestingly, in this experiment, the same sourdough batter rested for 24 hours yielded the worst result. More research would be needed to understand why.

I conducted further tests to determine the quantity of sourdough needed to achieve these same results. Using just one quarter of the amount of sourdough worked, proving that where a sour taste is not desired, less sourdough can be used. (I have so far experimented with using as little as 1 ounce of sourdough starter to 31 ounces of savory biscuit dough to achieve this same result.)

In each case, whole-wheat batters made without a rest traced a gentle glycemic curve, but phytic acid in the finished baked good may remain an issue.

Test results also indicated that the inclusion of sourdough in a batter—but without a rest—has no impact on the glycemic index. A rest is required, and resting time seems to matter.

There is more to learn. Most important, what is the ideal amount of sourdough and length of resting time needed to give the optimum result? Also, studies by others show that stone-ground flour (look for "stone-ground" on the package) is necessary for lowering blood sugar. My own tests confirmed this, but a closer look is warranted. Finally, in what other varieties of baked goods can we use sourdough to lower glycemic response, and where is this a palatable approach and where is it not? From a culinary perspective, I have used sourdough in other sweetened baked goods (cakes—including chocolate cakes—cookies, corn bread, muffins, and quick breads) and achieved a good result, often better than without. On the savory side, I have made sourdough pizza, pancakes, English muffins, and a variety of breads. All this is to say that sourdough offers delicious potential to lower the glycemic index of everyday baked goods.

SOURDOUGH BANANA BREAD

Makes 1 loaf

This is my favorite quick-bread recipe. It's based on a banana bread recipe that Peter Berley included in his wonderful cookbook *The Modern Vegetarian Kitchen*. When adding sourdough to a quick bread, which is easy to do with almost any quick bread or muffin recipe using the approach below, you will need to think ahead just as when adding it to a standard loaf. But once you make the batter and put it in the refrigerator to rest, nearly all of your work is behind you.

Managing Your Time

You will need about ½ hour to mix this batter. If you plan to rest it after mixing, as the recipe is written, allow up to 10 hours for refrigeration and 2 more hours to rest the batter on the countertop before baking. You will then need 1 hour to bake the loaf and 1 more hour to cool it before slicing. So, in total, you will need 14 hours after mixing the batter, with little active time required on your part. If, instead, you choose not to rest the batter, you can bake the loaf just after mixing. Simply allow 1 hour for baking and 1 hour to cool the loaf before slicing. That's 2½ hours total, again with little active involvement from you.

- 1 cup pecans or walnuts
- 1½ cups whole-wheat pastry flour
- 1½ cups white bread flour
- 1½ teaspoons cinnamon
- 1 teaspoon fine sea salt
- 1 tablespoon baking powder
- ½ cup sourdough starter
- 2 to 3 very ripe bananas (10 ounces), well mashed
- 1 stick butter, or 4 ounces homemade butter, melted and cooled somewhat
- ½ cup maple syrup
- 2 eggs
- 1 tablespoon vanilla

1. Preheat the oven to 350 degrees. Butter the sides and bottom of a loaf pan and line the bottom with a piece of parchment paper.

2. When the oven is preheated, place the nuts in a single layer on a baking sheet or in a pan and bake: 5 to 6 minutes for pecans or 8 to 10 minutes for walnuts. Let cool, chop medium-fine, and set aside. Turn off the oven, unless you want to bake the loaf without resting it first.

3. In a medium-sized bowl, combine the flours, cinnamon, salt, and baking powder and set aside. In a small bowl, combine the sourdough starter, mashed bananas, butter, maple syrup, eggs, and vanilla.

4. Add the wet ingredients to the dry ingredients and begin mixing. Then add the chopped nuts and continue mixing the batter until it's just combined. Spoon the batter into the prepared loaf pan. (If you want to bake the loaf without resting it, proceed from here to step 5.) To rest the batter, cover it and put it in the refrigerator until 2 hours before baking time. An ideal rest for this loaf is about 12 hours from the time it is mixed, but shorter or longer will also work.

5. About 30 minutes before baking, preheat the oven to 350 degrees. Bake the banana bread for 1 hour, turning the pan after 30 minutes for more even baking.

6. Transfer the banana bread to a rack and let it cool for at least 1 hour before slicing.

Note

- Some say that leaveners like baking powder and baking soda deactivate sourdough by killing the wild yeast and bacteria. I have not observed this firsthand, but it's information you may want to keep in mind as you work with this recipe and make the process your own. If you ever find this to be an issue—that is, if you fail to get the flavor, rise, or glycemic effect you're aiming for—simply hold off on adding any chemical leavener until just before baking. In this case, take care to mix well.

TO REST OR NOT TO REST?

In baking, you can use sourdough to moisten almost any batter or dough and give it a slightly sour tang. If these are your only goals, there is no need for a rest before baking. If, however, you want these benefits plus the health-giving benefits of fermentation—like improved flavor and digestibility, and the potential for a lower glycemic index—you will need to mix the ingredients and then allow for a rest in the refrigerator before baking.

SOURDOUGH COCOA CAKE

MAKES ONE 9-INCH CAKE

This cake provides an example of the way you can add sourdough to everyday baked goods to impart moistness and to enhance them in an almost indescribable way. The recipe calls for resting the sourdough mixture for 1 hour or, if you have time, for 12 hours; this longer rest can lower the glycemic effect of the cake (that is, limit its impact on blood sugar) and improve its healthfulness, just as a rest does for sourdough bread. The flavor and texture, however, will be the same no matter which rest you choose. Serve this cake alone or with lightly whipped cream and fresh berries.

Managing Your Time

Step 1 takes 5 to 10 minutes. You then have options depending on how long you want to rest the sourdough mixture before completing the batter: The minimum rest is 1 hour, but you can rest the batter in the refrigerator, covered, for 10 to 12 hours more before beginning step 2. Once starting step 2, you will need 20 to 25 minutes to finish the batter, with 1 hour more for baking plus 20 minutes to cool before turning the cake onto a rack. So that's 2 hours to finish the cake, with 25 minutes of active time.

½ cup sourdough starter
1 cup all-purpose flour
¾ cup plus 2 tablespoons whole-wheat pastry flour
⅔ cup whole milk
¾ cup natural cocoa powder, not Dutch process
½ teaspoon fine sea salt

1 teaspoon baking powder
¼ teaspoon baking soda
⅓ cup water
½ cup extra-virgin olive oil
1¾ cups maple crystals
4 eggs
1 teaspoon vanilla

1. In a medium bowl, mix the sourdough starter, flours, and milk until they are well combined. Use your hands to break up any lumps in the dough-like batter and knead for a moment to finish combining the ingredients; the batter may be sticky. Cover the batter and transfer it to the refrigerator to rest for 12 hours (in this case, incorporate time within the 12-hour rest to bring the batter to room temperature before moving on to step 2). Alternatively, you can rest the batter at room temperature for 1 hour and then move on to step 2.

2. About 15 minutes before the end of your chosen rest period, preheat oven to 350 degrees. Line the bottom of a 9-inch round cake pan with parchment paper, and oil both the bottom and sides of the pan.

3. In a small bowl, whisk together the cocoa powder, salt, baking powder, and baking soda and set aside.

4. Uncover the sourdough mixture and add the water. Using your hands, begin working the water into the batter and breaking up any clumps of dough (you will not be able to fully incorporate the water). Press and knead until you have a thoroughly wet mass. Set aside.

5. In a large mixing bowl or the bowl of a stand mixer, combine the olive oil and maple crystals and mix on medium speed until the crystals are coated with oil and have a sandy, granular appearance, 1 to 2 minutes. Turn the speed to low, add the cocoa powder mixture, increase the speed back to medium, and mix for 1 to 2 minutes more or until the granules are evenly coated with cocoa and the mixture resembles chocolate cookie crumbs. With the mixer still on medium, add the eggs one at a time. With the

last egg incorporated, turn the mixer to medium-high and beat for 2 to 3 minutes, scraping the sides and bottom once, until the mixture resembles chocolate pudding. Add the vanilla and mix a moment longer.

6. With the mixer on low, add half the sourdough mixture and mix just to combine. Then add the second half and mix for 1 minute more, scraping the beaters with a spatula to release any sourdough clumps.

7. Finish mixing with an immersion blender; I have so far found this to be the most effective way to break up the sourdough clumps and integrate them into the batter. Mix with the immersion blender for 1 minute. Scrape the sides and bottom of the bowl with a rubber spatula. Then mix and stir with the immersion blender for 1½ minutes more. In the end, the batter should be smooth and uniformly brown.

8. Pour the batter into the prepared cake pan, using a spatula to scrape the batter off the sides and bottom of the bowl.

9. Bake the cake for 55 minutes, or until a toothpick or cake tester comes out clean. Cool the cake in the pan for 20 minutes; then slide a thin knife around the edge of the cake and invert it onto a plate. Turn the cake right side up onto a cooling rack and serve it lukewarm or at room temperature. Lightly whipped cream and fresh berries make a nice addition.

Notes

- The trick with this cake, if there is one, is to smooth any clumps of sourdough in the mixture and integrate them into the batter without overworking it. Too much mixing and handling develops gluten, which is not our aim. With a cake, the goal is "tender," not "chewy." So while it's important to be sure there are no sourdough clumps left in the finished cake, you also want to avoid overmixing it. Practice will be your best guide.

- I made this cake dozens of different ways before settling on olive oil for the moisture it imparts. When choosing an olive oil, look for one labeled "mellow," "smooth," or "buttery." Avoid oils labeled "peppery" or "pungent." Better yet, taste a spoonful of olive oil and decide for yourself.

BOLD BAKING

If I could suggest one way to add assertiveness and boldness to the way you cook, it would be this: Every time you bake, replace up to half the white flour in your recipe with whole-grain flour. Don't stop to think about it; just do it, because nearly every baked good, whether savory or sweet, can handle this healthful substitution. You may need to add slightly more salt to make the change work, and you will know this by tasting the finished product and then adapting the recipe the next time.

In my experience, most people will not notice the switch, and those who do will often find the recipe improved. This is true even of finicky children, and it's because whole-grain flour has flavor, character, and integrity that are missing in white flour. This switch works for piecrust; it works for pizza dough; it works for muffins, cakes, quick breads, and pancakes. It works, period.

Here are suggestions for incorporating whole-grain flour into your baking:

• Whole-wheat bread flour, made from hard wheat, is best for pizza crust, bread, focaccia, and some pancakes. Whole-wheat pastry flour, made from soft wheat, is better for muffins, biscuits, popovers, scones, waffles, piecrusts, cakes, and many pancakes. It can also be used for pizza crust. Think of chew as a goal when you use whole-wheat bread flour; think of tenderness as a goal when you use whole-wheat pastry flour.

• Batters comprised of all or mostly whole-grain flour benefit from a rest before baking. A rest will improve the flavor; lighten the texture, making it smoother and less grainy; and give the flour needed time to absorb liquid in the batter. A rest can be as short as 15 to 30 minutes to be effective, but it can also be as long as overnight in the refrigerator. For a longer rest, baking powder remains potent, but baking soda should be left out and then mixed in thoroughly just before baking.

- If you completely eliminate the white flour in a recipe and replace it with all whole-grain flour, you will generally need slightly less flour than the original recipe called for. Three cups of all-purpose flour becomes about 2¾ cups plus 2 tablespoons of whole-wheat flour. In this case, the total flour has been decreased by 2 tablespoons (¼ cup equals 4 tablespoons).

- Converting a recipe to all whole-grain flour may increase the volume of batter. In a muffin recipe, for example, you may get more than the standard 12 muffins. In a cake recipe, you may need to allow for a slightly longer baking time.

- If you convert a recipe to all whole-grain flour and find the result too dense or "wheaty," try adding 1 tablespoon of orange juice in place of the same quantity of liquid to mellow the wheaty flavor. You can also add back a small portion of all-purpose flour. This will lighten the texture, increase the rise, and add strength to your baked goods ("adding strength," in this case, means your baked goods will hold together and not fall apart).

- Most cakes, banana breads, lightly textured blueberry muffins, and scones can be made with up to 50% whole-wheat pastry flour. Popovers can accommodate half or, for those with a more sensitive palate, about one-third whole-wheat pastry flour. Biscuits and hearty muffins—banana and bran, for example—can be made with all whole-wheat pastry flour. Pancakes and waffles work well with all whole-wheat flour, either pastry or bread, depending on the recipe.

- To achieve a light texture in sweetened baked goods, it's best to mix whole-grain batters until the ingredients are just combined and no longer so as not to overwork the gluten.

- Whole-wheat flour is an ideal match for bananas, so you might begin your experimentation by adding a portion of whole-wheat pastry flour when making banana bread, cake, or muffins.

- Oat flour pairs well with chocolate. You don't need to buy oat flour; simply put a portion of rolled oats (not quick oats) into a spice or coffee grinder and grind the amount you need, taking care to make it extra-fine. Use oat flour in place of all-purpose flour in a fudgy brownie recipe and see what you think (see page 201). Oat flour tends to keep baked goods moist without making them heavy or dense.

- Barley flour is fun to work with because it adds variety to your ingredients list and imparts a pleasing flavor. Since its gluten is weak, it doesn't promote a good rise, but you can successfully add it to recipes for muffins, cookies, and piecrusts. Using too high a percentage will cause baked goods to fall apart; I find it works well to substitute barley flour for up to one quarter of the all-purpose flour in a recipe.

- A final thought: Appreciating the character and integrity of whole-grain flour in baked goods may require our palates to adapt, slowly and over time. Baked goods made with a large percentage of whole-grain flour may not hold their own alongside airy confections made with white flour and refined sugar, but served alone and with confidence, they will be savored and, over time, they may even be preferred.

WHOLE GRAINS

"The most important fact about any food is not its nutrient content but its degree of processing." —Gyorgy Scrinis

While whole grains have gained attention in recent years, they remain an underdog in our modern culinary world—generally unappreciated and, for the most part, overlooked. Yet they can be irreplaceable allies in cooking and baking, especially for the home artisan, because they impart flavors and textures that are more interesting than those offered by refined white grains.

Whether taken alone or as the centerpiece of a meal, whole grains provide a welcome respite from richer foods, filling without overstuffing and satisfying for hours. Even nicer is that they're so easy to share. Whole grains enable generosity—urge us toward it, really—because with little effort we can multiply them, and they handle the challenge of feeding a crowd with economy and ease.

Like most people, my first flirtation with whole grains began with brown rice. Only later did I invite adventure into my kitchen in the form of quinoa, amaranth, millet, buckwheat, and other more exotic grains. If whole grains are new to you, it may help to know that what makes them different from refined white grains is their degree of processing. They come to us nearly as they grow, with their edible parts intact, so their flavors are more complex and they are more nutritious than their white counterparts. What makes whole grains similar to refined grains, however, is that, once you get used to preparing them, you can serve them simply or, if the occasion warrants, dress them into a fancier dish; and incorporating whole-grain flours into baking will add unexpected flair to finished baked goods.

Most of us don't think about whole grains as seasonal foods, but like vegetables and fruits, they're best when we vary our choice and cooking method according to what's happening outside. In colder months, slowly prepared oats, buckwheat, short-grain brown rice, and barley are warming and satisfy well. In the heat of summer, you may prefer uncooked oats (muesli) or a light pilaf of quinoa, couscous, or brown basmati rice. And for a twist in any season, you might consider wild rice, millet, farro, amaranth, or teff, all grains worth getting to know.

It's true that whole grains may, until now, have been an afterthought, but all that we eat, even everyday fare and including the most elemental grain, can be made more flavorful and better for us when gathered and approached with care. You might enjoy sourcing local grains raised by small growers, or heirloom grains that enable you to re-create flavors from generations past. If you have a grain mill, you can grind whole grains like buckwheat or spelt into flour for baking, or you can seek purveyors who mill grains to order. And you can tend the whole grains you cook with consideration for how you might bring out their innate goodness. This, after all, is part of the fun and challenge of handcrafting delicious food.

> We cook and eat quinoa as if it's a grain, so I refer to it that way in this section, but botanically speaking, it's a relative of spinach, beets, and chard and not a grain at all. Similarly, buckwheat is a fruit seed related to rhubarb, though for ease and because of how we consume it, I've included it in this section on whole grains.

In the recipes that follow, I've omitted the section Managing Your Time. The processes are simple enough, and the timing flexible enough, that detailed instructions seemed unnecessary.

FOR BREAKFAST

MORNING MUESLI

SERVES 2 TO 3

Muesli is my favorite year-round breakfast, and one that also happens to make a satisfying lunch, meal on the go, or dinner. The original muesli was developed in the early part of the last century by the physician Maximilian Bircher-Benner, who founded the Bircher-Benner clinic in Zurich, Switzerland. It has seen many incarnations since, including this one. While a crisp apple is a familiar addition, muesli is most special when it changes with the season. Try adding berries in early summer, followed by stone fruits in late summer, and pears in the fall. Use what you have on hand. No matter the combination, this recipe works and will hold you for hours.

1 organic orange
2 apples, unpeeled
1 cup thick rolled oats (not the quick-cooking variety); or ¾ cup thick rolled oats and ¼ cup steel-cut oats
⅓ cup raisins
2 tablespoons hazelnuts
2 tablespoons almonds
2 tablespoons sunflower seeds
⅓ cup plain yogurt
Optional: seasonal fruits or berries, 2 tablespoons freshly ground golden flaxseeds, 1 or 2 bananas, a sprinkling of cinnamon

1. In the evening, finely grate the zest of 1 orange into a bowl. Squeeze the orange juice into the same bowl.

2. Finely grate 1 apple into the bowl, reserving the second apple for morning. (For this task, I rely on a 6-sided box grater and use the side that has small horizontal slits with two small bumps above or below each slit. It best mimics the effect of Swiss apple graters.) The finely grated apple will be almost liquid.

3. Add the oats and raisins to the bowl, stirring until the mixture is well combined. Cover and refrigerate overnight, or for up to 2 days.

4. In the morning, preheat the oven to 350 degrees. Spread the nuts and sunflower seeds on a baking sheet and toast them for 10 minutes, or until golden brown. When they are cool enough to handle, remove the skins from the hazelnuts, and then coarsely chop the hazelnuts and almonds. Combine them with the sunflower seeds, and set aside.

5. Remove the muesli from the refrigerator. Dice the reserved apple into small pieces, stirring them into the muesli mixture. Also add any seasonal fruits or berries you want to include, slicing them into bite-size pieces, if needed.

6. Add the hazelnuts, almonds, sunflower seeds, flaxseeds (if using), and yogurt, and serve topped with sliced banana and a sprinkling of cinnamon, if you like.

Note

- The above recipe might feel ambitious for every day. I often reserve it for special breakfasts and rely on this simpler version of the recipe for everyday use. In the evening, or in the morning at least ½ hour before breakfast, combine 1 cup of rolled oats and ⅓ cup raisins with one finely grated apple and the juice of one orange if you have one. If not, the juice of one lemon also works. Let it sit for

30 minutes on the countertop or, if you're starting in the evening, let it sit covered in the refrigerator. Before eating, add 1 chopped apple, ¼ cup toasted sunflower seeds, ¼ cup toasted, peeled hazelnuts, and ¼ cup whole-milk yogurt. Fresh, seasonal berries or stone fruits, or apple and pear chunks make a nice addition, as do ground golden flaxseed and banana slices. Makes 2 to 3 servings.

BREAKFAST PORRIDGE: VARIATIONS ON A THEME

Serves 2 to 3

Breakfast porridge may seem old-fashioned, but it's a culinary tradition worth hanging on to and an easy way to introduce whole grains into your cooking. The porridge variations described below are uncomplicated and will grow especially welcome as you make them a regular part of your mornings. With each variation, remember that you'll need to soak the grains in the evening if you want to have porridge for breakfast the following morning.

Whole grains, as detailed below
1 tablespoon yogurt, lemon juice, or whey, optional
Pinch sea salt
1 tablespoon butter
Maple syrup to taste
1 tablespoon freshly ground flaxseeds, optional

Specifications by Grain Type:

Steel-cut oats: ¾ cup oats to 3 cups water. Add ⅓ cup raisins during soak. Cook covered for 15 to 20 minutes.

Millet: ¾ cup ground millet to 3 cups water. Grind in a grain mill or in a coffee or spice grinder. (You won't believe the way individualistic millet, whose each grain stands alone, becomes creamy when ground and soaked.) Cook covered for 15 to 20 minutes.

Amaranth: 1 cup amaranth to 3 cups water. Cook covered for 20 minutes.

Amaranth and teff: ⅔ cup amaranth plus ⅓ cup ivory teff to 3 cups water. Cook covered for 20 minutes.

Buckwheat, millet, and oats: 3 tablespoons each buckwheat, millet, and rolled or steel-cut oats plus ⅓ cup raisins to 3 cups water. Cook uncovered for 20 minutes, stirring more diligently toward the end of cooking. Add ¼ cup toasted sunflower seeds to finished porridge.

> Amaranth is remarkable in that it comes to us in two forms, and both are delicious: as a leafy green vegetable that cooks up like spinach or chard, and as a whole grain. It's the latter that we use for porridge, and it's a rich source of protein, fiber, and minerals. On top of that, it has a pleasant and satisfying taste that makes it a good introduction to whole grains.
>
> Teff is a species of love grass (so how can we not take to it?) that originated in Ethiopia. Like amaranth, teff is highly nutritious and a source of iron that is easily absorbed by the body. Ivory teff is better tasting, I think, than its darker brown sister.

1. In the evening, wash the grain of your choice and add it to a heavy lidded saucepan with the quantity of water called for. If using, add the yogurt, lemon juice, or whey. Cover and let it sit on the stove top overnight.

2. In the morning, add a pinch of sea salt and bring the mixture to a boil. Turn the burner to the lowest heat that will still allow a gentle simmer and cook, stirring now and then and following the guidelines for each grain type above, until the water is just absorbed. Turn off the heat and let the grains sit, covered, for another 5 minutes.

3. Add butter, maple syrup, and flaxseeds, if using, and serve warm.

Notes

- All whole grains contain phytic acid in their coarse outer bran layer. Much research suggests that phytic acid binds with the minerals in grains (calcium, magnesium, copper, iron, and zinc) and blocks their absorption by our bodies. So a diet high in unsoaked grains could lead to both mineral deficiencies and bone loss. Soaking grains is a traditional form of preparation that activates the enzymes in whole grains, breaking down their phytic acid and increasing the level of nutrients we are able to absorb. Soaking also improves the flavor of many grains and speeds their cooking. More delicate grains, like bulgur, couscous, and quinoa, need no soaking and yet can still be cooked in little time. Millet is a grain I soak only when I want it creamy for breakfast.

- I always add a spoonful of butter to cooked grains. Its taste complements most grains and adds to their goodness, and its saturated fat is thought to help with mineral absorption.

- Rolled oats are whole oats that are steamed and then flattened between rollers. They are not quite as flavorful as oats that are steel-cut, but they have their own charm, including the ability to cook up quickly after being soaked. Steel-cut oats are whole oats that have been cut during processing. They take longer to cook than rolled oats do, but their flavor is so good that they are worth making time for. Quick oats are rolled oats that are more heavily processed: flattened and thinned to cook in minutes, even without soaking. They become rancid, however, more easily than other oat varieties do.

FOOD THOUGHTS

HEIRLOOM GRAINS

There are everyday whole grains, like those we find on grocery store shelves, and there are heirloom varieties that are worth learning about and experimenting with. Heirloom grains make cooking with whole grains feel more interesting and worthwhile, and they're also better for us and better tasting than many of their modern counterparts.

Heirloom, or Old World, varieties of corn, rice, wheat, rye, and oats, for example, were routinely grown before the Civil War but are scarcely found today. Their flavors are complex and often remarkable, and because these grains perform in ways that modern varieties simply don't, there are some dishes we can't prepare without them.

I know little about our agricultural history, but at some point in time U.S. commercial farmers became dependent on soy, as well as on modern varieties of corn and wheat, to the exclusion of traditional grains that may require more care or that don't produce the large yields that modern industrial strains do. Thanks to the dedication of small farmers, however, heirloom grains like spelt, farro, and black barley, in addition to nearly forgotten varieties of corn, rice, and wheat, have been revived. These grains have interesting stories behind them: tales of teff from Ethiopia, or Appalachian blue cornmeal from pre-Columbian times. Many, like buckwheat, quinoa, and millet, are gluten-free, and most can be grown with fewer pesticides and less water than modern industrial varieties.

It's worth knowing that modern strains of wheat can be especially problematic for our health, and the way they are processed—at high speeds and using high temperatures—makes them more so. Breeding wheat to increase both yield and storage ability has changed it in ways that may explain rising rates of gluten intolerance.

As you begin to enjoy using whole grains in cooking, you may want to experiment with heirloom varieties. Many are visually beautiful and all will add interest to the foods you prepare. An ordinary pearled barley salad and a black barley salad, for example, are far removed from one another—so far that they are hardly the same dish.

Where to find heirloom grains? I've had luck at local farms, farmers' markets, and health-food stores. I also list mail-order sources in "Gathering Ingredients and Supplies" on page 315. Like learning a new word that you then hear spoken almost daily, once you put heirloom grains front and center in your mind, you will come to find them often and in unexpected places.

OATMEAL WITH WARM FRUIT TOPPINGS

Serves 3 to 4

Hearty, whole-grain oatmeal is a warm and nourishing standby, one that's good tasting and relatively quick to make. Oats can be rolled up thin or thick, and with some experience you may find you have a preference. Thin rolled oats cook more quickly, but thick rolled oats are chewier and tastier and, with a soak, still cook in about 10 minutes.

1½ cups rolled oats (not quick oats)
1 tablespoon yogurt, lemon juice, or whey, optional

Pinch sea salt

---

1. In the evening, combine oats with 3 cups cool water in a heavy lidded saucepan. Add yogurt, lemon juice, or whey (if using), and let the oats sit, covered, at room temperature overnight.

2. In the morning, add a pinch of sea salt and bring the mixture to a low boil. Stir and reduce the heat to very low. Simmer, covered, stirring now and then to prevent sticking.

3. After 8 to 10 minutes, turn off the heat and let the saucepan sit, covered, for a few minutes more. Serve warm with Prune-Orange Compote or Warm Maple-Glazed Apples (recipes follow) or other toppings of your choice (see "Notes").

Notes

- You may want to add any of these at the start of cooking: a handful of sunflower seeds; walnuts; raisins; ½ cup peeled, chopped apple; ½ cup peeled, chopped pear; ½ teaspoon ground cinnamon; or ¼ teaspoon vanilla extract. If you choose to add sunflower seeds or walnuts, you may want to toast them. As an alternative, you can soak them in water overnight (apart from the oatmeal) with ¼ teaspoon sea salt. This process is said to make nuts and seeds more digestible, and I find it gives them a pleasant, buttery feel. In the morning, strain the seeds and nuts, discarding the soaking water, then add them to the oats toward the end of cooking.

- To your cooked oats, consider incorporating a handful of dried cranberries, a dash of maple syrup, 1 to 2 tablespoons chopped dates, a knob of butter, or 1 to 2 teaspoons of ground flaxseeds. To ensure freshness, buy flaxseeds whole and keep them refrigerated until you're ready to use them. I prefer golden flaxseeds for their mellow presence, but the dark seeds also work. Before using, grind a small quantity in a spice grinder. You can cover leftover ground flaxseeds and store them in the refrigerator.

PRUNE-ORANGE COMPOTE

Serves 3 to 4

Zest from 1 organic orange
¾ cup pitted prunes
1½ cups freshly squeezed orange juice
1 cinnamon stick
½ vanilla bean, optional

1. Place the first 4 ingredients into a 2-quart lidded saucepan. Check prunes for pits as you do; even though you purchase prunes "pitted," you will often find some still there.

2. If you are using vanilla, slit the vanilla bean in half lengthwise. Using the back edge of a knife, scrape the tiny seeds from both halves into the compote and then add the bean pods as well.

3. Bring the mixture to a boil, lower the heat, and simmer, covered, for 45 minutes.

4. Remove the lid and continue to simmer the mixture, uncovered, for about 10 minutes more. When the sauce is thickened, the compote is ready. If the compote becomes too dry, you can add hot water to correct the consistency. Remove the cinnamon stick and vanilla bean pods (if you used them), and discard.

5. Serve the compote warm over oatmeal or bring to room temperature and store in the refrigerator, covered, for 2 to 3 days.

WARM MAPLE-GLAZED APPLES

Serves 4

2 tablespoons unsalted butter
1 large or 2 small apples—a mixture of Granny Smith and Gala is nice—peeled, quartered lengthwise, cored, and cut into ⅛-inch slices

½ cup maple syrup, divided
¼ cup heavy cream
½ teaspoon ground cinnamon
Pinch fine sea salt

1. Melt butter in a skillet over a medium-low heat.

2. Add apple slices and 2 tablespoons of the maple syrup. Cover and cook until the apples are tender, about 5 minutes.

3. Mix in remaining 6 tablespoons syrup, heavy cream, cinnamon, and salt and simmer, uncovered, for 3 to 5 minutes more—until the mixture thickens and coats the back of a spoon.

4. Serve warm over oatmeal or bring to room temperature and store in the refrigerator, covered, for 1 to 2 days.

MAPLE-NUT GRANOLA

Makes 5 to 6 cups

This granola has been my favorite for years, and it's good whether eaten dry by the handful or served in a bowl with yogurt and fresh fruit. It's easy to make, and one batch lasts for weeks or longer in the refrigerator. You can double the recipe to feed a crowd or if you want a supply that will last for months.

¼ cup virgin organic coconut oil
4 cups rolled oats (not quick oats)
½ cup pecans, coarsely chopped
½ cup almonds, coarsely chopped
½ cup unsweetened, shredded coconut (medium shred works well)
2 teaspoons ground cinnamon
1 teaspoon ground nutmeg
½ teaspoon fine sea salt
Zest from ½ organic orange
¼ cup maple syrup
¼ cup fresh orange juice
¾ cup chopped, pitted dates

1. Preheat oven to 350 degrees, and line a rimmed baking sheet with parchment paper.

2. In warm months, when coconut oil is naturally liquid, skip this step and move on to step 3. In cold months, scoop the solid coconut oil into a small pan and warm the oil on the stove top on the lowest heat until it's melted. Remove from the heat and set aside. (If you melt more than you need, you can add the extra back into the jar—one of coconut oil's most praiseworthy qualities.)

3. In a large bowl, combine the oats, pecans, almonds, coconut, cinnamon, nutmeg, salt, and orange zest.

4. In a liquid measuring cup or small bowl, combine the maple syrup, orange juice, and melted coconut oil.

5. Add the liquid ingredients to the dry ingredients and mix well, completely coating the oat mixture with the oil mixture.

6. Transfer the granola to the baking sheet and spread it in an even layer. Bake for 25 to 30 minutes, stirring 2 or 3 times to be sure it cooks evenly.

7. After removing the granola from the oven, mix in the chopped dates. Let the granola cool, and store it covered in the refrigerator, where it will keep for several months.

I don't pretend to be a great chef; rather, I'm a good and passionate cook and a joyful one. Being a great chef is not the point. I don't cook for status or to earn the admiration of others. I cook because it's a wholesome, meaningful way to spend time and because it's fun, productive, and necessary. It's also one of the truly great satisfactions in life. The meals I prepare are basic and traditional. They're also visually beautiful because I begin with fresh, seasonal ingredients and then doctor them little. I am well fed by the task, and when I share what I make, I nourish others. There's not much in life more gratifying than that.

AS SOUPS AND SIDES

BARLEY AND MUSHROOM SOUP

Serves 8

This recipe features maitake mushrooms, also known as hen-of-the-woods or dancing butterfly mushrooms. They are highly prized for their immune-stimulating properties, as well as their ability to balance blood sugar. The flavor of these mushrooms is robust and earthy; their texture is meaty; and they hold their shape well. If you happen to have other dried mushrooms on hand—porcini, or a combination of dried wild mushrooms—they will make an equally memorable soup and are a fine substitute.

1 cup whole or hull-less barley
1 ounce dried maitake mushrooms
2 tablespoons butter or olive oil
1 large onion, diced
1 teaspoon coarse sea salt
2 celery stalks, diced
1 medium carrot, sliced lengthwise and then crosswise into ¼-inch half moons
½ teaspoon dried thyme, or 2 to 3 sprigs fresh thyme
4 cloves garlic, peeled and thinly sliced
1 pound cremini mushrooms, thinly sliced
2 tablespoons all-purpose flour (if you want to substitute whole-wheat flour, use whole-wheat pastry flour here)
1 bay leaf
2 tablespoons heavy cream, optional
Fine sea salt and freshly ground pepper
2 tablespoons fresh parsley leaves, finely chopped

1. At least 6 hours or up to 24 hours before you plan to make the soup, soak barley in plenty of cool water. Just before cooking the soup, drain the barley and set it aside, discarding the soaking water.

2. Over a small bowl, break the maitake mushroom "fronds" into pieces with your fingers, leaving the center stem (if there is one)

WHOLE GRAINS • 169

whole. If you are using another variety of dried mushroom, there will likely be no center stem. Soak both the stem and mushroom pieces in 2 cups hot water for 30 minutes. Then lift the mushroom pieces out of the soaking water and set them aside. Strain the soaking water and set that aside also.

3. In a large soup pot, melt the butter or olive oil. Add the onion, salt, celery, carrot, and dried thyme, if using (if using fresh thyme, that will be added later), and cook over a medium-low heat until the onion is translucent and the vegetables are soft. Add the garlic midway through cooking.

4. Increase the heat to medium-high and add the fresh and dried mushrooms. Cook them, stirring occasionally, until most of the liquid they have given off evaporates.

5. Turn the heat to low, add the flour, and stir continuously as you cook for 5 minutes.

6. Add the reserved mushroom water, 8 cups fresh water, bay leaf, barley, and fresh thyme (if using) and bring the mixture to a boil. Turn the heat to low, cover, and simmer for 1 hour or until the barley is tender.

7. Remove the maitake mushroom stem from the soup, if applicable, and either discard it or chop it into small pieces and add it back to the pot. It will retain a somewhat firm bite, which you may not mind in soup. If you prefer a more delicate texture, discard the stem without worry; it has already done its work.

8. Add the cream, if using, and season with salt and pepper to taste. Add chopped parsley and serve warm.

BASIC BROWN RICE

Makes 3 cups

Brown rice works well for breakfast, lunch, or dinner, and it can be started ahead of time and cooked in half an hour. Even better, it pairs well with almost any companion on the plate: vegetables, beans, legumes, fish, eggs, and more. While I've been cooking brown rice for decades and in all sorts of ways, this basic approach is still the one I most enjoy.

1 cup short-, medium-, or long-grain brown rice
Pinch sea salt

1. From 6 to 24 hours before cooking the rice, wash and rinse the grains and add them to a heavy lidded saucepan with 1¾ cups cool water. Cover and let it sit at room temperature.

2. When you are ready to cook the rice, add a pinch of salt and bring the water to a boil. Turn the burner to the lowest heat that will still allow a gentle simmer, cover, and cook until the water is just absorbed; this will take 25 to 30 minutes. Turn off the heat and let the grains sit, covered, for another 5 to 10 minutes. This allows the grains to finish cooking while preventing them from sticking to or burning the bottom of the pot.

3. Serve the rice warm or at room temperature.

Notes

- Brown rice is chewier, nuttier, and richer in nutrients than its refined white counterpart. It can be approached seasonally, as the various lengths of grain affect our bodies differently. Short-grain brown rice is rounded and somewhat sticky when cooked; it is warming and so best served in cool weather. Long-grain brown rice is fluffier and cooks up lighter, which makes it ideal in the summer. In moderate weather, medium-grain brown rice might be your preference.

- As an alternative to stove top simmering, you can bake brown rice in a preheated 350-degree oven. In a heavy, lidded ovenproof saucepan, bring soaked rice to a boil. Add a pinch of salt, cover the pot, and place it in the oven to bake for 35 to 40 minutes. Remove the cooked rice from the oven and let it sit on the countertop for 5 minutes more. Uncover the rice, fluff it with a fork, and serve.

- This recipe calls for cooking rice in water, but it works equally well to cook rice in any variety of stock. In addition, you can toast rice dry or in oil before adding water or stock to the saucepan. The process of toasting separates individual kernels, adding texture, enhancing flavor, and imparting a nutty aroma. To toast rice that has been soaked, drain it well, then dry it thoroughly by heating it in the pan before beginning the toasting process.

- In recent years, there has been talk of high arsenic levels in brown rice. The arsenic appears to be absorbed from soil and, even more so, from water, as rice is grown in water-flooded conditions. While we still have much to learn, it seems that soaking brown rice reduces arsenic levels. It's also a good idea to discard the soaking water and then cook rice in plenty of fresh, cool water, just as we do pasta, draining off any excess at the end of cooking. This approach is an alternative to the more precise cooking method described above and it may give a healthier result.

- Brown rice pairs well with other grains in the cooking pot. A ratio that works well is ¾ cup brown rice to ¼ cup other grain, with no change to the quantity of cooking water. Likewise, you can add lentils to brown rice because they cook in about the same amount of time; simply soak and cook the two together. Another brown rice adaptation is to add additional ingredients to the cooking water. You might try dried mushrooms (soak them before adding and use the strained soaking water as part of your cooking liquid), cubed winter squash, or chopped greens (these should be added toward the end of cooking).

- Starting rice in cool water gives cooked grains a creamy texture. Heating the cooking water before adding rice maintains the individuality of each kernel, making this a good way to prepare rice that will become part of a salad or stir-fry.

- Leftover brown rice is easy to reheat. Place about ⅛ inch water in the bottom of a lidded saucepan. Add the rice and sprinkle a small amount of water over the top layer, taking care not to wet the grain too much. Bring the heat up until the water simmers, then turn it to low and cover the pot. Steam for 4 to 5 minutes, toss with a fork, and serve. Leftover rice is also ideal for use in a stir-fry and keeps in the refrigerator for 3 to 4 days.

- This same recipe for cooking rice works for all sorts of grains. You might need more water or an altered cooking time, but once you master this way of cooking grains, it becomes easy to make substitutions.

- There is a method for almost completely removing phytic acid from brown rice. Remember, phytic acid is said to be present in the coarse outer bran layer of most grains, beans, nuts, and seeds. According to obesity researcher and neurobiologist Stephan

Guyenet, to remove phytic acid, measure the quantity of brown rice you want to make. Add cooking water and soak the rice for 24 hours at room temperature. At the end of soaking, pour the cooking water off into a liquid measuring cup and take note of the volume. Save 10 percent of this volume and store it in a covered jar in the refrigerator; then discard the remaining soaking liquid. Add the same measure of fresh water to the rice that you first poured off and cook as usual. The next time you make rice, follow this same procedure, incorporating the reserved soaking liquid as part of the new batch of soaking water. Each time you repeat this cycle, the effectiveness of the treatment will improve until nearly all phytic acid is removed after a 24-hour soak. This process seems to work because soaking cultivates microorganisms that produce phytase, an enzyme that breaks down phytic acid. (I should confess, so as not to put you under undue pressure, that this method can be cumbersome and I most often make brown rice without this step. Still, it's an approach you might want to be aware of if phytic acid is a particular concern.)

ADORNMENTS FOR A BOWL OF RICE

There are many ways to add flourish to a bowl of warm brown rice:

A spoonful of butter

A raw egg stirred into just-cooked rice

A sprinkling of gomasio (see page 293)

A handful of tamari toasted pumpkin seeds (see page 294)

Slivers of toasted nori (cut them with a pair of scissors)

An egg, served sunny-side up; a layer of cooked spinach under the egg is also good

Grated sharp cheddar cheese

Sautéed leafy green vegetables; adding toasted walnuts makes this especially good

A fillet of salmon, panfried in butter, with the butter drizzled over the top of the rice.

DITTO THE BEAN

Nearly every word I have written about whole grains could also be written about their humble relation, the bean, a culinary workhorse and perhaps the ultimate plant food, one that is justifiably a part of almost every cuisine in the world—from the Mediterranean's elegant cannellini and rosy borlotti to Japan's delicate, deep-red aduki. Beans are dependable and sturdy. You can call on them in a pinch because, when dried, they are always ready to do your bidding and in an endlessly adaptable way. One pot of beans can be eaten as is on Monday, glad to take center stage. Then, on Tuesday, you can give it a bit part in a soup, only to enhance its role in a bean spread on Wednesday and a burger on Thursday. What friend bends and gives in this way, and so willingly?

Beans are also glad to take the role of understudy, which is another reason to appreciate them. So many are interchangeable that if a recipe calls for navy beans and what you have are great northern or cannellini, you can substitute them and your meal will still be delicious. Or, if your lentil soup requires French lentils and in your pantry are black beluga, make the substitution and then savor the elegant soup these small jewels help you create. This flexibility makes beans wonderful for the playful cook, or for the one who is caught unawares on a busy day and in need of a fine stand-in.

While beans will acquiesce, generally allowing you to do with them as you wish, there are a few steps you will need to take no matter your ultimate plans for them:

Washing. Before you cook them, all beans need a good rinse. It works best to put them in a bowl full of water and swish. Then pour off the water and repeat until the discarded water runs clear.

Sorting. After you wash the beans, you'll need to sort them by putting them in the cooking pot or on a plate or tray. Sift through them with your hands, discarding any that are cracked. Also, look for small stones, bean wannabes that will try to work their way into your cooking. Discard these as well.

Soaking. Like whole grains, beans contain phytic acid, which is said to bind with minerals and make them unavailable for absorption. You can reduce phytic acid by soaking beans, and this immersion in water also activates the enzymes that break down complex carbohydrates into more digestible starches. This is why soaking beans reduces or eliminates their gassiness. To soak, put rinsed beans in a bowlful of cold water and let them sit for 6 to 24 hours. Your goal is for them to be generally softened. If you find beans uncomfortable to digest, a longer soak will help. On a hot, sultry day, you may want to do this long soak in the refrigerator. If the moment arrives when you find yourself cooking beans on short notice, there's a quick-soak method that can rescue you: After washing and sorting, put the beans in a pot and cover them with water by 3 to 4 inches. Bring the water to a boil and simmer the beans for 1 to 2 minutes. Remove the pot from the heat and let it sit, covered, for 1 hour before proceeding with cooking.

Cooking. No matter which soaking method you use, pour off the soaking water and discard it. This step is key to cooking digestible beans. Then cover the beans with fresh water. In general, use 4 to 6 cups water for each cup of dried beans if you are making soup; use 3 to 4 cups water if you are making the beans as an entrée or side dish. Bring the beans to a boil and skim and discard any foam that rises to the top. Add a piece of kombu, if you like, and about ½ teaspoon coarse sea salt for each cup of dried beans. It's a myth that we shouldn't salt beans until after cooking. Salted beans cook faster, are more tender, and have a deeper, fuller flavor than those cooked without salt. Check the beans from time to time to see if more water is needed; beans should remain submerged during cooking.

A POT OF SOUP THAT YOU CAN MAKE WITH ANY LENTIL, PEA, OR BEAN

"Do you have a kinder, more adaptable friend in the food world than soup? Who soothes you when you are ill? Who refuses to leave you when you are impoverished and stretches its resources to give you hearty sustenance and cheer? Who warms you in winter and cools you in summer? Yet who also is capable of doing honor to your richest table and impressing your most demanding guests? . . . Soup does its loyal best, no matter what undignified conditions are imposed upon it. . . . You don't catch steak hanging around when you're poor and sick, do you?" —Judith Martin (Miss Manners)

SERVES 4 TO 6

2 tablespoons butter or extra-virgin olive oil
1 onion, diced into ¼-inch pieces
1 teaspoon coarse sea salt
1 carrot, cut lengthwise into quarters, and then cut crossways into ¼-inch pieces
2 celery stalks, diced into ¼-inch pieces
2 to 3 cloves garlic, chopped well
Herbs, spices, and additional ingredients as detailed under each bean type

1½ cups lentils, peas, or beans, soaked for at least 6 hours in plenty of cool water (if necessary; see below for each bean type)
1 piece kombu, optional
Fine sea salt and freshly ground pepper to taste
Chopped fresh parsley or basil, fresh lemon juice, optional

Specifications by Bean Type

These are basic variations for making a pot of soup. There are countless ways to experiment and embellish these variations, but even if you stick to basics and leave out the extra ingredients, your soup will be delicious.

WHOLE GRAINS • 179

French, green, or black beluga lentils

Cooking water: 7 to 8 cups

Cooking time: 35 to 40 minutes

Possibilities: Add 1 bay leaf and a sprig of fresh thyme to the soup when you add the lentils. You can also add 1 to 2 cups chopped spinach or green Swiss chard in the last 2 to 3 minutes of cooking; these greens need only enough time to wilt. Soaking lentils is optional, though I generally soak mine before adding them to the soup pot.

Red lentils

Cooking water: 8 to 9 cups

Cooking time: 45 to 60 minutes

Possibilities: Add ½ teaspoon each dried thyme, basil, and oregano when you add the onion. Red lentil soup can also be good with 1 to 2 cups chopped spinach or green Swiss chard (see lentils above). Red lentils should not be soaked.

Green split peas

Cooking water: 9 to 10 cups

Cooking time: 2 to 3 hours, during which you can put your feet up and read a good book or accomplish about half a dozen tasks

Possibilities: Add ½ teaspoon celery seeds when you sauté the onion. Add 1 bay leaf when you cook the split peas. Add ½ pound peeled, diced sweet potatoes or unpeeled blue potatoes in the last hour of cooking. Consider replacing ½ cup of split peas with ¼ cup barley and ½ cup dried cannellini or navy beans. It's best to soak barley, beans, and split peas, and you can combine them in the same soaking bowl.

Cannellini, navy, or great northern beans

Cooking water: 8 cups

Cooking time: About 1 hour

Possibilities: Add a sprig each of fresh thyme and rosemary, as well as 1 bay leaf, when you add the beans. You can also add a 2- to 3-inch piece of fresh Parmesan cheese rind if you like. If you don't plan to make a thick puree, white beans pair well with blanched kale or escarole added 5 to 10 minutes before the end of cooking. It's nice to finish this soup with a squeeze of fresh lemon juice or with freshly grated Parmesan cheese. White beans require soaking.

Black beans

Cooking water: 7 cups

Cooking time: 1 to 1½ hours

Possibilities: Add ½ teaspoon dried thyme and 1½ teaspoons dried oregano when you sauté the onion. If you like the flavor of gentle heat, also add ½ finely chopped and seeded jalapeño pepper at this time. Add 1 bay leaf when you add the beans. Finishing this soup with chopped parsley leaves or cilantro adds a splash of color. A squeeze of fresh lemon juice will brighten the soup as well. Black beans require soaking.

Mung beans

In Traditional Chinese Medicine, these homey beans are thought to stimulate detoxification, and they're one of the most cherished foods in India's Ayurveda healing system.

Cooking water: 7 to 8 cups

Cooking time: 45 minutes to 1 hour

Possibilities: Add a sprig of fresh thyme when you add the beans. As with lentils, you may also want to add 1 to 2 cups chopped spinach or green Swiss chard toward the end of cooking. Finishing the soup with chopped parsley will also enhance the color of the soup. I soak mung beans, but it is optional, as they are easy to digest.

1. In a heavy soup pot, warm the butter or olive oil over a medium-low heat. Adding this small amount of high-quality fat will help capture the essence of your soup, carrying its aroma and personality throughout.

2. Add the onion, which will be the foundation of your soup, and the salt, which will help draw out its flavors. I suggest coarse sea salt because it's less expensive, but fine sea salt will work just as well; simply use a little less of it. If you take your time and caramelize the onion slowly, cooking it gently until the pieces become translucent and then brown, your soup will have a round and robust flavor. You can use this knowledge to affect the intensity of your soup, cooking the onion for less time to achieve a more delicate result.

3. In this step, you have a choice to make. You can add the carrots and celery to your soup shortly after you begin cooking the onion. A longer cooking time will result in a more assertive flavor. Or you can add them to the pot just before the onion is finished cooking and warm them for just a few minutes before adding the water. Again, it depends on how intensely flavored you want your soup to be. This is also the step in which you will add the chopped garlic and most dried herbs, if you are using them.

4. Once the onions and vegetables are cooked to your liking, add the beans (discard the soaking liquid), kombu (if you are using it), and water to the pot. Then bring the soup to a boil, skim and discard any white foam that appears, lower the heat, and simmer the soup, partly covered, for the amount of time listed above. If,

toward the end of cooking, you have more liquid than you want, you can uncover the soup while it cooks to allow for evaporation and a deeper concentration of flavors.

5. As you approach the end of cooking, taste the soup to see if it's ready. The sign you are looking for is tender lentils, beans, or peas. Since cooking times depend on both the type and age of the bean you use, there is no firm rule. A taste will tell.

6. When the soup is ready, remove and discard the kombu and fresh herb stems if you used them. Also, discard the bay leaf, unless you want to follow our family tradition: Whoever finds the "lucky leaf" in his or her bowl gets a kiss and lots of good luck!

7. Taste the soup to decide what else it may need. This is best determined when the soup is not too hot, so you may want to turn off the heat and let it sit, uncovered, for a few minutes. If you made the soup with white or black beans, do you want to puree some or all of them? The easiest way to do this is with an immersion, or stick, blender. Just put it into the pot and puree the soup until you achieve the texture you desire. If you're using a regular blender, be sure the soup has cooled somewhat, and leave the center hole of the lid partly open during blending so the contents don't explode. If you are not going to puree your soup, would it benefit from the addition of chopped fresh greens? If so, stir them into warm soup and allow 5 minutes or so for them to wilt. No matter how you finish the soup, remember to check the seasoning. You will likely need to add salt. Keep in mind, however, that you don't want the taste of salt in the finished soup; you want to use just enough to brighten the flavors and that's it. You might also consider freshly ground pepper, fresh lemon juice, or chopped fresh herbs. Any of these can enliven a soup and finish it with a flourish.

CORN POLENTA: VARIATIONS

Serves 2 to 3

I stayed away from cooking polenta for years because it seemed the antithesis of my favorite handcrafted foods—sourdough bread and yogurt, to name just two. When I prepare these foods, I am able to rely on a team of invisible microbes that move their creation along, requiring little active time on my part. Polenta, on the other hand, necessitated that I stand alone at the stove top, stirring and stirring—that is, until I learned this basic approach by Martha Rose Shulman (followed by several of my own variations) that put an end to interminable stirring. I have enjoyed polenta ever since; it is, perhaps, the quintessential comfort food.

1 cup polenta
4 cups water
1 teaspoon coarse sea salt
1 tablespoon butter

1. Preheat the oven to 350 degrees.

2. In a medium-sized baking dish or lidded pot, combine the polenta, water, and salt. Stir the ingredients to wet the grain, scraping down the inside of the pot to be sure all the polenta is submerged in water. Bake in the oven for 50 minutes.

3. Remove the pot from the oven, stir in the butter, and return it to the oven for 10 minutes more.

4. Remove from the oven and serve immediately.

VARIATIONS

TOMATO SAUCE AND PARMESAN CHEESE

In a medium saucepan, combine one 28-ounce can diced tomatoes, 1 teaspoon dried basil, 2 peeled garlic cloves, 2 tablespoons olive oil, a pinch of red pepper flakes, and ½ teaspoon sea salt. Simmer uncovered for 30 minutes. Puree and season with sea salt and freshly ground pepper. When the polenta comes out of the oven, stir in ¼ cup freshly grated Parmesan cheese. Then spoon the polenta into 2 to 3 wide bowls. Using a spoon, make a slight indentation in the center of each serving of polenta, and ladle in about ⅓ cup tomato sauce. Sprinkle with additional Parmesan cheese and serve.

CREAMY MUSHROOM SAUCE

Wash and slice 8 ounces cremini mushrooms and 4 ounces wild mushrooms. Heat 1 to 2 tablespoons olive oil in a skillet, add the mushrooms with a pinch of sea salt, and cook over medium heat. When the mushrooms begin to release their juices, increase the heat and simmer until their juices cook off. Then lower the heat, add ¾ cup heavy cream, 1 to 2 sprigs fresh thyme, and 1 crushed garlic clove. Cook until the cream thickens into a sauce, stirring occasionally and taking care not to let the cream simmer over. Once done, lift out the thyme sprigs and garlic clove, and season with sea salt, freshly ground pepper, and a pinch of nutmeg. Spoon the cooked polenta into 2 to 3 wide bowls. Make a slight indentation in the center of each serving of polenta, and ladle in a helping of the mushroom sauce. Garnish with chopped fresh parsley and serve.

FRIED EGGS AND SAUTÉED GREENS

Wash a small bunch of green Swiss chard (red chard will color the polenta). Dry the greens well, cut the leaves into bite-size pieces, and set them aside, reserving the stems for another use. Heat 1 to 2 tablespoons olive oil in a skillet and add 1 small chopped onion. Sauté until the onion is translucent, then add 1 to 2 cloves minced garlic; sauté 1 minute longer. Add the Swiss chard pieces and sauté until the greens are tender, about 10 minutes. Transfer the greens to a plate, and in the same skillet, fry 2 to 3 eggs in 1 tablespoon butter. Spoon cooked polenta into 2 to 3 wide bowls. Make an indentation in the center of each serving of polenta, and into each place fresh greens with a fried egg on top. Season with sea salt.

PANFRIED POLENTA TRIANGLES

While the polenta cooks, lightly oil an 8 x 10-inch baking dish. When the polenta is ready, pour it into the baking dish and spread it evenly with a spatula. Let the polenta cool; then cover the dish and refrigerate the polenta for at least several hours or until it firms up. Cut the polenta into squares, then divide each square into 2 triangles. Panfry the triangles in 1 to 2 tablespoons butter or olive oil until they're lightly browned and crisp on both sides. Serve unadorned as a side dish, or use in any of the variations described above.

Notes

- While I prefer to soak most grains before cooking them, I don't soak polenta. Soaking doesn't shorten the cooking time as it does with other grains, and it doesn't improve texture either. In fact, soaking seems to make the texture watery.

- I have found that it works well to cook polenta in a wide, shallow cooking pot with a lid, if you have one. The ample cooking area thickens the finished polenta.

QUINOA IN SHIITAKE MUSHROOM STOCK

Serves 3 to 4 as a side dish

Quinoa is my own version of "fast food," because unlike most other whole grains, it cooks quickly and requires no soak. I prefer the taste and texture of brown quinoa to its red cousin, but you can generally use them interchangeably. Brown quinoa is coated with bitter-tasting saponins, however, that should be thoroughly rinsed off before cooking. Saponins serve as a natural protectant that make brown quinoa taste bitter to birds; as a result, it requires little protection as it grows. Red quinoa, if you use it, does not have the same saponin issue, and so a quick rinse is enough. My own hunch is that because red quinoa is less delicate—sturdier, if you will—it is naturally less palatable to birds and so requires no bitter layer of protection.

FOR THE STOCK:
1 ounce dried shiitake mushrooms
1 piece kombu, optional

FOR THE QUINOA:
2 cups shiitake mushroom stock
1 cup quinoa, rinsed well

1 tablespoon extra-virgin olive oil
1 tablespoon shoyu
1½ teaspoons brown rice vinegar
⅛ teaspoon fine sea salt
¼ cup chopped parsley
Freshly ground pepper

1. In a medium-sized lidded pot, combine the dried mushrooms with 3 cups water, and soak the mushrooms for 30 minutes to 2 hours.

2. Add the kombu, if using, and bring the mixture just to a boil. Lower the heat and simmer, partly covered, for 5 minutes.

3. Remove the kombu and strain the stock, pressing the mushrooms to extract all the liquid. Discard or reuse the mushrooms and kombu,

and pour 2 cups of stock back into the pot. If you have more than 2 cups, save the extra to use in cooking soup, grains, or beans. If you have less than 2 cups, make up the difference with water.

4. Place the quinoa into the pot and bring it to a boil. Lower the heat and simmer, covered, for 20 minutes.

5. While the quinoa is cooking, combine the olive oil, shoyu, brown rice vinegar, and salt in a bowl. Chop the parsley and set it aside.

6. When the quinoa is cooked, turn off the heat and crack open the lid to pour off any remaining stock. Then let the quinoa sit, covered, for 5 to 10 minutes more.

7. Uncover the quinoa, pour the dressing over it, and toss with a fork. Then spoon the quinoa into a serving bowl, add the parsley and freshly ground pepper, and toss with a fork once more.

8. Serve warm or at room temperature.

Notes

- An alternative method for cooking quinoa is to approach it as you do pasta: Boil it in a pot of salted water. After 15 to 20 minutes, test for doneness, strain, and serve.

- Another option for finishing cooked quinoa is to add toasted pine nuts, chopped fresh herbs, and olive oil to coat. Season to taste with sea salt and freshly ground black pepper.

A Quick Approach for Chopping Fresh Parsley Leaves

To easily chop parsley, start by separating the leaves from the stems; the simplest way to do this is to hold a bunch of parsley by the stems in one hand, and rest the leaves on the cutting board. Take a large chef's knife in the other hand, and with the knife at an angle, scrape the leaves off the stems, almost as if you are peeling the parsley. Rotate the parsley so that all the leaves come off onto the cutting board, and you will be left with a handful of bare stems that you can discard or use for making stock. Move the leaves into a pile and chop them until they are as fine as you would like them to be.

IN BAKING

BUCKWHEAT-OAT SCONES WITH ORANGE AND CURRANTS

Makes 8 scones

This is a tender scone, delicately speckled from the buckwheat and mildly sweet. It makes a good breakfast or a fine companion to a mug of tea. Unlike many other recipes for baked goods, this one relies on ingredients that are cold—butter, egg, and buttermilk—to produce a lighter, flakier scone. It also incorporates a short rest for the dough, a whole-grain baking technique that gives the flour needed time to absorb the wet ingredients.

½ cup rolled oats
½ cup buckwheat flour
1¼ cups all-purpose flour
1½ teaspoons baking powder
¼ teaspoon baking soda
¼ teaspoon fine sea salt
1 stick butter, or 4 ounces homemade butter, cold and cut into chunks

⅓ cup currants
Zest of 1 orange
¼ cup maple syrup
1 egg, cold
⅓ cup cold buttermilk, plus extra for brushing

1. Preheat the oven to 375 degrees, and line a baking sheet with parchment paper.

2. In 2 batches, put the oats into a coffee or spice grinder and grind them into fine flour. As each batch is ground, add it to the bowl of a food processor.

3. Add the remaining flours, baking powder, baking soda, and salt to the oat flour in the food processor and pulse to mix.

WHOLE GRAINS • 189

4. Add the butter chunks to the flour mixture and pulse several times until the butter is broken up and dispersed throughout.

5. Transfer the mixture to a medium-sized bowl. Add the currants and orange zest and mix with a fork.

6. In a small bowl or liquid measuring cup, combine the maple syrup, egg, and buttermilk and mix with a fork until the yolk is broken up. Then use the fork to stir the liquids into the dry ingredients until just combined. Cover the dough and let it sit on the countertop for 15 minutes or until the liquids are absorbed. In a warm kitchen, you might want to rest the dough in the refrigerator.

7. Uncover the dough and knead it several times inside the bowl to pick up any stray bits of flour. Then transfer the dough to the countertop and pat it into an 8-inch round. Cut the round into quarters and then cut each quarter in half, giving you 8 triangles.

8. Place each triangular scone on the parchment-covered baking sheet, leaving 2 inches of space around each, and brush the tops with a thin coating of buttermilk. Bake for 18 to 20 minutes, or until the scones are puffed and golden brown.

9. Transfer to a rack to cool. Serve warm or at room temperature.

APRICOT UPSIDE-DOWN SKILLET CAKE

Makes one 10-inch round cake

I adapted this recipe from one published in *Gourmet* magazine, and it has long been my favorite summer cake. It's so beautiful, moist, and delicious that I return to it year after year when apricots are in season and I want to make something special and sweet. The cake is best when made with small, local apricots, rather than with the large grocery store variety, but it is so good and will be so appreciated that you should not overlook the recipe if large apricots are all that's available where you live.

FOR THE TOPPING:
1 stick butter or 4 ounces homemade butter
¾ cup maple crystals
6 to 7 apricots, halved lengthwise and pitted

FOR THE CAKE BATTER:
¾ cup whole-wheat pastry flour
1 cup all-purpose flour
1½ teaspoons baking powder
½ teaspoon baking soda
½ teaspoon fine sea salt
1 stick butter, or 4 ounces homemade butter, at room temperature
¾ cup maple crystals
1½ teaspoons vanilla extract
¼ teaspoon almond extract
2 large eggs
¾ cup well-shaken buttermilk

1. Preheat the oven to 375 degrees.

2. Prepare the topping. In a 10-inch cast-iron skillet (at least 2 inches deep), heat the butter over low heat until the foam subsides. Sprinkle the maple crystals evenly over the melted butter and cook, undisturbed, for 2 minutes. Turn off the heat, and arrange the apricot halves on top of the maple crystals, cut side down. Resist the temptation to fill the pan to the edges with apricots. You will achieve a nicer result by leaving the outer inch or two of the pan

free for cake batter. Depending on the size of your apricots, you may have some halves left over.

3. Prepare the cake batter. Into a small bowl, sift the flours, baking powder, baking soda, and salt. Discard any chaff remaining in the sifter.

4. In a large bowl or the bowl of a stand mixer, combine the butter, maple crystals, and extracts. Beat at medium speed until light-colored and fluffy, at least 3 to 4 minutes. Add the eggs one at a time, scraping the sides and bottom of the bowl after each addition. Mix at medium speed for 2 to 3 minutes until the volume has nearly doubled. Using the lowest mixing speed, add the flour mixture in three batches, alternating with the buttermilk. Beat only until combined, and finish mixing gently with a rubber spatula.

5. Spoon the batter over the apricots and spread evenly, though not quite to the outer edge of the skillet. Place the skillet in the middle of the oven on a rimmed baking sheet to catch any overflow, and bake for about 40 minutes, rotating once. When the cake is ready, a toothpick inserted into the center should come out clean.

6. Turn off the oven, remove the cake, and let it cool in the skillet for 15 to 30 minutes. Then place the cake back into the still-warm oven for 2 to 3 minutes, just long enough to loosen the apricots from the bottom of the pan.

7. Using oven mitts, place a large plate over the skillet and, keeping the plate and skillet pressed firmly together, invert the cake onto the plate. Gently lift the skillet off the cake and replace any fruit that may still be stuck to the bottom of the skillet.

8. Cool and serve.

APPLE CRISP: VARIATIONS

Serves 6

The nature of a crisp is simple: fruit piled high as a bottom layer, baked under a crunchy topping, usually a coarse mixture of oats, nuts, and flour held together with a good quality fat and some sweetener. As for apples, a mix of both tart and sweet is best. One classic and easy-to-find combination is Granny Smith and Golden Delicious, but other apples work just as well and can make for an interesting change. Consider tart apples like Idared, Macoun, Macintosh, Cortland, Gravenstein, Jonathan, or Northern Spy. Sweet baking apples include Gala, Baldwin, and Stayman Winesap.

FOR THE FILLING:
- **6 apples**, peeled and cut into either ¼-inch slices or ¾-inch chunks
- **2 tablespoons whole-wheat pastry flour**
- **2 tablespoons maple syrup**
- **2 tablespoons apple juice**
- **Juice of 1 lemon**, plus zest if organic
- **1 teaspoon ground cinnamon**
- **Pinch fine sea salt**

FOR THE TOPPING:
- **¾ cup rolled oats** (not quick oats)
- **¾ cup whole-wheat pastry flour**
- **¾ cup almonds, walnuts, or pecans**, coarsely chopped
- **½ teaspoon fine sea salt**
- **½ cup maple syrup**
- **5 tablespoons butter**, or 2 ½ ounces homemade butter, softened; or 3 tablespoons melted virgin organic coconut oil

1. Preheat the oven to 375 degrees and set aside an 8 x 8-inch baking dish.

2. Make the filling. In a medium-sized bowl, combine the filling ingredients and pour them into the baking dish.

3. Make the topping. In the same bowl (there's no need to rinse it), combine the topping ingredients. Using your fingers or a wooden

spoon, work the fat into the topping, taking care to fully coat the oats and nuts. For the best flavor and presentation, disperse the fat evenly throughout.

4. Crumble the topping over the filling and bake the crisp for 45 to 60 minutes. You will know it's done when the topping is golden brown and the fruit is bubbling around the edges. If the crisp is brown on top but the filling isn't ready, cover it lightly with foil, shiny side down, to finish the cooking. Serve warm or at room temperature.

VARIATIONS

Here are simple ways to vary and embellish an apple crisp. Keep in mind that since fruit sizes vary, the quantities listed are approximate. What you're looking for is a nice full baking dish of fruit, with room for an ample quantity of crisp topping.

ADD DRIED FRUIT: Combine either ¾ cup raisins or ½ cup chopped dried apricots with the apple juice and lemon juice already called for in the recipe and simmer the fruit, covered, until it's soft. Cool somewhat before adding the fruit and juice to the rest of the filling ingredients.

ADD PEARS AND CRANBERRIES: To 4 medium apples (instead of 6), add 3 medium pears (Bosc, Bartlett, or d'Anjou are nice, and there's no need to peel them) and ½ cup fresh or frozen cranberries. Also add 1 teaspoon vanilla extract and ½ teaspoon ground ginger to the filling.

ADD HARVEST FRUITS: To 3 medium apples (instead of 6), add 3 medium pears (as above, Bosc, Bartlett, or d'Anjou work well and don't need peeling), 1½ cups seedless red grapes, 1 cup fresh or frozen cranberries, 2 teaspoons ground cinnamon, 1 teaspoon ground ginger, and ½ teaspoon ground cloves.

ADD BLUEBERRIES: To 4 medium apples (instead of 6), add 8 ounces fresh or frozen blueberries.

ADD PLUMS: To 5 medium apples (instead of 6), add 8 sliced plums. Italian plums give an especially good result, but all plums work. Also, replace the lemon juice and zest with the juice and zest of 1 orange.

Notes

- Crisps are almost endlessly adaptable. If you're baking for 3 or 4 people, you may want to cut this recipe in half and bake it in 4 ramekins. In this case, you'll need to shorten the baking time to 30 to 40 minutes. If you're feeding a crowd, you can double the recipe and use a large baking dish, keeping the baking time about the same.

- The filling calls for little sweetener because the topping itself is sweet, though keep in mind that if you use mostly tart apples, you may need more maple syrup to balance the flavors. As for the flour in the filling, its purpose is to thicken the juices the apples give off when baking.

- As the ingredients list indicates, the choice of how to cut the apples is yours to make. Chunks have a rustic, down-home appeal and the advantage of taking less time to chop, while slices create a more refined presentation and cook faster.

- To peel or not to peel? This is often a question in cooking and baking fruits or vegetables. This recipe works better if you peel the apples. If you're in a hurry and getting the optimum result is not as important as your time, then by all means skip the peeling. The crisp will be just fine. But one of the qualities of an especially good crisp is the way some of the apples break down and become almost saucy, while others hold their shape. When you include the peels in a crisp, they hold the apples together and stand in the way of this delicious development.

- Step 4 suggests placing the foil shiny side down. This is because aluminum can react with the acid in fruit and can break down, finding its way into your food. The shiny side of foil is more stable, which means it breaks down more slowly than the dull side does. Heavy-duty foil is also said to break down more slowly than ordinary foil does. My usual routine is to place a piece of parchment paper between foil and food, which is another way of addressing this issue.

COCONUT CARROT CAKE

Makes one 9-inch round cake

The fat used in this cake is coconut oil, which makes it tender, flavorful, and dairy-free. You'll want to use virgin coconut oil, which is relatively unprocessed and retains both sweetness and a subtle coconut flavor that really shine in this cake.

¾ cup pecans
½ cup unsweetened, medium-shred dried coconut
1¼ cups whole-wheat pastry flour
1¼ cups unbleached all-purpose flour
2½ teaspoons baking powder
1 teaspoon fine sea salt
1 teaspoon ground cinnamon
¼ teaspoon ground nutmeg
¼ teaspoon ground cloves
1½ cups maple crystals
4 eggs
1 cup virgin organic coconut oil, melted and slightly cooled
4 cups grated carrots
½ cup dried currants

1. Preheat the oven to 350 degrees. Line the bottom of a 9-inch round cake pan with parchment paper. Lightly coat the parchment paper and the inside of the pan with melted coconut oil.

2. Spread the pecans on a cookie sheet and toast them in the oven for 5 minutes. Cool, chop medium-fine, and set aside.

3. In a small dry skillet, toast the shredded coconut over medium heat for 2 to 4 minutes or until lightly browned. Set aside.

4. In a large bowl, whisk together the flours, baking powder, salt, cinnamon, nutmeg, cloves, and maple crystals.

5. In a small bowl, whisk together the eggs and melted coconut oil.

6. Stir the wet ingredients into the dry ingredients, mixing with a

WHOLE GRAINS

wooden spoon until the dry ingredients are just moist. Then stir in the carrots, currants, pecans, and coconut. The batter will be heavy and you will need to mix it with care (it may help to use your hands) to be sure the ingredients are evenly combined. Transfer the batter to the prepared pan and spread it evenly over the bottom.

7. Bake until a toothpick inserted into the center comes out clean, 65 to 70 minutes. Then cool the cake for 10 minutes in the pan before turning it onto a rack, where it should finish cooling.

8. Serve the cake at room temperature. Its flavor improves on day 2, and it can be kept covered on the countertop for up to 4 days.

MINIATURE CHOCOLATE CUPCAKES

Makes 12 miniature cupcakes

These small cupcakes have an intense chocolate taste without being overly sweet. They take little time to make and they are appreciated as much by adults as they are by children.

¼ cup unsweetened cocoa powder, not Dutch-processed	¼ teaspoon vanilla
1 ounce fine-quality (70% cacao) bittersweet chocolate, coarsely chopped	1 large egg
	Pinch fine sea salt
	2 tablespoons whole-wheat pastry flour
⅓ cup pitted dates, coarsely chopped (check for pits and discard)	2 teaspoons butter or virgin organic coconut oil
3 tablespoons maple syrup	*Special equipment:* 12-cup mini-muffin tin
¼ teaspoon baking soda	

1. Preheat the oven to 325 degrees.

2. Place the cocoa powder and chocolate pieces into the bowl of a food processor.

3. In a small saucepan, bring ⅓ cup water and dates just to a boil. Remove from the heat and let cool for a moment. Then add the dates and water to the food processor and pulse once or twice to combine. Uncover the food processor and let the mixture cool for a couple of minutes.

4. Add the maple syrup, baking soda, vanilla, egg, and salt to the food processor and puree until smooth. Then add the flour and pulse until just mixed. Gently finish mixing with a rubber spatula and let the mixture sit for 15 minutes.

5. While the mixture is resting, liberally oil a 12-cup mini-muffin tin with butter or coconut oil. The fat is an ingredient in the cupcakes as well as a lubricant that prevents the cupcakes from sticking, so don't worry if there seems to be an ample amount in each cup.

6. Divide the mixture evenly between the muffin cups—each cup will hold about 1½ tablespoons batter—and bake, rotating once, for about 20 minutes. The tops should be firm to the touch. Let the cupcakes cool in the tin for 10 minutes, then remove the cupcakes to cool on a rack.

7. Serve warm or at room temperature. The cupcakes will keep for 1 day, covered, at room temperature.

COCOA BROWNIES

Makes 16 brownies

To my palate, these are the best brownies: soft, fudgy, and indescribably good. The credit goes to Alice Medrich—she created the recipe and I adapted the process. I also revised the ingredients list to make it healthier. What you'll get is still a brownie, but one you may feel better about eating. Use the finest cocoa powder you can buy: unsweetened and natural. Dutch-processed may also work, imparting a more pudding-like quality, but I always use natural cocoa powder for this recipe. Dutch processing, incidentally, is said to significantly reduce cocoa powder's healthful compounds, known as flavonoids.

½ cup pecan or walnut pieces, optional
1¼ sticks butter, or 5 ounces homemade butter
1¼ cups maple crystals
¾ cup plus 2 tablespoons unsweetened cocoa powder
¼ teaspoon fine sea salt
½ teaspoon vanilla
2 large eggs, cold
½ cup oat flour (see "Note," page 202)

1. Place a rack in the lower third of the oven, and preheat to 325 degrees.

2. Put the nuts, if using, into an 8 x 8-inch baking dish and toast them in the oven: 5 to 7 minutes for pecans and 8 to 10 minutes for walnuts. Transfer the nuts to a cutting board to cool, then chop them coarsely and set aside.

3. Line the bottom of the cooled baking dish with two sheets of parchment paper, one in each direction, with the long ends hanging over. Lightly butter the sides and bottom of the parchment paper.

4. Put the butter in a medium heat-proof bowl (stainless steel works well) and set it over a wide pot filled with 1 inch of barely simmering water. If you have one, you can use a double boiler for this step. When the butter melts, add the maple crystals, cocoa powder, and salt and stir until smooth. Continue stirring until the mixture is hot enough that you want to remove your finger quickly after dipping it in to test the batter.

5. Remove the bowl from the pot of water and set it aside until the mixture cools somewhat. When it's warm but not hot, stir in the vanilla. Then add the eggs one at a time, stirring vigorously after each addition. When the batter looks shiny and well blended, add the oat flour and stir well, until there is no visible trace of flour. Then beat the mixture vigorously with a wooden spoon for 40 strokes. Stir in the nuts, if you are using them.

6. Transfer the batter to the prepared baking dish and let it rest on the countertop for 15 minutes. Then bake the brownies for 25 minutes, or until a toothpick inserted into the center comes out only slightly moist with batter.

7. Cool the brownies in the baking dish on a cooling rack before slicing into 16 squares; if you cut them before they have fully cooled, they will not hold together well.

Note

- To make oat flour, place ½ cup rolled oats (not quick oats) into a spice grinder and grind them until they are finely textured; then use as directed. Using ½ cup rolled oats should give you ½ cup of oat flour. Steel-cut oats may yield slightly more.

VEGETABLES

"The things most worth wanting are not available everywhere all the time."
—Alice Waters

Memorable home cooking is, at its best, based on fresh, seasonal ingredients, and nowhere is this truer than in the realm of vegetables. The beauty and challenge of using them, however, is that every vegetable is unique and, like the people we know, each must be approached with consideration for its innate personality. You cannot interact with a cucumber in the same way you do a parsnip. Their talents and tastes vary and, in the kitchen, their demands differ.

Another challenge, especially when handcrafting foods at home, is that most of us share a wish and a need to serve plenty of fresh vegetables daily and in ways that please. Yet we are already spending time and energy on bread baking and yogurt making—on handcrafting foods that cannot be had any other way.

My aim in including a chapter on vegetables, then, is not to suggest that you undertake the task of creating elaborate vegetables dishes. On the contrary, it is to offer you a new way of seeing how fresh vegetables might fit into your own home kitchen and, at the same time, free you to put your energy where it matters most. There are foods that, if you want them, you must craft by hand and with care because this is the only way; it is the only path to fresh cultured butter, homemade pickles, or other handcrafted specialties. But there are other foods, and I count vegetables among them, that don't necessitate your putting the same level of energy into their preparation.

What I am suggesting is this: Vegetables need to be artfully sourced, and this is where your investment of time and thought might best be spent. As for their preparation, when you bring the vibrant flavors of fresh, seasonal produce into your kitchen, a light touch often works best. So take this chapter as a lesson in strategy. It begins with four easy ways to prepare and serve a variety of vegetables, and if you never go further than that, you will be fine. Just-picked vegetables have incomparable flavors and look beautiful no matter how you serve them. I've also included some of my favorite, yet still relatively simple, recipes for when you want vegetables to play a more prominent role in a meal.

If you're feeling skeptical about your ability to source freshly picked produce, a trip to a farm stand, farmers' market, or community-supported garden can give you a boost. The small window of freedom they offer from grocery-store fare makes these the worthiest of destinations. Of course, buying vegetables locally means buying what's in season, so you may have to do without some of what you've grown used to having. It's generally not possible to harvest tomatoes in New York in January. Yet it's a worthy exercise to learn to love what we have—an attitude and a virtue that will carry over into other parts of our lives.

Rest assured that during each month of the year, it's possible to find vegetables that are filled with flavor, and the gift that platters of fresh, seasonal vegetables bring to us is one of deep nourishment, abundance, and lightness of heart. It's a gift that beckons us daily and joyously to the table.

·············· **A LIGHT TOUCH** ··············

There are hundreds of interesting ways to cook vegetables, but simple is what we are after. Using basic methods to prepare an abundance of fresh vegetables is, in fact, an artisanal approach. This is because the key to preserving their incomparable flavors is to gather these ingredients at their peak and then prepare them simply. A light touch matters most, as it is freshness itself that will elevate your cooking, turning vegetables into memorable meals and side dishes. What follows are four easy and traditional approaches for preparing and serving a variety of vegetables in ways that will best preserve and enhance their unique flavors.

RAW

Carrots, cucumbers, garlic, salad greens, tomatoes

Raw vegetables stimulate digestion, add crunch and texture, and prepare you for the rest of your meal. They're especially good when you serve them properly dressed. Here is an all-purpose vinaigrette, along with ways to adapt it. A general rule of thumb for making vinaigrette is to use 1 part vinegar or lemon juice to 3 to 4 parts oil.

ALL-PURPOSE VINAIGRETTE

Mix 1 tablespoon red wine vinegar with ¼ teaspoon sea salt and a few sprinklings of freshly ground pepper. Then whisk in 3 tablespoons good-quality extra-virgin olive oil and taste. Does it need more salt? More oil? More zing (vinegar)? Taste it as you make it and stop when it seems right. For a twist, consider adding a clove of minced fresh garlic, up to ½ teaspoon Dijon mustard, freshly squeezed lemon juice (instead of vinegar), or fresh herbs like parsley, basil, tarragon, chives, or thyme. Introduce any of these options, except the herbs, before you mix in the oil.

Note

- You may have noticed that certain vegetables are excluded from the "raw" list, and this is because they should ideally be cooked. Cruciferous vegetables (broccoli, cabbage, kale, cauliflower, kohlrabi, and more) contain goitrogens that are said to potentially depress thyroid function. Spinach, beets, and Swiss chard contain oxalic acid that may block your absorption of calcium and iron. You can reduce both goitrogens and oxalic acid by cooking the vegetables that contain them. Raw mushrooms are indigestible and potentially toxic, so these should also be cooked before eating.

STEAMED

Beets, broccoli, cabbage, carrots, fennel, green beans, leeks, parsnips, peas, snap peas, snow peas, sweet potatoes, winter squash, yellow squash, zucchini

Light steaming is a wonderful way to soften vegetables while preserving their "aliveness." I used to have a metal steamer basket that I relied on for steaming vegetables; then one day, on a whim, I bought myself a set of bamboo steamer baskets that wasn't expensive but felt indulgent. The sight of beautifully colored vegetables against the natural bamboo is one I still appreciate.

To steam vegetables, take out whatever steamer basket you have and place it in a pot over 1 inch of water. Cut evenly sized vegetable pieces, about ½ to ¾ inch, and place them in a layer that's not too thick. Then bring the water to a boil. Turn the heat down to low, cover the pot or basket, and steam until the vegetables lose their raw edge but still retain a firm bite. Often 5 to 10 minutes of steaming is enough. For delicate new peas, you'll need less than that, and sturdy vegetables like beets, cabbage, fennel, and squash may require 20 minutes or more.

ROASTED

Asparagus, beets, broccoli, carrots, cauliflower, celeriac, eggplant, fennel, garlic, green beans, kohlrabi, mushrooms, onions, parsnips, rutabaga, sweet potatoes, turnips, winter squash, yellow squash, zucchini

Roasting vegetables is so easy and gives an especially good result, offering concentrated flavors that are more intensely sweet than what you may be used to. To roast vegetables, preheat the oven to 425 degrees. Cut evenly sized pieces—1-inch chunks roast well, but almost any size works—and toss them in a bowl with olive oil and sea salt to coat. There should be no oil left puddled in the bottom of the bowl when you're done tossing. If you like, add sprigs or chopped leaves of fresh rosemary, thyme, or sage. You can also add whole peeled garlic cloves in the last half hour of cooking.

Spread the vegetables and any herbs you are using in a single layer on a parchment-lined baking sheet; if you overlap the vegetables, they will steam rather than roast. Then put the baking sheet into the oven and roast until they are nicely browned and tender—20 to 30 minutes for delicate vegetables and up to 1 hour for sturdy roots—stirring the vegetables once or twice as they cook.

Here are a few specific roasting pointers:

Asparagus: Snap off the thick bottom ends and keep asparagus spears whole for roasting. For an elegant look, use a vegetable peeler to taper the bottom ends.

Beets: Roast beets whole by scrubbing them, wrapping 2 or 3 unpeeled beets together in a piece of parchment paper, and then overwrapping the parchment paper in foil. Increase the heat and roast at 450 degrees for 1 to 2 hours, depending on their size. Beets will be fork-tender when ready. Peel and serve.

Cauliflower: Roast the green outer leaves along with the florets. When roasted, the leaves become crisp and flavorful.

Eggplant: Cut into ¾-inch slices, drizzle both sides with olive oil, and sprinkle with sea salt before roasting.

Fennel: Cut off feathery fennel stalks (you can save them to use in making stock), and slice the fennel in half from top to bottom to make removing the core easier. (For small fennel bulbs, you can skip this step.) Then slice or dice and roast.

USING FRESH GARLIC

The simplest way to peel a whole garlic clove is to place it on a cutting board and, using the flat side of a large knife, press on it gently, so as not to crush it. The skin will crack open for easy peeling. To peel a quantity of garlic cloves, place them into a saucepan of rapidly boiling, salted water and blanch the cloves for 30 seconds. Strain and plunge them into cold water. The skins will practically slip off. To puree fresh garlic, place it on a cutting board, mince it, and sprinkle sea salt over the surface. Then, using the flat side of a large knife, mash the garlic and salt together. After a few minutes of mashing, you will have garlic puree.

If you find a light green shoot inside a clove, remove it before using the garlic; it's the sprout of a new young plant and it imparts a bitter taste. (If you find a shoot inside one clove of garlic, you will likely find it inside all the cloves of that bulb.)

Winter squash: To roast with little cutting, slice the squash in half lengthwise; scoop out the seeds; coat the cut sides with olive oil; sprinkle with sea salt and freshly ground pepper; and place cut side down on a parchment-lined baking sheet to roast. To eliminate cutting entirely, coat a whole squash with olive oil (this draws the heat inward and speeds cooking), place it in a baking dish, and roast. Midway through cooking, cutting the squash becomes effortless. As an alternative, prick the squash with a fork and roast it whole until it's cooked through.

SAUTÉED

Beet greens, bok choy, broccoli*, broccoli rabe*, Brussels sprouts, cabbage, cauliflower*, collard greens, fresh corn off the cob, eggplant, fennel, garlic, green beans*, kale*, leeks, mushrooms, mustard greens*, onions, peas, peppers, snap peas, snow peas, spinach, Swiss chard, tatsoi (Asian mustard green), turnip greens, yellow squash, zucchini

*Before sautéing, these sturdy or strong-flavored vegetables benefit from blanching— steaming or boiling in 1 to 2 cups salted water for 3 to 4 minutes (bring the water to a boil before adding veggies). Then drain well, chop (if appropriate), and sauté.

Technically, to sauté vegetables means to cook them quickly over a high heat in a small amount of fat. So here I am more correctly referring to "sweating" vegetables in a small amount of fat, but not necessarily quickly or over too high a heat, as you don't want the oil to smoke. If it does, it means the fat has broken down and could act as a carcinogen in your body, so wipe your skillet clean and start over. Olive oil works well for sautéing vegetables, as does ghee (see page 291). Butter will often smoke.

To sauté greens, start by removing any thick ribs and tear or cut the leaves into bite-size pieces. To sauté other vegetables, cut them into evenly sized chunks, about ½ to ¾ inch in size. Then place a heavy skillet on the stove top. I like to use a cast-iron skillet, but any sturdy, wide pan with low, angled sides will do the job.

Add enough fat to coat the pan, which will keep the vegetables from sticking. If they start to stick as they cook, add more fat or a tablespoon of water. If you like, add sliced garlic and/or anchovies to flavor your oil. The anchovies will dissolve, and you can remove the garlic to a plate before adding the vegetables; it can be added back at the end of cooking.

Bring the heat up and add chopped vegetables in a quantity that you can toss or stir. If you like, add capers or red pepper flakes and cook them along with the vegetables. Taste the vegetables to determine when they are ready. Previously blanched vegetables should be warm and full of flavor, tender greens take 5 to 10 minutes, and firmer vegetables can take as long as 20 to 30 minutes.

Here are a few additional sautéing pointers:

Collard greens: It works well to discard the ribs and then slice collard leaves into very thin ribbons (chiffonade). Then sauté them, adding water partway through cooking—enough to nearly cover the greens, but not so much that they are submerged. Simmer the greens, uncovered, until the water is nearly cooked off, and serve with a sprinkling of sea salt.

Eggplant: You may notice that eggplant absorbs oil. As a remedy, you can add extra oil to the skillet. Or you can salt the eggplant before cooking to make it less absorbent and easier to cook. In this case, cut the eggplant into cubes, sprinkle it with salt, and drain it in a colander for 30 minutes. Rinse the eggplant, pat it dry, and proceed with sautéing.

Red Swiss chard: Red chard bleeds just as beets do. Keep this in mind if you're adding sautéed red chard to other foods—a frittata or soup, for example. Green chard may be a better option.

A FINISHING TOUCH

Here are easy additions, beyond sea salt and freshly ground pepper, for adding flavor and texture to just-cooked vegetables:

- Toasted fresh bread crumbs. Finely chop one or two slices of bread in a food processor (homemade sourdough bread works especially well), then crisp the crumbs in a skillet with butter or olive oil and sea salt.

- Toasted pine nuts. Place pine nuts on a cookie sheet and bake them at 325 degrees for about 5 minutes. Or toast them in a small skillet on the stove top, stirring until they are golden brown.

- A squeeze of fresh lemon juice or a splash of balsamic vinegar. Add either of these just before serving. If you add them too far in advance of eating, bright green vegetables may darken and appear drab.

- Melted butter and freshly grated Parmesan cheese.

·········· IN SOUP ··········

GOLDEN STAR SOUP

Serves 4 to 6

This light broth is a year-round favorite. You can add nutrients and flavor by including the optional vegetables and herbs (see "Notes"), but it works just as well with only the basics, and most of the ingredients are easy to store in your pantry or the refrigerator for when you need them. Take note that turmeric, which you'll see in the ingredients list, has a long history of use as a powerful anti-inflammatory in both Chinese and Indian systems of medicine. It needs pepper for your body to assimilate it well, so be sure to include the peppercorns (you'll strain them out at the end).

2 tablespoons extra-virgin olive oil
1 onion, peeled and roughly diced
½ teaspoon turmeric
1 carrot, roughly chopped
1 celery stalk, roughly chopped
1 clove garlic, peeled and crushed
½ cup yellow split peas, unsoaked or soaked 6 to 24 hours

6 peppercorns
1 piece kombu, optional (see "Notes")
1 teaspoon agar flakes, optional (see "Notes")
Fine sea salt
2 ounces tiny star or other shaped noodles

1. In a medium soup pot, heat the oil and add the diced onion and turmeric. Cook until the onion begins to soften; then add the carrot and celery, garlic, and split peas. Continue cooking and occasionally stirring until the onion is translucent.

2. Add 8 cups water, along with the peppercorns, kombu, and agar flakes (if using), and any extra ingredients you may want to include

(see "Notes"). Bring the soup to a boil; then lower the heat and simmer gently, uncovered, for 45 minutes.

3. Strain the soup and return the broth to the pot, discarding the cooked vegetables. Add salt to taste.

4. Meanwhile, in a small saucepan, bring 4 cups of water to a boil. Add a pinch of sea salt and noodles. Cook the noodles according to the instructions on the package. Then drain and set aside in a bowl with a bit of soup broth to keep them moist.

5. To serve, fill soup bowls with warm broth and add a portion of noodles to each. If you have leftovers, it's best to store broth and noodles separately in the refrigerator.

Notes

- To add nutrients and flavor to the soup, add any of the following: 1 leek, both white and green parts, roughly chopped; 1 piece Swiss chard, both leaf and stem; 1 small bunch parsley, both leaves and stems; a few sprigs fresh thyme; a handful of green beans; 1 zucchini, roughly chopped; a chunk or two of winter squash.

- Kombu is a mineral-rich sea vegetable that won't change the flavor of the soup but will make it more nutritious by adding minerals. There's no need to wash or wipe kombu. Just add 1 piece, 4 to 6 inches long, to the soup pot when you add the water.

- Agar is another sea vegetable that works as a natural, flavorless gelatin. Adding agar flakes to this recipe gives the broth more body. Because it thickens as it cools, the flakes may cause the refrigerated soup to congeal in the same way that animal-based gelatin does. As with animal-based gelatin, it will become liquid again when warmed.

ZUCCHINI SOUP WITH BUTTERMILK AND FRESH HERBS

Serves 6 to 8

Zucchini is summer's hoi polloi; in July and August, gardeners everywhere will beg you to take theirs. For nothing. Please! But turned into a light soup, zucchini becomes elegant. For a celebratory meal, try garnishing each bowl of soup with a tiny dice of sautéed yellow squash or, later in the summer, sautéed corn kernels and sliced scallion greens. Since zucchini continues to offer up its gifts as summer turns into fall, you can adapt this recipe with ingredients that are warming in chilly weather: butter instead of olive oil and cream instead of buttermilk.

1 to 2 tablespoons extra-virgin olive oil
1 large onion, diced
1 bunch scallions, all the whites and half the greens, sliced into ¼-inch pieces
2½ teaspoons coarse sea salt, divided
2 cloves garlic, coarsely chopped
5 to 6 sprigs fresh thyme
⅓ cup fresh parsley leaves
1½ pounds zucchini, cut into ½-inch-thick slices
2 tablespoons arborio rice
5 cups vegetable stock, divided, or quick stock (see page 278)
2 cups chopped spinach or green chard leaves
⅓ cup buttermilk
Fine sea salt and freshly ground pepper
A squeeze of fresh lemon juice, optional

1. In a large soup pot, heat the olive oil over medium heat. Stir in the onion, scallions, and ½ teaspoon salt. Cook until the onions are soft, 5 to 10 minutes.

2. Add the garlic and cook 2 to 3 minutes longer. Then add the remaining 2 teaspoons salt, thyme, parsley, zucchini, rice, and 2

cups of the stock. Bring the mixture to a boil, lower the heat, cover, and stew for 10 minutes.

3. Add the remaining 3 cups stock. Bring the soup to a boil, lower the heat, and simmer, partly covered, for 20 minutes more.

4. Remove the thyme stems and, if you are making the soup ahead of time, stop here and resume with step 5 just before serving.

5. To the warm pot of soup, add spinach or chard leaves and heat until just wilted.

6. Using an immersion blender, puree the soup until smooth. (If you prefer to use a traditional blender, keep the hole in the lid partially open so pressure from the hot soup doesn't force the lid off and cause the soup to splatter.)

7. Add buttermilk and correct the seasoning with salt and pepper. If you like, add a squeeze of fresh lemon, and serve warm.

SEASONING SOUP WITH SALT AND PEPPER

Every soup recipe seems to end with these words: "Season to taste with salt and pepper." But what precisely does this mean? When it comes to salt, it means you shouldn't taste it in the finished soup. When the soup is otherwise ready, add salt in small increments until the flavor of the soup brightens, then stop. With full attention and some practice, you will know when this has happened. If in doubt, let the soup sit for a few minutes and then come back to it. It's easiest to taste the soup when it's not too hot, and it's best to season it at serving temperature, so let the soup cool somewhat before salting it. If you add too much salt, you may be able to thin the soup with stock, water, cream, or buttermilk.

As for pepper, you need it to give many soups an edge, but too much can ruin the dish. It's best to grind your own from whole peppercorns and, unless you are seeking assertiveness and boldness, add it at the end of cooking.

······· FOOD THOUGHTS ·······

Inspiration

"Cooking is an art and patience a virtue. . . . Careful shopping, fresh ingredients, and an unhurried approach are nearly all you need. There is one more thing—love. Love for food and love for those you invite to your table."

—Keith Floyd

Meals that are shared have a way of punctuating the day, and when those meals are filled with fresh foods, especially generous platters of fresh vegetables, they suggest a degree of caring. Although I know this, I sometimes surprise myself by feeling flat and uninspired when faced with cooking vegetables. It's true that I grow a wide variety in my garden, but it must be for that joy alone, as I don't always get around to cooking them. Like flowers, I keep them for the beauty and fragrance they add to my patch of earth.

My occasional lack of inspiration has taught me that having a reliable method for putting fresh vegetables on the table is essential, because when we learn how to prepare and serve them with ease, we come closer to mastering the art of making good nutrition a pleasure and of elevating a meal from ordinary to special. We all know that vegetables are alive with energy and packed with nutrients that help keep us strong and well. But the way they lift a meal, the way they entice us, is through their essential loveliness.

Have you ever really thought about the dazzle of a ripe, warm summer tomato? Or the softness of fresh baby lettuce leaves, or the way young snap peas dangle just so from their delicate vines? When I tug at a leek in the ground, I'm positive I have never met a more dignified gentleman. And I'm always touched by the surprising generosity of the winter squash that plant themselves yearly as volunteers alongside my fence. I have to race my goats to get them first. I deeply appreciate each one of these vegetables—I just don't want to labor over them. At times, I'd rather meet them in a sunny garden than in my kitchen.

After some reflection, I think I know why I feel this way. I suspect it's because there's so little bang for the buck with vegetables; the time and attention they demand can be monotonous, and they offer few efficiencies. I don't mind hard work in the kitchen, but I want it to be for a longer-lived purpose. When I make a quart of yogurt or bake a loaf of sourdough bread, as I do each week, they last me. But every meal of washing, chopping, and cooking vegetables is followed by another meal of washing, chopping, and cooking vegetables.

> One foundation of cooking well is knowing how to approach ingredients with a keen eye. By this, I mean knowing when and how much to act on ingredients and understanding what is required for each to reach its potential on a plate. I rarely, for example, cook or bake with the fresh strawberries I harvest from my garden because it's not what these berries call for. They are already far too alive with flavor to impose on them any treatment other than washing just before serving. So freshly picked strawberries get no more than a pretty bowl and a topping of lightly whipped cream, and here I see no contradiction with an artisanal approach. Remember, the goal is to start with the finest ingredients and work with them just enough to capitalize on their essence. And if there is any place in the artisanal home kitchen in which it's easy to do this, it's in your treatment of fresh seasonal produce, which is often already nearly the best that it can be.

The process is relentless, reminiscent of Sisyphus and his rock and hill.

This challenge has helped me develop a conviction, and it's one that I live by. When it comes to cooking vegetables, the simplest approaches are often best. Cooking a meal full of fresh foods like these shouldn't have to take hours, especially when I'm already crafting so many of the foods on my table. Since it can be a trick to serve and eat many vegetables, my goal is to reduce the fuss of preparing them. That way I can enjoy them in abundance, for lunch and dinner, and getting them on the table is more fun. Once we come to expect fresh vegetables, a meal without them feels oddly empty, like eating a plateful of air. So while I hunger for vegetables, my goal is to get the most nourishment for the least effort, and I say this with the utmost gratitude for a garden bounty that bursts with beauty and goodness.

CAULIFLOWER AND LEEK SOUP

SERVES 8

This soup is so creamy and good that you won't believe it's made with little more than cauliflower and leeks. I make it as often as I can in the fall and early winter, when cauliflower is readily available at farmers' markets, and I never tire of it. As an option, you can garnish the soup with rosemary-orange almonds (see step 5). The soup feels complete without them, but they do dress it up for a special meal, and the nutty crunch provides a nice contrast to the soup's smooth texture.

FOR THE SOUP:
2 **medium heads cauliflower,** 3 pounds total, separated into florets
2 **tablespoons butter**
6 **small or 3 large leeks,** tough green stalks discarded, white and light-green portions cut into 1-inch pieces and thoroughly rinsed
½ **teaspoon coarse sea salt**
6 **cups vegetable stock** or quick stock (see page 278)
Fine sea salt

FOR THE ROSEMARY-ORANGE ALMONDS:
½ **cup whole almonds with skin,** coarsely chopped
4 **tablespoons butter,** or 2 ounces homemade butter
4 **teaspoons fresh rosemary leaves,** coarsely chopped
Zest from ½ organic orange

1. Add 1 inch of water to the bottom of a large pot fitted with a steamer basket. Place the cauliflower florets into the basket and bring the water to a boil. Lower the heat and steam, covered, for 15 minutes. When ready, remove the cauliflower from the steamer basket and set it aside.

2. Meanwhile, warm the butter in a heavy soup pot over medium

heat. Add the leeks and stir to coat, seasoning with coarse sea salt and cooking until very tender, 8 to 10 minutes. Adjust the heat as needed to prevent browning.

3. Add the steamed cauliflower and the stock to the leeks, and bring the mixture to a boil. Lower the heat and simmer, covered, for 25 minutes or until the cauliflower is soft and cooked through.

4. Using an immersion blender, puree the soup until it's smooth, or use a slotted spoon to transfer the leeks and cauliflower to a blender or food processor and puree them with a little of the stock until smooth. Then return the puree to the pot and add fine sea salt to taste. (If you prefer to use a traditional blender, keep the hole in the lid partially open so pressure from the hot soup doesn't force the lid off and cause the soup to splatter.)

5. Make the almonds (optional). In a small, dry skillet, toast the chopped almonds over medium-low heat, stirring often, until fragrant and light brown, 4 to 5 minutes. Remove the skillet from the burner, let it cool for a moment, then add the butter before returning the skillet to the burner. Lower the heat and cook the almonds for 3 minutes more. Turn off the heat, add the rosemary leaves, and stir once to combine. With a slotted spoon, transfer the almonds and rosemary to a paper towel to drain.

6. Sprinkle the almonds with orange zest and use to garnish each bowl of soup.

BUTTERNUT SQUASH SOUP

SERVES 6

I offer thanks to Myra Kornfeld, who included this simple recipe in her cookbook *The Healthy Hedonist*. As she wrote: "Creamy squash soups sing of autumn." I would add that it sings of winter, too. No matter how many ways I've varied this recipe over the years—and there are a couple of tweaks below that were included by me—I always return to this version that is, in all important ways, her original.

---

1 butternut squash, about 2½ pounds
2 tablespoons butter or extra-virgin olive oil
6 cloves garlic, peeled
1 leek, white and light green parts, washed and thinly sliced
1 teaspoon coarse sea salt

1½ teaspoons ground cumin
1 medium orange sweet potato, peeled and cut into ½-inch rounds
½ cup apple juice or apple cider
Fine sea salt and freshly ground pepper

---

1. Preheat the oven to 375 degrees, and line a rimmed baking sheet with parchment paper.

2. Trim and discard the stem end of the squash. Slice the squash in half lengthwise and place it cut side down on the baking sheet. Bake until tender, 45 to 50 minutes. Remove the squash from the oven and let it cool until it's easy to handle.

3. While the squash is cooling, warm the butter or oil in a medium-sized lidded pot. Add the garlic, leek, coarse sea salt, and cumin and cook, uncovered, until the leeks are softened, about 10 minutes.

4. Add the sweet potato, apple juice or cider, and 5 cups water to the pot. Increase the heat and bring the soup to a boil.

5. While the soup is heating, use a large spoon to scoop the seeds out of the roasted squash and discard them. Then scoop the flesh out of the squash and add it to the soup pot, taking care not to let the hot liquid splatter.

6. When the soup reaches a boil, lower the heat and simmer, covered, for 15 to 20 minutes or until the sweet potatoes are cooked through.

7. Using an immersion blender, puree the soup until smooth, or transfer the mixture to a blender and puree, but keep the hole in the lid at least partially open so pressure from the hot soup doesn't force the lid off and cause the soup to splatter.

8. Return the soup to the pot and season to taste with fine sea salt and freshly ground pepper.

> Whether you start a pot of soup with butter or olive oil, it will taste good. I tend to use butter during colder months because it adds richness to soup and, as a saturated fat, has warming qualities. In warmer months, I most often use olive oil.

FOOD THOUGHTS

CRAFTING A SALAD

Salads made with the bounty of each season have intense and robust flavors; they also have a vitality that can be energizing. In contrast, when we compose salads using out-of-season produce, the flavors lack luster. There is a sameness to our meals and to the months of the year, with little to distinguish December from June, or this week's salad from one we ate months ago. Rich contrasts we may remember from another time and place, from childhood perhaps, are replaced with a steady humdrum of kitchen staples: lettuce and carrots, celery and cucumbers.

It's good to remind ourselves that there is beauty to be found in the salad bowls of every season, and it's more interesting and delicious when our salads reflect and connect us to what's happening outside at this very minute. When they do, they deepen our appreciation for the seasons and the cycles of cooking and eating they bring to our kitchens, and they overlay an order on what would otherwise be a jumble of days.

Autumn and winter, for most of us, inspire long, slow days in the kitchen and make cooking feel leisurely because time is ours in abundance. Salads made from slow-roasted root vegetables suit the mood well. But winter's chill eases into spring and summer, with warm days that inspire simple salads that come together easily, perhaps lightly-dressed greens or sliced tomatoes and basil.

In my work and at home, I savor a variety of salads as the seasons push round and round. A steadfast reliance on autumn's sturdy greens turns into an appreciation for winter's earthy root vegetables, then spring's asparagus and tender baby lettuce, and finally summer's brimming bounty of just about everything. This circling around sustains me, and composing salads in a kitchen that changes as the seasons do helps me move forward in pace with the passing year.

IN A SALAD

SOURDOUGH BREAD AND ROASTED SUMMER VEGETABLE SALAD

Serves 3 to 4

This salad makes an elegant presentation on the table and takes full advantage of late summer's high-season harvest. Who knew stale sourdough bread and ripe garden vegetables could be this good?

3 cups 1-inch-cubed Sourdough Wheat and Rye Bread (page 97) or other hearty day-old bread, hard crusts removed

1 red onion, cut in half through the middle, then into ¼-inch slices cut along the grain

1 red pepper, diced into ¾-inch pieces

1 zucchini, diced into ¾-inch pieces

1 yellow summer squash, diced into ¾-inch pieces

1 small eggplant, diced into ¾-inch pieces

3 plum tomatoes, each cut lengthwise into 8 thin wedges

½ cup extra-virgin olive oil, divided

2 to 3 sprigs fresh thyme, leaves only

3 to 4 leaves fresh basil

1½ tablespoons red wine vinegar

¼ teaspoon fine sea salt

⅛ teaspoon freshly ground pepper

4 ounces goat cheese, crumbled

1. Preheat the oven to 425 degrees.

2. On a large rimmed baking sheet, spread the bread cubes in a single layer and toast, stirring once or twice, until crisp, 5 to 10 minutes. Remove the bread cubes from the oven and set them aside on a plate or cooling rack.

3. Line the warm baking sheet with parchment paper. In a medium bowl, combine the vegetables and tomatoes with ¼ cup of the olive oil and toss to coat. Spread the vegetables evenly across the baking sheet and roast until they're cooked through and starting to brown, 15 to 20 minutes. Remove the vegetables from the oven and set them aside to cool.

4. Finely chop the thyme and basil leaves and place them in a small bowl with the remaining ¼ cup olive oil, red wine vinegar, salt, and pepper.

5. Transfer the roasted vegetables to a serving bowl, pour the dressing over the top, and toss to coat. Add the bread cubes and toss once more. Add the goat cheese and serve at once.

Note

- Although the recipe, as written, is for a salad served at room temperature, it also works to serve it warm. Simply make the dressing and toast the bread cubes first. Then, as a final step, roast the vegetables, letting them cool only slightly and adding them to the dressing. Toss in the bread cubes and goat cheese, the latter of which will melt into the vegetables to create a nice effect.

TRADITIONAL GREEK SALAD

Serves 4 to 6

This simple salad is best in the summer, when long days pull us outdoors and off in many directions. Days like these call for foods that are fresh, light, and easy to prepare. Greek salad is all of these and more.

FOR THE DRESSING:
- 1 teaspoon coarse sea salt
- 2 teaspoons red wine vinegar
- Freshly ground black pepper
- 3 tablespoons extra-virgin olive oil

FOR THE SALAD:
- 1 medium red onion, peeled, cut in half through the middle, and sliced thinly against the grain
- ½ head romaine lettuce, torn into bite-size pieces
- 1 pound ripe tomatoes, each tomato cut into eighths
- 1 cucumber, peeled, cut in half lengthwise, and thinly sliced
- ¾ cup kalamata olives, pitted if you prefer
- 1½ cups feta cheese

1. In a small bowl, combine the salt and red wine vinegar with a dash or two of freshly ground pepper. Add the olive oil and mix well to combine.

2. Place the onion slices into the bowl with the dressing and leave them to marinate for 30 to 60 minutes, tossing now and then.

3. Once the onions have marinated, place the lettuce into a large salad bowl. Add the tomatoes, cucumber, olives, and marinated onions, along with the dressing. Crumble the cheese over the top and toss to combine. Serve at once.

HOW TO WASH LEAFY GREENS

One hazard to relying on really fresh greens in cooking is that, on occasion, a bug might make its way into your food. Since many people find this generally unpleasant, and to the cook it can be embarrassing, here is the best way I know of to wash leafy greens: Fill a large bowl or the bowl of a salad spinner with salad or cooking greens. Then cover them completely with water so that they float (you may have to work in batches to leave enough room for swishing the greens around). Let them sit for a moment or two, to allow any grit to settle. Then lift the leaves out of the water into a strainer; don't pour the gritty water off or the dirt will once again mix with the greens. While the leaves drain, clean the bowl and then place the leaves into it once again. Refill the bowl with water and repeat this same process two more times. When you have cleaned the leaves for the third time, spin them dry, wrap them in a dish towel, and refrigerate until serving or cooking time. If you want to store washed greens for longer than a couple of hours, place them between paper towels inside a resealable plastic bag.

TOMATO SALAD WITH CHIVE OIL

Serves 4

This salad is centered around two ingredients, tomatoes and chives, so the quality of these ingredients matters. If you have them, the salad is beautiful made with colorful heirloom tomatoes. Regardless, really fresh seasonal ingredients are a prerequisite.

1 bunch chives (1 ounce), coarsely chopped into 2- to 3-inch lengths
6 tablespoons extra-virgin olive oil
Pinch fine sea salt, or to taste
4 medium-sized ripe tomatoes

1. Place the chives into the bowl of a food processor.

2. With the food processor running, add the oil through the chute and pulse until the chives begin to break down and are well mixed with the oil. Scrape the sides and bottom of the food processor with a small rubber spatula and pulse once or twice more.

3. Season the chive oil with salt to taste.

4. With a serrated knife, cut the tomatoes into ½- to ¾-inch slices and arrange them on a plate. Spoon the chive oil over the tomatoes and serve.

5. Cover any leftover oil and store it in the refrigerator for up to 2 days.

·Notes

- Tomatoes are best kept on the countertop at room temperature because the refrigerator imparts a mealy texture and will cause them to lose their fresh flavor.

- Chive oil also makes a delicious dressing for warm potatoes.

NEW POTATO SALAD

Serves 8

This is a happy recipe that tastes old-fashioned, conjuring up visions of sunshine and red-checkered picnic blankets. While you can update it by adding roasted beets or baby greens just before serving, I like it best served as is.

2¼ pounds small red potatoes
Pinch coarse sea salt
Juice of ½ lemon
4 hard-boiled eggs, peeled
⅔ cup mayonnaise (see page 295)
1½ tablespoons Dijon mustard
2½ tablespoons apple cider vinegar
⅓ cup finely chopped onion
2 celery ribs (no leaves), sliced into ¼-inch pieces
Fine sea salt
Freshly ground pepper

1. Place the potatoes into a large pot and cover by 2 inches with cold water. Add a pinch of coarse sea salt and lemon juice, which helps keep the potatoes from falling apart as they cook through. Bring the water to a boil, lower the heat to a gentle simmer, and cook, uncovered, until the potatoes are fork-tender, 15 to 30 minutes, depending on their size. Drain and set aside to cool slightly.

2. While the potatoes are cooking, place the egg yolks into a small bowl and set the whites on a cutting board. Using a fork, mash the yolks with mayonnaise and mustard. Set aside.

3. Coarsely chop the egg whites and leave them on the cutting board.

4. Into a large bowl, measure the apple cider vinegar. When the potatoes have cooled enough to handle, slice them thinly, put them into the bowl with the vinegar, and toss to coat. There is no need to peel

the potatoes as you slice them, though it's best to discard any loose peels.

5. To the potatoes and vinegar, add the egg yolk mixture, egg whites, onion, and celery.

6. Season to taste with fine sea salt and pepper and serve chilled.

Notes

- There are many ways to enhance this recipe. Roasted beets, for example, make a good tasting and beautiful addition. With colors that bleed, it works best to add them just before serving. You can also experiment with summer varieties of beet, which come in colors that don't run, adding them in step 5. Dill pickles are nice, and even better if you have homemade pickles on hand (see page 244). Scallions, baby greens, and fresh herbs like chives, basil, dill, parsley, or tarragon also work well in this salad.

- You can substitute white potatoes for red, but the colored skin on red potatoes makes the salad more visually pleasing. You can also substitute larger potatoes for smaller ones; just halve or quarter them before slicing in step 4.

IMPLICIT IN VINAIGRETTE

"I see no reason whatsoever for using a bottled dressing, which may have been sitting on the grocery shelf for weeks, even months—even years. With your own dressing, everything is fresh—the best oil, your own choice of vinegar, fresh lemon—and a really good salad dressing is so quick and easy to make."
—Julia Child

Not all salad dressings are equal, and the ways they differ can be important and altogether unexpected. While quality matters, I am referring to differences that run deeper and are perhaps more significant. There are dressings that empower us, and there are those that undermine our ability to think and do for ourselves. That's a lot to claim about so small a dish. Let me explain.

Over the years, I've enjoyed spending time in Italy, where salad is served daily in every sort of restaurant. Alongside bowls of undressed greens, four ingredients are placed on the table: extra-virgin olive oil, balsamic vinegar, salt, and pepper. The last two are in mills so you can grind them yourself. The offering of these ingredients is based on two underlying assumptions. First, that anyone big enough to eat a salad is also big enough to dress it, without measuring spoons and without a recipe. And second, that our personal preferences vary.

The power to dress a salad—that is, the power to choose and do for oneself—is granted and taken daily. Implicit in the granting is a message so ennobling that it's worth pausing to consider: Without a recipe, anyone can dress a salad using ingredients that are simple and real, and make it taste good. We all have that ability.

How different salads are for many of us, having lost self-reliance in the kitchen to an industry that has reduced personal choice to an array of inferior bottled dressings. It is not too strong to say that this is emblematic of the larger ways, in the realm of cooking, that we have let our power go, giving it to an industry that generally has profit, rather than our well-being, as its motive.

Making a good vinaigrette is a worthwhile step toward self-reliance. It is so easy and takes so little time that I wonder how we've been persuaded to spend money on bottled dressings that cost more and are comprised of mostly poor-quality oils and artificial ingredients.

The concept of a vinaigrette is as simple as combining a fat with an acid, and the ways you can then embellish it are almost endless. You can vary your choice of oil—from neutral to intense, or fruity to peppery. You can alternate vinegars, choosing red wine, balsamic, sherry, or a different acid altogether, like orange or lemon juice. And you can experiment with texture, making your vinaigrette thin or, if you prefer, creamy like mayonnaise. For everyday use, you might rely on a standard recipe of vinegar and oil, combined with shallots, mustard, salt, and pepper. You can also add fresh herbs for color and flavor.

As you experiment with various approaches, keep in mind that quality and proportion matter most. You will want to use a fine fresh oil, delicious vinegar, and good sea salt. A standard ratio is three parts oil to one part acid. Also remember that vinaigrette can be prepared in the moment, or made a day ahead to give the flavors a chance to meld.

Vinaigrette is, most of all, a can-do creation that allows you to imprint your preferences and personality onto everyday dishes. It asks so little and gives so much, and I'll illustrate this point by concluding with a story about my daughter, Rebecca.

One day, when Rebecca was four years old, I asked her to help me finish making a vinaigrette, the one I toss with almost every green salad I make. I needed someone else to taste it. It turns out that Rebecca has an impeccable palate, which I do not. She seasoned and finished it so beautifully that I would no longer dream of making this vinaigrette without her. It has become Rebecca's signature dressing. She makes it for company. People ask her for the recipe and for advice on duplicating her results in their own kitchens. All this from a young girl who doesn't give a whit about cooking.

That's the beauty of vinaigrette; it allows even a child to sparkle and shine. For those of us who let it, it works its magic for us, too.

REBECCA'S EVERYDAY VINAIGRETTE

1 small clove garlic, minced
½ teaspoon coarse sea salt (use half that amount or less if your sea salt is finely ground)
½ teaspoon shoyu (naturally brewed soy sauce)
Scant ¼ teaspoon honey
1 tablespoon lemon juice
3 tablespoons good quality extra-virgin olive oil
Freshly ground black pepper

1. In a small bowl or in a salad bowl, mash the garlic with the salt.
2. Add the shoyu, honey, and lemon juice and mix.
3. Add the olive oil in a slow stream, stirring as you go.
4. Taste the dressing and correct the seasoning. It may need more sea salt or more lemon juice. When you have it right, the flavors will pop. This dressing can be made just before serving, but it tastes even better if you give the flavors several hours or as long as overnight to meld.
5. Grind fresh pepper over the dressed salad just before serving.

CAESAR SALAD TWO WAYS

Serves 6 as a side dish

Here are two ways to make Caesar salad dressing. The first is a traditional method, which bases the dressing on raw egg yolk. With our modern food sensibility, this version begs the question of whether you can instead cook the egg or use a substitute of some sort. You can, of course, because you're cooking to please your own palate and sense of what's good for you, and the result might be very good; it just won't be Caesar dressing. This version is the real McCoy. For the faint of heart, however, I've also included an egg-free "Caesar-ish" salad dressing.

SALAD WITH TRADITIONAL CAESAR DRESSING

FOR THE DRESSING:
1 small clove garlic
3 anchovy fillets
1½ tablespoons fresh lemon juice, at room temperature
½ teaspoon Worcestershire sauce
¼ teaspoon fine sea salt
Freshly ground pepper
Yolk from 1 large egg, at room temperature
3 tablespoons extra-virgin olive oil
2 tablespoons freshly grated Parmesan cheese

FOR THE SALAD:
1 large head romaine lettuce, leaves torn into bite-size pieces
2 tablespoons freshly grated Parmesan cheese
Croutons, optional (see page 237)

1. Place the garlic, anchovy, lemon juice, Worcestershire sauce, salt, and a dash of freshly ground pepper into a blender.

2. Cover the blender and mix on low speed to finely chop the garlic and anchovy fillets.

3. Add the egg yolk to the blender. With the center hole partly open and the motor running on "stir" or on a similarly low speed, blend in the egg yolk. Then, with the motor still running, slowly drizzle the olive oil into the mixture.

4. Pour the dressing into a bowl and mix in the Parmesan cheese by hand. You have the option of covering and chilling the dressing for up to 3 days before moving on to step 5.

5. Fill a salad bowl with romaine lettuce, pour the dressing over the lettuce leaves, and toss. Sprinkle with Parmesan cheese and garnish with croutons, if desired (see next page). Serve at once.

SALAD WITH EGG-FREE CAESAR-ISH DRESSING

FOR THE DRESSING:
1 small clove garlic
3 anchovy fillets
½ teaspoon red wine vinegar
½ teaspoon Worcestershire sauce
½ teaspoon Dijon mustard
¼ teaspoon fine sea salt
Freshly ground pepper
3 tablespoons extra-virgin olive oil
2 tablespoons freshly grated Parmesan cheese

FOR THE SALAD:
1 large head romaine lettuce, leaves torn into bite-size pieces
2 tablespoons freshly grated Parmesan cheese
Croutons, optional (see next page)

1. Place the garlic, anchovy, red wine vinegar, Worcestershire sauce, mustard, salt, and a dash of freshly ground pepper into a blender.

2. Cover the blender and mix on low speed to finely chop the garlic and anchovy fillets. With the center hole partly open and the motor still running, slowly drizzle the olive oil into the mixture.

3. Pour the dressing into a bowl and mix in the Parmesan cheese by hand. You have the option of covering and chilling the dressing for up to 3 days before moving on to step 4.

4. Fill a salad bowl with romaine lettuce, pour the dressing over the lettuce, and toss. Sprinkle with Parmesan cheese and garnish with croutons, if desired (see right). Serve at once.

Notes

- Many classic recipes for Caesar salad dressing include egg white, but I omit it from the Traditional Caesar Dressing because raw egg white is difficult to digest and it's not essential.

- Caesar salad becomes a meal when topped with grilled, baked, or broiled chicken or fish.

Homemade Croutons

Croutons are the ideal finishing touch for Caesar salad, and making homemade croutons takes no more than 20 minutes, which means you can bake them while you're making the dressing. Preheat the oven to 325 degrees. Cut stale sourdough bread or a baguette into ¾-inch cubes. Coat the cubes in olive oil and sprinkle with sea salt, freshly ground pepper, and, if you like, dried herbs like thyme, oregano, or basil. As an option, you can add a clove of minced garlic to the oil. Spread the bread cubes on a tray in a single layer and bake until they're toasted, turning once halfway through cooking; they take about 15 minutes to finish. Homemade croutons also make a nice garnish for a bowl of soup.

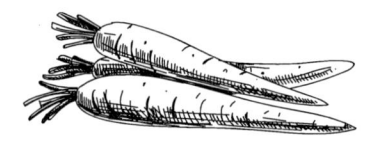

FOOD THOUGHTS

Homegrown

"A tomato grown by a friend has more appeal than one from the store. There is an undeniable beauty in having sprouts and lettuce grown at home rather than shipped across a continent. If we know that our provisions were grown on healthy soil, they are even more beautiful." —William Coperthwaite

There may be few pursuits more gratifying than growing your own food. It's a path to freedom that opens wide the gates that hold you captive to ordinary grocery fare. More special, perhaps, is the way meandering through a seed catalog in deepest winter can lead to a summer garden full of incomparably beautiful and delicious produce.

If you've never grown vegetables, or herbs or fruits, for that matter, you may be reluctant to take on a challenge that feels so ambitious and new. But growing produce doesn't have to be overwhelming. Your pace can be slow and measured and the learning and doing can be fun. There are many plants you can grow in large pots or containers: lettuce, green beans, carrots, tomatoes, berries, herbs, and more. And if you later decide to expand beyond pots, a small garden plot might be enough. No matter the size of your planting space, produce requires six hours of sunlight and protection from deer, rabbits, woodchucks, and the like. These animals don't know how to share.

I can assure you of this: If you have never done it, you cannot fully imagine the deep pleasure you will feel harvesting your first tomato or tugging your first carrot out of the soil—like spinning flax into gold, this turning of seed into food.

If you want to take gardening one step further, you can make compost to enrich the soil. It requires little daily effort, because compost happens whether you do anything or not. All you need are leaves and grass, with food scraps added if you like. As for equipment, a pitchfork for turning the pile is the most I ever use. Composting bins, in my experience, are not nearly as effective as a looser approach. The basic method is simple. Gather leaves into a rectangular-shaped pile. Then add a layer of grass clippings, and another layer of leaves. It helps to sprinkle a handful of lime over each leaf layer, and you can work in food scraps as you have them or build them in as a separate layer.

What about weeds, the albatross of any gardener? One hour a week of active weeding is usually enough to keep them under control in even a large backyard garden. A weed mat positioned under pathway mulch can help.

Keeping a garden or, more specifically, growing your own food, is one of life's enduring satisfactions. Watching seeds turn into sprouts that then flourish in sunlight and rain, and then harvesting mature produce when it is at-the-moment ripe and at its peak nutritionally—this is empowering and never stops feeling like magic. Even better, growing your own means you will always have a gift derived from your own curiosity and hard work to share around your table.

·········· **ON THE SIDE** ··········

SAUTÉED RAMPS

Serves 4

As one who appreciates the inward pull of winter, I greet spring each year with some hesitation. But then April arrives and ramps appear at the farmers' market, and because I'm wild about ramps, I get a little lift, one I need to embrace the new season. If ramps are new to you, imagine a small and slender wild leek with a delicate white bulb that's peppery and oniony. Its long green leaves, when sautéed, balance the bulb's pungent edge. (Ramps, when harvested sustainably, are gathered and prepared without the white bulb and are equally delicious.) If you are anything like I am, ramps will brighten your mood around mid-spring, and if April makes you smile, ramps will give you one more reason to celebrate a season you already enjoy.

2 bunches (8 ounces) ramps
2 tablespoons extra-virgin olive oil
Fine sea salt

1. Trim the hairy roots off the white bulb end of each ramp and discard.

2. Early in the season, when the white bulbs are small and delicate, keep ramps whole and move on to step 3. Mid-season, when bulbs are mid-size, slice into the cut end of each white bulb using an "X" pattern, stopping where the white bulb meets green leaves. Late in the season, when bulbs are large, separate each white bulb from the green leaves. Cut the bulbs into halves or quarters, depending on their size, and set the leaves aside.

3. In a sauté pan or wok, warm the olive oil over low heat. If you are working with whole ramps, add them to the warm oil and sauté until the white bulb is translucent and the leafy greens are well cooked, about 10 minutes. If you are working with bulbs and leaves that have been separated, add bulb pieces to the warm oil and sauté until nearly translucent. Chop the leafy greens or keep them whole, add them to the bulbs, and cook until the greens are wilted and cooked through.

4. Season to taste with salt and serve warm or at room temperature.

Note

- Ramps are in season for such a short while that I rarely look for new ways to prepare them—they aren't here long enough to lose their appeal. There is one variation I'm glad for, however: ramp butter. Begin with 2 ounces whole ramps. Clean them well, trim hairy roots off the white bulb ends, and blanch them for 30 seconds in salted water at a rolling boil. Drain the ramps, and squeeze them or use a salad spinner to remove any remaining water. Chop them as finely as you can, season with sea salt and freshly ground pepper, and combine the ramps with 1 stick, or 4 ounces, softened butter. Ramp butter is especially nice over cooked fish, in mashed potatoes, or as the base for cooking scrambled eggs. It keeps in the refrigerator for 2 to 3 days.

TAMARI GREEN BEANS

Serves 4 to 6 as a side dish

The inspiration for this recipe came from a friend, Audrey Silverberg, and it has been a favorite ever since. It's at its best in the summer when thin, tender green beans are available in backyard gardens and at farmers' markets. But even with autumn's stout green beans, it makes a simple, ideal side dish, one you will call on often.

1½ pounds green beans
1½ tablespoons olive oil
2 tablespoons tamari

1. Snap the stem end off each bean.

2. Fill a wide, lidded skillet or wok with half an inch of water. Bring the water to a boil, add the green beans, lower the heat, and simmer, covered, for 5 minutes or until their color brightens and the beans are just tender.

3. Drain the beans and run cold water over them. Drain again and set aside.

4. Place the skillet or wok back onto the stove top and heat the oil over medium-low heat. Then add the beans and cook, using tongs to turn and stir, for 5 minutes.

5. Add tamari to the green beans and cook, turning often, for 5 to 10 minutes more. Taste the beans to be sure they're as tender as you like them to be before moving on to step 6.

6. Increase the heat to medium-high and cook the beans until the sauce thickens and the beans are well coated, 1 to 2 minutes. Serve warm or at room temperature.

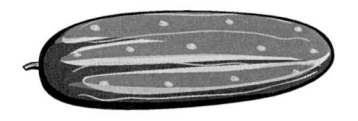

THE ALLURE OF SUMMER PICKLES

As the pace of our days has quickened, we rarely make room for anticipation in our lives anymore. Experiences move past us one after another, with little time to hope or wonder about the future, and even less time to reflect on pleasures of the past. Yet in our flurry, we may be missing an aspect of life that is beautiful and essential. Planning, looking ahead, and preparing for what's to come enlarges our experience and, as it does, deepens every satisfaction.

It pays to look for ways to welcome anticipation back into our lives, and in the summer kitchen, making pickles is one way to do this. The process of making pickles slows us down because it unfolds over days or weeks and can't be rushed. It is a process that has a beginning, middle, and end, and with each phase expectation builds.

There is, of course, a familiar and circular challenge: Making pickles takes time when we have little to spare. But pickle making is unique among many kitchen endeavors in that it allows us to rely on an invisible team of helpmates, the bacterial cultures that make fermentation happen. These cultures move our labors along and toil for us as we tend to other tasks. Once we establish a home for them, we have the pleasure of observing their work—marveling at their bubbles, smelling, poking, and tasting from time to time.

What's better is that if you enjoy being at home as much as I do, you will appreciate experiencing adventure without ever leaving your kitchen because pickle making is an endless source of mystery and wonder. The process is fascinating. It is also the cherished source of a quiet and particular kind of excitement.

MAKING PICKLES

Homemade pickles are easy to make. The recipe is as foolproof as a fermentation recipe can be, which is a confession of sorts. Once a summer, when it's really hot and my kitchen is especially inviting to an army of microbes, I have a batch that fails. The reason why remains a mystery, but then how cucumbers become pickles is a mystery, too.

Here, then, is a recipe for you to use and enjoy. It's my own adaptation of a recipe by fermentation guru Sandor Katz.

3 to 4 pounds small pickling cucumbers
6 tablespoons coarse sea salt
3 to 4 heads fresh flowering dill, or 1 small bunch fresh dill
2 to 3 heads fresh garlic, scrubbed with loose peels discarded and cloves separated (there is no need to fully peel the cloves)

1 handful fresh oak, horseradish, cherry, or grape leaves (I most often used fresh grape leaves)
6 to 8 whole black peppercorns

1. Rinse cucumbers and scrape off any remaining blossoms. If you are using cucumbers that were not just picked, soak them for a couple of hours in cold water to freshen them.

2. In a large bowl, mix the salt with ½ gallon filtered water to create a brine solution. Stir until the salt is thoroughly dissolved and set aside.

3. To make pickles, select a large ceramic crock or use 2 to 3 half-gallon glass canning jars. At the bottom of the crock or jars, place the dill, garlic, fresh leaves, and peppercorns.

4. Place the cucumbers in the crock or jars and gently cover them with either fermentation weights or a plate. Add enough brine to cover the cucumbers by several inches. If you don't have a large enough quantity of brine, mix more using the same ratio of ¾ tablespoons coarse sea salt to 1 cup water.

5. Loosely cover the crock or jars and check for mold every few days. Skim any mold from the surface, but don't worry if you can't get it all. It only matters that it not touch the cucumbers as they ferment.

6. Taste the pickles 7 to 10 days after starting them. If you like the flavor, enjoy them from the crock or jars as they ferment over several weeks. Or remove them and store them, covered, in the refrigerator. In this case, strain the brine you used for pickling and add it to the storage jar, covering the pickles completely. If you are fond of garlic, you can also collect the whole garlic cloves from the crock and cover them with brine *in a separate jar* and store them in the refrigerator to eat as you do the pickles.

Notes

- It is best to make pickles from small cucumbers, usually Kirby, that are the freshest you can find. If they are not recently picked, soak them in cold water to revive them. Fresh Kirbys are easy to get at farmers' markets all summer long. They don't all need to be the same size, but look for the smallest, "tightest" (meaning least juicy) cucumbers and forgo those that are large—even if they are labeled Kirby—as you will not get a good result. Juicy cucumbers are not a pickle maker's friend.

- Since proper crunch is essential, it is important to know that the secret behind it seems to be the tannin in the leaves you add to the pickling crock with the rest of your ingredients. I used to use oak leaves. My preference is now fresh grape leaves.

- Homemade pickles are fermented, and later preserved, in a salty brine. After getting a batch or two of pickles that didn't preserve well, I tried making a fresh brine for storing finished pickles. This new brine ruined the pickles, and I have not yet been able to attain the correct ratio of salt to water for this method to work. To avoid the heartache that comes with ruining perfectly good pickles, strain your pickling brine and use it to store your finished pickles.

- Most pickle recipes call for dill heads; these are flowers that form at the end of dill stalks as they grow in the garden. If you like to grow herbs and you allow your dill to go to seed, you will have all the dill heads you need. If you don't have a garden, you can use a fresh bunch of purchased dill and this will work, too.

- Knowing that beneficial compounds in garlic are released when cloves are cut or crushed, I tried cutting the garlic that I added to my brine, and this approach ruined several batches of pickles. It is not a good idea to create such a potent garlic flavor if you want to keep your friends and family close to you; whole garlic cloves give a more pleasing result.

- Cucumbers are held under weight in the pickle-making crock. It took me years to learn that this weight should not put any real pressure on the cucumbers. On the contrary, it should be placed gently on top, as its only purpose is to submerge the cucumbers under the brine.

- Mold, alas, is part of the pickle-making process. Do not fear it. You can skim and toss it if there's a lot. As long as mold stays on the surface of the brine and doesn't touch the tops of the cucumbers, you will get good pickles. When you are ready to store the pickles, skim the mold. Then strain the brine into your storage container.

- If you want to make a smaller batch of pickles, you can use a ½-gallon glass mason jar. Scale the ingredients down and use a single grape leaf (or leaf of your choice) to cover the ingredients, just under a loose-fitting lid. I get little or no mold growth using this approach. When the pickles are ready, strain the brine and set it aside. Discard all but the pickles. Then rinse the jar, replace the pickles and brine, and store the pickles in the refrigerator.

- In my kitchen, pickles predictably take 10 days to mature. You might eat yours earlier or later depending on the flavor you seek. They improve, for a time, after you store them in the refrigerator. I have had success keeping pickles with their crunch for a couple of months, but generally not longer than that.

ITALIAN BROCCOLI

Serves 4 to 6

The technique with this dish is one you might also use for kale or mustard greens: to blanch or steam the greens and then sauté them. Prepared this way, broccoli is the best that it can be. When making this recipe, be sure not to overlook the stem, as it's really the most flavorful part. You'll need to slice off the woody bottom and peel the outer layer, but what's underneath is worth the extra effort. While you're at it, when you can get freshly picked broccoli, cook the leaves, too—either with the broccoli or in a soup. When tender and fresh, they will only enhance the pleasure this simple dish provides.

1 bunch broccoli (1½ to 2 pounds)
3 tablespoons extra-virgin olive oil
1 large or 2 small cloves garlic, peeled and cut into ⅛-inch slices

Pinch red pepper flakes
Fleur de sel for finishing
Fresh lemon juice, optional

1. Cut off the woody ends of the broccoli stalks and discard them. Separate the stem ends from the florets, and cut the florets into bite-size pieces. Then trim the outer layers of the stem pieces and cut them into ½-inch slices.

2. Place the florets and stem pieces into a steamer basket. Put the steamer basket into a large pot or wok. Cover the bottom of the pot or wok with ½ inch of water and bring it to a boil. Lower the heat, cover the steamer basket, and cook the broccoli over medium-low heat for 4 to 5 minutes, or until the color brightens. Uncover the

steamer basket, remove the broccoli from the heat, and set it aside.

3. In a large sauté pan or wok, warm the olive oil over a low heat. Add the garlic and red pepper flakes and simmer gently for 1 minute. Remove the garlic and set it aside.

4. Increase the heat to medium-low, add the steamed broccoli, and cook for 8 to 10 minutes, tossing from time to time. Keep in mind that, because the broccoli was precooked, there is flexibility with this step; sauté it until it's as tender as you like it to be.

5. Season to taste with fleur de sel. If you like, finish with a squeeze of fresh lemon juice to brighten the flavor. Serve warm or at room temperature.

Notes

- If the broccoli is freshly harvested, you may want to soak it in salted water before cooking, which will cause any hidden bugs to float to the surface. Rinse the broccoli in several changes of cool water before steaming in step 2.

- Another good way to prepare this dish is to substitute butter for olive oil; you may need 1 to 2 extra tablespoons to fully coat the broccoli. Omit the garlic and red pepper flakes and instead add ⅓ cup freshly grated Parmesan cheese in the last minute of cooking. Season to taste with fleur de sel and serve at once.

CRISPY POTATO RÖSTI

"Our garden's earthy signature—the coldness of the ground in spring, the run-off from the alley, water from our hose, and the dirt my father sweetened with manure from my grandparents' farm—was as familiar as the salt I licked from the sun-browned skin on my forearms. They were our potatoes, and I had helped make them. I had seen their beginning in the moon's frail light."

—Lorna Crozie

SERVES 2 AS A MAIN COURSE OR 4 AS A SIDE DISH

The potato is a roustabout among vegetables, the working stiff we rely on yet so often take for granted. All that changed for me, however, when I was in college and on a backpacking trip in Europe. At the end of an open-air train ride through the Swiss Alps, I found myself in the picturesque village of Bergün. It was there that I, famished, stumbled into a small restaurant and was served my first plate of rösti, a humble comfort food so warming and good that I couldn't wait to learn how to make it myself.

1 pound unpeeled Yukon Gold potatoes	¾ teaspoon fine sea salt
1 teaspoon coarse sea salt	Freshly ground pepper
Juice of ½ lemon	2 tablespoons butter, divided

1. Place the potatoes into a large pot and cover by 2 inches with cold water. Add coarse sea salt and lemon juice (lemon juice prevents the potatoes from falling apart as they cook through). Bring the water to a boil, lower the heat to a gentle simmer, and cook, uncovered, until the potatoes are fork-tender, 30 to 35 minutes. Drain, cool,

and refrigerate, covered, for at least 4 hours or as long as 2 days.

2. When you are ready to prepare the rösti, use the large holes of a box grater to grate the potatoes into a mixing bowl. Discard any large pieces of peel that come off, but leave any small pieces in the bowl.

3. Sprinkle the mixture with fine sea salt and a few grinds of pepper and toss with a fork to combine.

4. Add ½ tablespoon of the butter to a nonstick skillet and warm it over low heat. Pour half the potato mixture into the buttered skillet and use a rubber or silicone spatula to flatten and shape it into a large, flat pancake. Cook for about 10 minutes; it should be golden brown on the bottom and crispy around the edges. If it's not, next time turn the heat up or down accordingly.

5. Slide the rösti onto a large plate, taking care to keep it whole. Then cover the rösti with another large plate and flip the two plates over. Add another ½ tablespoon butter to the skillet. Then lift off the top plate and slide the rösti, uncooked side down, into the skillet, cooking for 10 minutes more. When it's ready, slide the cooked rösti onto a serving plate and repeat the process with the second batch of potatoes. If you prefer, you can slide the first rösti "pancake" onto a baking sheet and hold it in a 200-degree oven until the second one is ready.

6. Use a pizza cutter to slice the rösti into crisp wedges and serve warm.

Note

- It is not sacrilege to take liberties with this basic recipe, so have fun and make it your own. Try adding sautéed onions to the potato mixture, or thinly sliced scallions. Or place a thin layer of the potato mixture in the pan, then grate sharp cheddar cheese on top of it and cover that with another thin layer of potatoes. Another option: Add a beaten egg to the potato mixture. All of these possibilities and more will work.

CREAMED SPINACH GRATIN

Serves 6 to 8

Who makes creamed spinach anymore—and with béchamel sauce, no less—except those of us still unafraid of butter and cream? Carry on undaunted! This is old-fashioned comfort food at its best.

3 pounds fresh spinach leaves, stems discarded

FOR THE BÉCHAMEL SAUCE:
2 cups whole milk
3 tablespoons (1½ ounces) butter
3 tablespoons all-purpose flour
Fine sea salt and freshly ground pepper

FOR THE GRATIN:
¼ cup heavy cream
Pinch freshly grated nutmeg
Fine sea salt and freshly ground pepper
1 cup fine bread crumbs
3 tablespoons (1½ ounces) butter, cut into small pieces

1. Preheat the oven to 350 degrees, and set aside an 8 x 10-inch gratin dish or shallow baking dish.

2. Wash and drain the spinach, and with water still clinging to the leaves, transfer it to a large, dry pot. Cook the spinach over medium-high heat, partially covered, using tongs to turn it every so often until the leaves wilt. This will take about 4 minutes for baby leaves and 6 to 7 minutes for large leaves. Drain the spinach, run cold water over it to stop the cooking and cool the leaves; then drain once more. Squeeze the spinach to remove as much excess water as you can and set it aside to dry.

3. Make the béchamel. In a small, lidded saucepan, heat the milk to just under a boil. Turn off the heat and cover the milk so that it

stays warm. In another saucepan, melt the butter over low heat. Add the flour, and stir constantly with a wooden spoon for 2 minutes. Avoid letting the flour brown. In a slow stream, add the warm milk to the flour mixture and, with a whisk, stir continuously until the sauce thickens and any lumps are broken up. Increase the heat and bring the mixture to just under a boil. Then lower the heat and simmer for 5 minutes, whisking occasionally. Remove the sauce from the heat, season to taste with salt and pepper, and set aside.

4. Coarsely chop the cooled spinach leaves and combine them with the sauce and heavy cream. Add a pinch of nutmeg, less rather than more, and season to taste with salt and pepper.

5. Transfer the spinach mixture to the baking dish and spread it in a smooth layer, about ¾ inch deep. Cover the spinach mixture with bread crumbs and dot the crumbs with pieces of butter.

6. Bake for 30 minutes, or until the spinach is bubbling and hot throughout. Broil 1 to 2 minutes, or until the bread crumbs are well browned, and serve hot out of the oven.

Notes

- If you have any slightly stale Sourdough Wheat and Rye Bread, finely chop 2 slices in a food processor. It makes an especially good bread-crumb topping for the gratin.
- The cooked mixture of equal portions butter and flour in step 3 is called a roux. It forms the basis of this and almost any cream sauce, and can also be used to thicken soups.

ROASTED SWEET POTATOES WITH THYME

Serves 3 to 4

These sweet potatoes are easy to make and good to eat. They're crispy on the outside, creamy on the inside, and full of caramelized sweetness.

---

2 medium sweet potatoes (1½ pounds), peeled and cut on the diagonal into ½-inch thick rounds

2 tablespoons extra-virgin olive oil
1 teaspoon coarse sea salt
3 tablespoons fresh thyme leaves

---

1. Preheat the oven to 425 degrees and line a baking sheet with parchment paper.

2. In a medium bowl, combine the ingredients and mix well. Transfer the mixture to the baking sheet and arrange the sweet potatoes in a single layer.

3. Bake for 35 minutes. When ready, the sweet potatoes should pierce easily with a fork and be brown around the edges. Serve warm or at room temperature.

You will feel, most especially, the power of fresh vegetables in elemental dishes like roasted vegetables or sautéed greens. Freshness by itself elevates staple dishes and makes them memorable. As always, the idea is to gather ingredients with care and prepare them simply.

MAPLE-GLAZED BRUSSELS SPROUTS

SERVES 6

This is a perfect side dish to make in the autumn, especially around Thanksgiving, and if you live in the sort of climate where Brussels sprouts grow, you will appreciate the difference freshness makes. That's because Brussels sprouts improve in flavor when harvested in cool, frosty weather. Also, the fresher the sprouts are, and the smaller and more compact the heads, the lighter and better their flavor. If you remember or imagine Brussels sprouts as mushy or bitter, take a chance on this recipe. Properly harvested, stored, and cooked, Brussels sprouts are delicate and far more interesting on the plate than some of their more common crucifer cousins.

2 to 3 stalks Brussels sprouts, or 2 pounds loose Brussels sprouts
¼ cup extra-virgin olive oil
6 tablespoons butter
3 tablespoons maple syrup
1 teaspoon Dijon mustard
1 tablespoon apple cider vinegar
¼ teaspoon fine sea salt

1. If you are starting with Brussels sprouts still on the stalk, use a small, sharp knife to remove the sprouts from the stalk at their base. Wash the sprouts; then use a towel to dry them well.

2. Cut the Brussels sprouts into quarters lengthwise through the base, and set them aside.

3. In a heavy or cast-iron skillet, warm the olive oil over medium heat. Add the Brussels sprouts and toss them to coat with oil. Then let them cook, without stirring, for 2 to 3 minutes.

4. Shake the skillet, or use a wooden spoon or firm spatula to turn

the sprouts. Then add butter to the skillet and let it melt, stirring the sprouts to coat them.

5. While the sprouts are cooking, combine the maple syrup and mustard in a small bowl. Add this mixture to the skillet and stir to coat the sprouts. Continue cooking, stirring every few minutes, until the sprouts are lightly browned and tender but still toothsome. This should take about 10 minutes more. Using a slotted spoon, lift the sprouts from the skillet and place them in a serving bowl, taking care to leave in the skillet any remaining buttery mixture.

6. Add cider vinegar and salt to the skillet and simmer over medium-low heat for a moment or two. Then pour the mixture over the Brussels sprouts and serve warm or at room temperature.

BUTTERNUT SQUASH GRATIN

Serves 6

What I love about butternut squash is its almost endless adaptability, the way it waits patiently on the countertop all fall and winter to bring your imaginings to life. Butternut squash makes a wonderful soup or puree, and it's delicious roasted or in a pie. But on cold winter nights, I think a gratin is an elegant, deceptively simple, and deservedly indulgent way to enjoy this vegetable.

---

1 butternut squash, about 2½ pounds, peeled and cut into ¾-inch cubes
⅔ cup heavy cream
2 to 3 fresh sage leaves
¾ teaspoon sea salt
⅔ cup freshly grated Parmesan cheese, divided

---

1. Preheat the oven to 400 degrees.

2. In a square 8 x 8-inch pan, or in a similarly sized shallow baking dish, toss the butternut squash with the cream, sage, and salt. Cover the squash with a layer of parchment paper, and then cover the baking dish with foil. Bake the squash for 30 minutes.

3. Remove the baking dish from the oven and add ⅓ cup of the Parmesan cheese and stir into the squash. Sprinkle the remaining ⅓ cup cheese evenly over the squash and return the baking dish to the oven, uncovered. Bake for 20 minutes more, or until the sauce is bubbling and the squash is cooked through. Serve warm.

Note

- Cutting squash can be hard on kitchen knives. I find it works best to slice the top and bottom off the squash, and then peel the remaining portion that you will be using. You can then slice the squash lengthwise through the middle, and scoop out the seeds and stringy pulp before cubing the squash for this recipe.

Artfully crafting food becomes easier if you cultivate the habit of observing, and then capitalizing on, nature's rhythms. Learning when foods are fresh and in season, and then basing your meals around what you can get right here, right now, will make food gathering and cooking more interesting. How does squash in the summer differ from squash in the winter, and what does it ask of you that you may not have given before? Try to observe and then respond. If you can stay flexible in the kitchen, and adapt your approaches to seasonal rhythms, your cooking will become more fluid, and this is an important aim for the home artisan.

PURE WATER

Water flows from high in the mountains.
Water runs deep in the Earth.
Miraculously, water comes to us,
And sustains all life.

—Thich Nhat Hanh

....

When one of my daughters was a toddler, each time she sipped water she would sigh with an expression of pure pleasure, an emotion experienced and expressed less often by adults than by children new to the world. It was a charming and reflexive response, and one that might inspire us all.

My sense that we need inspiration stems from the reality that there are many beverages we've grown accustomed to drinking that we would be better off without: sodas and sugared drinks are just two. There is also fruit juice, which is merely concentrated sugar; there can be as much in a glass of orange juice as in a frosted cherry Pop-Tart or a dish of ice cream. Have a look at the labels and you'll see. Even many vegetable juices, if prepared with mostly carrots and beets or if consumed too often, can have more sugar than we would want on a regular basis. They are also missing the fiber that helps slow the absorption of their sugars into the bloodstream.

I recognize that I've blithely cast aside the beverages that seem to quench thirst for many of us, which leaves us with the water that so satisfied my daughter. If you're willing to consider this your drink of choice, or the starting point for your drink of choice, keep in mind that there is no perfect source. Yet it's unlikely you'll go wrong by filtering the water that comes out of your kitchen faucet, and there are many good filters on the market.

As for how much to drink, we've all heard the conventional wisdom that we should consume six to eight glasses of water every day, but for many of us this feels like too much. That may be because a good deal of the liquid we need in a day is provided by fresh foods: soups, beans, grains cooked in stock or water, vegetables, and fruits. A good rule is simply to drink when we're feeling dry.

What follows are little recipes for beverages that will give you a boost when you've fallen low and that use water as a starting point. To call these "recipes" may be an overstatement, because in various versions they have

---

> It's funny to think about "handcrafting" anything made primarily from water. But remember that artisanal cooking is focused on using pure, fresh ingredients to enhance the goodness of the foods that come out of your kitchen. Looked at this way, the connection makes more sense.
>
> It's good to keep in mind, too, that there is nothing real about the beverages that line our store shelves. No mater how costly or how beautiful the labels, these are mostly factory-produced, sugar-laden beverages that have no place alongside carefully crafted food. It's true that wine can be a good choice for the table, but perhaps not always. And so it pays to look at how we might maximize water's essential goodness by using it as a starting point for a variety of simple drinks that are worthy of standing side-by-side with the food on your table.

been around for as long as people have been cultivating and gathering fresh ingredients. The beverages in this section may remind you of the old expression: "There's nothing new under the sun." With regard to many of the foundations of exceptional home cooking and lasting good health, this may be more accurate than we know.

CUCUMBER WATER WITH LEMON SLICES AND FRESH MINT

Makes 1 to 1½ quarts

Cucumber water is especially refreshing on a summer afternoon. There's no need to peel the cucumber, though it's a good idea to use one that is organic or, at least, unsprayed and unwaxed.

½ cup cucumber, peeled or unpeeled and thinly sliced

½ organic lemon, thinly sliced

1 to 2 sprigs fresh mint

1. Place cucumber and lemon slices into a pitcher. Add mint sprigs and fill the pitcher with 4 to 6 cups of cool water.
2. Cover and chill for 2 to 3 hours. Then serve strained or unstrained. If you like, you can garnish each glass with fresh mint or a lemon slice.

STARTING WITH COLD WATER

Water that runs hot from the tap can pick up impurities from the pipes in your house, as well as from the hot-water heater. For this reason, it's always best to start with cool water from the tap, and to let the tap run for a moment or two if you haven't taken water from it in several hours. Letting water run is a good idea because contaminants leach into water, even cold water, as it sits in pipes without moving.

PINK RASPBERRY LEMONADE

Makes 1 quart

This pale pink lemonade is unique in that it uses the whole lemon. This means fewer lemons are needed, and there's no squeezing involved. It also imparts a pleasing bitter edge to the lemonade that makes it somewhat adult and offers a good counterbalance to its inherent sweet and sour goodness.

2 organic lemons, cut into eighths, plus extra lemon juice to taste
⅔ cup maple crystals, plus extra to taste
⅓ cup raspberries
1 to 2 sprigs fresh mint, optional

1. Place the lemon pieces into a food processor and process until they're well chopped and the mixture is juicy.

2. Add the maple crystals and raspberries and process for 5 to 10 seconds. Add 2 cups water and mix for 5 to 10 seconds more.

3. Place a fine mesh sieve over a pitcher and pour the lemonade through it; then pour through an additional 2 cups water.

4. Discard the solids. Taste and correct the flavor of the lemonade, adding lemon juice, maple crystals, or water if needed.

5. Serve, garnished with a sprig or two of fresh mint, if you like.

It's true that local, seasonal ingredients are fresher than their shipped-across-miles counterparts, and they are therefore more flavorful and nutritious. And while eating what's fresh right now is both a principle and a habit, I am known to cheat when I must. This is why there are lemons in my kitchen all year long. Lemons are not local, not seasonal, but of crucial importance and, so, a compromise.

SPARKLING SOUR CHERRY LEMONADE

Makes 1 quart

When you have sour cherries on hand, I know of no better use for them. This is a lively, memorable, beautiful pink pitcher of lemonade, and there's no cherry pitting to contend with because the recipe calls for the whole cherry. Also, note that because this recipe relies on agave nectar for sweetening, the lemonade should not cause blood sugar to spike; this may make it suitable for diabetics or those with blood-sugar issues. If you prefer, you can substitute another sweetener, but expect to increase the quantity, as agave is highly concentrated.

1½ pounds fresh sour cherries
1½ cups fresh lemon juice, strained of pulp and seeds
⅓ cup agave nectar
4 to 5 cups sparkling water
Mint leaves or lemon slices, optional

1. Stem the cherries and place them into a blender. Process them at low speed until they break down.

2. Place a fine mesh sieve over a pitcher and strain the blended cherry mixture through it, pressing to release all the juices. Discard the solids.

3. Add the remaining ingredients to the pitcher, stir gently, and serve garnished with mint leaves or lemon slices, if you like.

Note

• If you want to make this lemonade ahead of time, prepare it through

PURE WATER • 265

step 3, but leave out the sparkling water. Cover and refrigerate the mixture and add sparkling water just before serving. Alternatively, make the lemonade without fizz using regular drinking water, and this way you can make the full pitcher in advance.

THE DIFFERENCE BETWEEN CLUB SODA, SELTZER, AND SPARKLING MINERAL WATER
Club soda is made from water that's charged with carbon dioxide to make bubbles. So is seltzer water. Many brands of sparkling mineral water come by their delicate effervescence naturally from the underground springs that are their source and contain more minerals than the other two do.

ROSEMARY LEMONADE

Makes 2 quarts

This is a lovely, subtle summer beverage; it's also a personal favorite.

1 bunch rosemary sprigs, equal to about 1 cup
¾ cup maple crystals
1 cup fresh lemon juice, strained of pulp and seeds

Lemon slices, optional

1. Place the rosemary sprigs in a small, lidded saucepan and cover with 3 cups cool water. Bring the water to a boil, turn off the heat, cover, and steep for 20 minutes.

2. Using tongs, remove the rosemary sprigs as well as any loose pieces of rosemary from the water, and discard. Add the maple crystals to the hot rosemary water and stir to dissolve.

3. Pour the sweetened rosemary water into a pitcher. Add 4 cups cool water, along with the fresh lemon juice. Chill and serve garnished with lemon slices, if you like.

················ FOOD THOUGHTS ················

SUN TEA

There is little that's easier than harnessing the sun's power to brew a pitcher of tea. The process feels almost primitive, and I mean that in the nicest way.

On a hot, clear day, fill a pitcher or jar with cool water; I use a half-gallon glass mason jar, but any nonreactive container will do. To the water, add whatever tea bags, tea leaves, or fresh herbs you like. Nearly any variety will give you a good result. The goal is to use the sun to heat the water, extracting the essence of the tea leaves in the same way that boiled water does, only more gradually. As a general guide, use either 2 to 4 tea bags, ¼ cup dried tea leaves, or 1 handful fresh herbs for ½ gallon of water. Mint leaves are nice. So are hibiscus flowers or rose hips. My current favorite is a combination of peppermint and hibiscus, but almost any fresh herb will make a pleasing sun tea, so allow your imagination free reign.

Once the herbs and water are combined, place the jar in direct sunlight and keep it there until the tea is as strong as you want it to be; over time, experience will be your guide. On a very hot day, several hours in the sun is usually enough. On a partly cloudy day or on one that is not especially hot, your tea may take up to 8 hours to brew. The timing depends on how strongly flavored you want your tea to be. There is no right or wrong.

When the tea is ready, strain out the herbs, squeezing the tea leaves or bags to extract any remaining goodness. If you prefer sweetened tea, add 1½ to 2 tablespoons good-quality honey to sun-warmed tea and stir until it dissolves. Serve warm or cold as you please.

ICED HIBISCUS TEA

Makes 2 quarts

This zingy herbal iced tea takes only minutes to make, and although hibiscus has the tendency to stain, it's worth taking the risk for—it's that refreshing and good.

6 hibiscus tea bags	1 cinnamon stick
½ organic orange	2 tablespoons honey
½ organic lemon	**Orange slices**, optional

1. Place the tea bags into a ½-gallon pitcher or jar. Add the orange, lemon, and cinnamon stick and set the pitcher or jar aside.

2. Bring 8 cups water to just under a boil. Pour the water over the tea ingredients and steep for 15 minutes.

3. Using tongs, remove the tea bags, orange, lemon, and cinnamon stick. Add honey and stir to dissolve.

4. Chill and serve, garnishing the tea with orange slices, if you like.

GREEN TEA

Serves 1

Green tea gives me a gentle lift each morning, and offers the added reward of being an immune-boosting powerhouse. To get the most health benefits from of a cup of green tea, you'll need to extract the full complement of polyphenols (antioxidants that may help prevent cancer and other diseases). This means steeping tea leaves for about 10 minutes per cup. Although optimum steeping time depends, in part, on the tea leaves you're using, my experience is that this approach works beautifully with fine-quality Japanese or Chinese green tea leaves. But if you're drinking the sort of green tea sold in most grocery stores, this long steep may cause the tea to be bitter. In this case, try steeping the same tea leaves three different times over the course of a day, for about 3 minutes each time, to maximize the health benefits.

Keep in mind that, with this last approach, only the first cup of tea is fully caffeinated. This is information you can use if you prefer your tea to be mostly caffeine-free. In this case, simply steep tea leaves for 1 minute in just enough water to cover them; then discard the water. Cover the same tea leaves with enough water to make a full cup of tea and allow time for the leaves to steep. Since caffeine is released into water quickly, the tea made from resteeped tea leaves will have little, if any, discernible caffeine.

With or without caffeine, it's best to drink green tea within 1 to 2 hours of steeping to benefit from its full polyphenol punch. Over time, sitting on the counter, it tends to oxidize.

1 teaspoon green tea leaves, or 1 green tea bag

1. Heat 6 to 8 ounces cool water to 140 to 175 degrees (see "Notes").

PURE WATER • 271

2. While the water is heating, put green tea leaves into a ceramic or glass teapot. Or, if you're using a tea bag, put it into a cup or mug. Then pour hot water over the tea leaves or tea bag and steep for 10 minutes. (Keep in mind that tea bags often contain powdery leaf "dust" that requires less steeping time than tea leaves do.) If you're using a tea bag, move it up and down in the mug as it steeps to increase the extraction of polyphenols.

3. Strain the tea into a cup or mug, or if you're using a tea bag, remove it. Enjoy your tea within 1 to 2 hours.

Notes

- Water temperature plays a meaningful role in eliciting optimum flavor from tea leaves. Too hot, and water tends to "cook" leaves and make green tea bitter; it can also destroy the delicate aroma of green tea. Yet heat is needed to extract polyphenols and flavor, so it's a balancing act. As a general guideline, it's best to brew green tea in water ranging from 140 to 175 degrees. The ideal temperature for each variety of tea will depend on when the leaves were harvested and on the grade of tea. It may work best to experiment, brewing leaves for 2 to 3 minutes at 140 degrees, and then increasing the time and temperature until you get the cup of tea you like best. In general, steeping time and water temperature should be balanced: The lower the water temperature, the longer you can steep the leaves.

- Many tea merchants believe that Japanese green teas are generally best steeped for 2 minutes, and Chinese green teas for 3 minutes. This is because Japanese green tea leaves are smaller, so their essence can be extracted more quickly. These experts, however, are most concerned with the ideal treatment of tea leaves for flavor rather than health benefits; the latter would require a longer steeping time. For years, I have also read that nearly all caffeine in tea is fully extracted in the first 30 seconds of steeping. Tea merchants suggest that it takes 8 minutes of steeping to remove caffeine from tea leaves. My own experience is that discarding the tea I extract in the first 60 seconds of steeping, and then resteeping the leaves, gives me a tea with no discernible caffeine. The beauty of differences of opinion like these is that they free you to exert dominion over your own pot of tea, so experiment and decide for yourself.

GINGER TEA

Serves 1

If you want a tea that's caffeine-free, good for digestion, and nice for a change of pace, this may be what you're looking for. It's my own version of Korean ginger tea, and I never tire of drinking it. You can serve ginger tea simply or, for a special occasion, garnish each serving with thin slivers of fresh ginger and a spoonful of lightly toasted pine nuts.

½ **cinnamon stick**
1 knob fresh ginger, peeled and thinly sliced (about 2 teaspoons), plus extra for garnish
Honey, optional

Toasted pine nuts, optional

1. Into a small, lidded saucepan, place the cinnamon stick and sliced ginger. Cover with 15 ounces cool water and bring to a boil. Lower the heat, cover, and simmer gently for 30 minutes.

2. Strain the tea, add honey to taste, if you like, and garnish with slivers of fresh ginger and toasted pine nuts. Serve warm or at room temperature.

BY YOUR OWN HAND

"The only real stumbling block is fear of failure. In cooking you've got to have a what-the-hell attitude." —Julia Child

Handcrafting basic staples for the kitchen—like stocks, sauces, spreads, and condiments—can move your food from good to exceptional by adding to it layers of personality and flavor. When made with fresh ingredients, these homemade extras brighten a plate and enliven a meal, with the bonus of being easier to prepare than you might expect. These elements are often left out of home cooking, perhaps because they seem too time-consuming to make, yet you can pull most together in minutes rather than hours. In the case of stocks, they practically make themselves once you assemble the ingredients. Homemade staples are worth extending yourself for because knowing how to make them, and when and how to use them, will elevate your cooking a notch or two. It will also reward you with the ability to create more memorable meals.

It's interesting to note that kitchen staples may themselves be more important than the foods you put them on or with. I've always viewed the banana bread I bake as a vehicle for the ricotta spread I gladly slather over it; in fact, I make the spread first and the banana bread as an afterthought. And an everyday omelet beautifully showcases fresh, homemade tomato sauce, not the other way around.

What's wonderful is that many of the recipes presented here involve cooking on such a small scale that they provide the perfect opportunity, a training ground, if you will, for shifting your focus to finding the freshest ingredients you can and preparing them well. You will also become skilled at pairing them with compatible dishes, so experimenting with handcrafted staples is your chance to be a culinary matchmaker.

Unlike other foods made with fresh ingredients, many of these recipes keep well, some for weeks or even months. This quality gives you the ability to work magic, to pull a rabbit out of a hat, producing a stock or condiment from the refrigerator when its qualities are exactly those needed to add kick to a dish.

This ability to wait and be ready is unique to these elements, and it makes them valuable commodities in the home kitchen. Without your exerting much effort in the moment, they perk up a bowl of brown rice with chicken stock one night and toasted pumpkin seeds the next. They also add nutrition to our meals with the vegetables, herbs, seeds, nuts, cheese, and meat they're often made from.

What may be most worth appreciating, however, is the way these handmade staples bring all corners of the world into the kitchen. Gomasio from Japan, pesto and olive spread from the Mediterranean, and barbeque sauce from Mongolia open wide the doors of our homes and welcome the influence of many cultures. They offer up the grace of the finishing touch to Asia one night and the Middle East the next. There's a refreshing openness to this way of crafting meals.

VEGETABLE STOCK

Vegetable stock, when seen with fresh eyes, can be a lovely piece of culinary music, an improvisation rather than a classical composition, developed note by note from that which you once readily tossed away. As vegetable odds and ends sit on the countertop, there is nothing to suggest the possibility of a transformation. But, as with music, when you lift your attention from the individual notes and appreciate the larger whole, you tap into a melody.

Like any piece of music, vegetable stock can have a "long line," or theme around which it is built: It might emphasize mushrooms, asparagus, garlic, or leeks. Or you can improvise a less formal melody, a stock to suit any mood or purpose. Either way, vegetable stock will fill your kitchen with a heavenly aroma that, like music's pure notes, might just wend its way into the secret places inside of you.

Makes 4 to 6 cups

1 onion, loose outer layers peeled, cut in half through the middle in either direction
Carrot pieces, equal to about 2 whole carrots
Celery pieces, equal to about 2 celery stalks
4 to 6 cloves garlic, crushed and loose outer layers peeled
4 to 6 whole peppercorns
Small handful parsley leaves or stems
2 to 3 thyme sprigs
1 bay leaf

1. Warm a heavy soup pot over medium-low heat. Place the cut sides of the onion halves facedown in the dry soup pot and cook them for 5 to 10 minutes, or until the cut sides are lightly browned.

2. Add 8 cups water, along with the remaining ingredients, including

any optional ingredients (see "Notes"). Bring the stock just to a boil, lower the heat, and simmer very gently, uncovered, for 45 to 60 minutes.

3. Strain the stock and use it at once. You can also cover and refrigerate it for up to 5 days. Broth keeps frozen for up to 6 months.

QUICK STOCK

There is a meaningful difference between stock that you make yourself and stock that you buy. Even so, making homemade stock can take time you may not always have. When you begin a soup recipe that calls for vegetable stock, try this shortcut for making stock as you prepare your soup. Simply follow your soup recipe and, where the recipe calls for "stock," add the same amount of water plus 1 onion, 1 carrot, 1 celery stalk, and a few parsley stems or thyme sprigs. You can also add 1 to 2 crushed garlic cloves. Use tongs to lift these ingredients out when the soup has finished cooking, and you will have soup made with homemade stock.

Notes

- As you cook with vegetables, their tops and bottoms will crowd your counter or compost bin. Both tradition and thrift suggest that you put these lost treasures to use, making something, in a sense, from almost nothing. Turning scraps into stock will stretch your food dollars; add layers of flavor, easy-to-assimilate nutrients, and living energy to the foods you cook; and give you full control over your ingredients list.

- There are many optional ingredients you can add in step 2: leek pieces (both white and green portions), Swiss chard stems, Jerusalem artichoke pieces, parsnip pieces or peels, shallots, mushroom stems, soaking water from dried mushrooms, scallions (both white and green portions), potato peels, celeriac pieces or peels, squash ends (both winter and summer squash work well), lettuce bottoms, spinach, tomatoes, eggplant, green beans, rosemary, marjoram, basil, or chives.

- For accent, add 1 to 2 of the following: asparagus stems, fennel fronds or pieces, corncobs, pea pods, cilantro, or lovage.

- For complexity, any or all of the following: ½ cup yellow or green split peas, 2-inch piece Parmesan cheese rind, 1 piece kombu, 1 teaspoon agar flakes. You might also roast tomatoes, garlic, onions, carrots, celery, or leeks before adding them to the stock. Toss them in olive oil and spread them on a parchment-lined baking sheet; 45 minutes at 450 degrees will roast them well.

- The most important piece of information you need for cooking any sort of stock is this: It prefers to be left alone. Its simple request while cooking is "Do Not Disturb."

SHIITAKE MUSHROOM STOCK

Makes 3 to 4 cups

It is a wonder that we can make mushroom stock from only two ingredients other than water: kombu and dried shiitake mushrooms. This stock has more depth and complexity than you would imagine, and it imparts a special warmth. Shiitake mushroom stock makes a good base for cooking grains or serving Japanese udon noodles; if there is any leftover, try adding it to soup.

Several pieces kombu, about 12 inches total
1 ounce dried shiitake mushrooms

1. Place the kombu and mushrooms, along with 4 cups cool water, into a medium-sized pot. Soak them at room temperature, covered, for at least 2 hours or as long as 24 hours.

2. At the end of the soak, bring the water to a boil. Reduce the heat to low and simmer, covered, for 5 minutes. Turn off the heat and let the mixture sit, covered, for 5 minutes more.

3. Strain the stock, squeezing the mushrooms to remove all the liquid.

4. The stock will keep for 2 to 3 days in the refrigerator. You can also freeze it, though it may lose its pleasing aroma.

RICH CHICKEN BROTH

Makes 2 quarts

Broth made from chicken bones is a rich source of minerals, including calcium. When made well, it is also a wonderful source of gelatin. In folk medicine, and more scientifically today, chicken broth is a prized treatment for colds and flu and helps maintain an overall state of health. Uncovering broth while it cooks allows for a deeper concentration of flavors. Simmering it over the lowest heat, so there's "barely a smile," as the French like to say, ensures clarity and preserves gelatin.

1 chicken, 3 to 4 pounds, whole or in parts; or the same measure of chicken bones, necks, and skin (and feet, if you are lucky enough to get them)
1 onion, loose outer layers peeled, cut in half
4 to 5 medium carrots, cut in half
2 to 3 celery stalks (with leaves), cut in half
6 to 8 cloves garlic, loose outer leaves peeled, well scrubbed and cut in half
1 leek, both white and green parts, cut in half
Handful parsley leaves or stems
3 to 4 thyme sprigs
1 bay leaf
6 to 8 whole black peppercorns

1. Wash the chicken pieces or bones, and place them into a stock pot with 10 to 12 cups cool filtered water. Heat the water slowly, gradually bringing it to a low boil. Then reduce the heat to the lowest simmer; the surface of the broth should ripple only slightly.

2. Skim any foamy scum that rises to the surface, as it contains impurities. When the surface is relatively clear, add the remaining ingredients and simmer, uncovered, for 6 hours.

3. Strain the broth through a fine mesh strainer. If you want a really

clean broth, you can line the sieve before straining with a double layer of cheesecloth or with a smoothly textured dishcloth. Discard the bones and cooked vegetables, and allow the broth to cool before refrigerating.

4. Once cool, refrigerate the broth, which will ideally become thick and gelatinous. Before reheating, you may want to remove some or all of the fat from the top of the broth. Then apply a gentle heat to restore its liquid consistency.

5. Chicken broth keeps for about 5 days in the refrigerator, or longer if you boil it before reusing. Broth keeps frozen for up to 6 months.

Notes

- Some people believe that onion peels lend a bitter flavor to broth, but this has not been my experience; I like the flavor and rich color they impart. When adding unpeeled onions to broth, remove any loose outer layers of peel, rinse what remains, and add the unpeeled onion to the soup pot.

- If you are making broth with both meat and bones and you want the meat for your finished soup, keep in mind that boiled meat is relatively spent after 6 hours of cooking. In this case, follow steps 1 and 2, but simmer the meaty bones for only 1 hour and then remove them from the pot to prevent the meat from overcooking. Let them cool enough to handle, and while the broth is simmering, remove the meat from the bones. Break the meat into bite-size pieces, set it aside to add back to the finished broth, and add the bones and skin back to the pot for the remainder of the cooking time.

- To turn broth into soup, simply slice 1 carrot and 1 celery stalk into bite-size pieces and simmer them in salted water until softened, about 10 to 15 minutes. Add a handful or two of egg noodles to the vegetables and continue boiling until cooked. Strain, and add the vegetables and noodles to the broth, along with any reserved meat pieces. You will need to add little, if any, salt because the long cooking time draws sodium from the bones and leaves you with a naturally well-salted broth.

- To turn broth into a "medicinal" tonic, you can add the Chinese herb *Huang qi* (astragalus) in step 2 (see Gathering Ingredients and Supplies on page 315). It works well to add 3 pieces for a full pot of soup—it has no discernible flavor.

- Some other broth-making tricks that you may want to try: Parboiling and rinsing the bones before cooking and cooking over a low heat both help reduce the quantity of residue, producing a clear broth. To parboil bones, place them in the soup pot and cover them with cold water. Bring the bones to a low boil, reduce the heat, and gently simmer until they have released all their scum. Drain and discard the water, rinse the bones, and begin the recipe with step 1. Also, cutting or breaking bones before adding them to the cooking water is thought to add nutrients to the finished broth.

You will find no recipe for veal stock on the pages of this book, artisanal though it may be, because I can teach only what I know. Since childhood I have chosen not to eat veal. I don't feel comfortable with how the veal calf lives any part of its life, and so I forgo anything it might do for me in the kitchen. I realize that this introduces politics into my cooking, but perhaps gathering ingredients and cooking them *should* be political for the home artisan. Crafting food by hand is such a deliberate way of putting meals on the table—details matter, especially details surrounding how the animals we eat are raised. Perhaps, over time, you will come to believe, if you don't already, that each meal we prepare and all that we eat can be a vote cast in favor of a more considerate and responsible world.

FISH STOCK

Makes 4 to 6 cups

Fish stock is especially nutritious. Because it's made from fish bones, it puts iodine in your diet, and other minerals, too, including calcium. It can also be a source of gelatin, which aids digestion and confers other health benefits. And if you add fish heads to your stock, which fishmongers often give away for free, it becomes nourishing for the thyroid gland. I most often use fish stock as the basis for a memorable fish soup (see "Notes").

1 to 2 back bones from any white fish that is nonfatty and nonoily: red snapper, sea bass, sole, and whiting work well
1 to 2 fish heads, optional (be sure the gills are removed)
2 tablespoons extra-virgin olive oil
1 onion, peeled and coarsely chopped
2 carrots, coarsely chopped
2 celery stalks, coarsely chopped
2 tablespoons apple cider vinegar, optional
Several sprigs fresh thyme, optional
1 bay leaf
1 tablespoon whole black peppercorns

1. In a large bowl, carefully wash the fish bones (and heads, if using) in cold water. Drain and repeat, washing until the water runs clear. Drain the bones once more and set them aside.

2. Add olive oil to a heavy soup pot and warm it over a low heat. Add the onion, carrots, and celery and cook until the onions are translucent, 8 to 10 minutes.

3. Add the fish bones (and heads, if using) along with 8 cups of water, and gradually bring the stock to a low boil. Then reduce the heat to the lowest simmer; the surface of the broth should ripple only slightly.

4. Skim any foamy scum that rises to the surface as it contains impurities. When the surface is relatively clear, add the remaining ingredients and simmer uncovered for 30 to 60 minutes.

5. Strain the broth through a fine mesh strainer. If you want a really clean broth, line the sieve with a double layer of cheesecloth or with a smoothly textured dishcloth before straining. Discard the bones and cooked vegetables, and allow the stock to cool before refrigerating.

6. Store broth covered in the refrigerator for 3 days, or frozen for up to 3 months.

WHY ADD APPLE CIDER VINEGAR TO STOCK?

Stock is all about the bones, and a key goal in preparing it is to draw as many nutrients as possible out of the bones and into the finished stock. If your aim is to create a stock rich in gelatin, it may be best to omit the apple cider vinegar, which in my experience seems to inhibit gelatin formation. If, on the other hand, your goal is to draw out as much calcium and as many other minerals as possible from the bones, add the vinegar and rest assured that its acidity will help extract the minerals you want, and you won't taste it in the finished stock.

Notes

• On occasion, there may be a conflict between maximizing healthfulness and maximizing culinary appeal. Fish stock is just such a case. Cooking it for hours extracts more nutrients from the bones. But a more palatable fish stock is cooked quickly; longer cooking makes it cloudy and the flavor becomes less appealing. So, what to do? The answer may depend on how you plan to use the stock. If you'll turn it into a light soup, a short-cooked stock might be best. But a chowder made with added ingredients might be more forgiving and allow for a longer cooking time. While I tend to use chicken stock for medicinal purposes—as a way of consuming minerals and gelatin, for example—I generally make fish stock with culinary goals in mind, and so I most often cook it for an hour or less.

- Every so often, I make an ambitious and delicious fish soup. But for everyday fare, I have Mark Bittman to thank for this simple recipe: In a couple tablespoons of olive oil, soften a chopped onion, a smashed clove of garlic, and a half teaspoon of paprika for about 2 minutes. Add 4 cups fish stock, 1 can chopped tomatoes with their juice, a pinch of saffron, salt, and pepper. Bring the soup to a boil, reduce it to a simmer, and cook it for 5 minutes. Add 1 to 1½ pounds white fish, cut into chunks, and simmer until the fish is cooked through, about 5 minutes more. Serve garnished with chopped parsley and slices of toasted baguette.

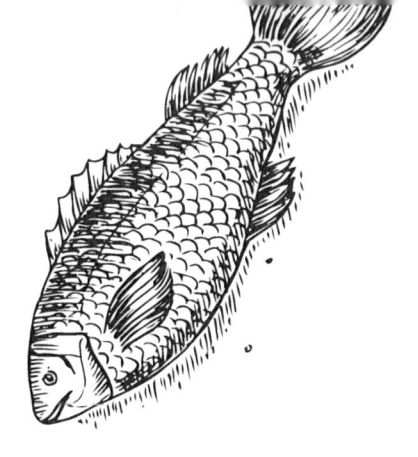

········· FOOD THOUGHTS ·········

POULTRY, RED MEAT, AND FISH

"Animals eat plants, so, ultimately, we are all grass, pretty much."

—*Carl Safina*

There are no recipes for poultry, red meat, or fish within these pages, other than recipes for stock made from fish and chicken, because, to be honest, there are others who know more about preparing these foods in an artful way than I do. While I am not a vegetarian, I tend to get most of my animal protein from dairy and eggs because these are what I have in plenty and can gather without reaching beyond my front yard. But I can tell you this: As with fresh vegetables, it is worth spending time sourcing the highest quality meats and fish you can get, gathering them carefully, and then, if you like, preparing them using simple recipes and techniques.

There is, as you likely know, a lot of hype around the "certified organic" label. When it comes to sourcing animal foods, however, I overlook those that come from large companies raising thousands of animals and calling their products good because the grain they feed is organic, and because they don't inject any hormones or antibiotics. Their animals live confined lives and eat grains that are indigestible for them and bad for us. Instead, when I do buy animal products, they come from small businesses or farmers I trust who avoid antibiotics and hormones, rely on minimal processing, and feed their livestock grass. These products are available to most of us if we seek them out.

Poultry and red meat, if you buy them, are best when they come from unmedicated animals, even if the resulting foods are not "certified organic." And poultry, after spending its early weeks in a brooder, should live on grass. Note that a "free range" label says nothing about whether an animal lives outdoors on pasture, even though it sounds as if it does. It simply means the animal is not caged and that somewhere in its pen is a door to the outside, even if the animal is unaware of it. Unlike many other forms of livestock, poultry do eat grain, but grass and bugs form a crucial part of their diet. If they live among cows, they may also consume whey, skim milk, or yogurt. You have the option of seeking poultry that have no soy in their diet if that's an ingredient you wish to avoid. It's even easier to find poultry fed grain that's free from genetic modification. If you buy it at a store, the carton will be labeled "GMO-free" or "certified organic." Cows and other red meat animals should be grass-raised and grass-finished (on confinement farms it is customary to fatten and finish cows on grain in order to get nicely marbled meat).

The most important question to ask about poultry is this: "Was it raised on pasture?" And about red meat: "Was it grass-finished?" Labels for poultry and red meat, or farmers from whom you buy, must specify "pasture-raised" or "grass-finished" for you to know it meets these standards.

Seafood has its own set of considerations. In general, the fish we eat should ideally come from waters that are as close to pristine as still exist. They should also, whenever possible, be wild and small—either a small species of fish (anchovies, sardines, or herring, for example) or a young fish within a species that, in maturity, grows large.

Wild fish are better for us because they provide us with more high-quality fats than do their farmed counterparts. This is because wild fish eat leafy green plants that grow in the water, which, like grass, are a rich source of beneficial omega-3 fats. Farmed fish eat grain and processed pellets that contain a variety of unhealthful ingredients. Interestingly, when wild fish live in water that is cold—in the Pacific Northwest, for example—they have a richer content of omega-3 fats. This is because for fish to flourish in cold water, their bodies must produce more oily fat.

Size is also important because fish, like people, store toxins in their fat. Large fish eat smaller fish, which in turn eat very small fish. So large fish consume a lot of toxic fatty tissue that they then store in their flesh; it's a compound effect that's part of any food chain. In addition, large fish within a species are older and have therefore had more time to accumulate toxins. So, when eating fish that tend to live long lives—for example, tuna, halibut, sablefish, or mackerel—it's important to eat those that are harvested young.

As with all aspects of careful food gathering, the slope tends to steepen as your knowledge grows. Over time, you may decide to seek meat that comes from animals killed on site. On-farm slaughter is a way of avoiding the stress animals experience in transport before death. The stress hormones that are released are thought to toughen meat and impact an animal's well-being in the end. Or you may want to eat only local fish caught within a day of purchase. How far you go, how steep your slope becomes, is personal and depends on the level of time and energy you want to commit in pursuit of quality. It also depends on how you come to define quality for yourself and those you feed.

The most important idea to remember, whatever your vantage point, is that if an animal food is to truly nourish you, it must come from an animal that was well nourished itself. At the very least, this means it must come from animals that are fed with what nature provides—grass or, in the case of fish, green plants—and that are tended with respect and care.

GHEE

Makes 1½ to 2 cups

Ghee is a type of clarified butter—butter without moisture and milk solids—that has gone further than simple clarification; the milk solids are lightly browned, which gives it a slightly nutty flavor. You can use it when you want to impart a buttery flavor, yet need a fat for stove-top cooking that's more heat-tolerant than butter is. A common misconception is that you can achieve this same effect by using a mixture of butter and oil, but the addition of oil doesn't increase the temperature at which milk solids burn and smoke. It's good to know that you can substitute ghee 1:1 in place of vegetable oil when you bake. Butter cannot be substituted in as simple a way.

1 pound unsalted butter

1. Line a sieve with cheesecloth or butter muslin (see Gathering Ingredients and Supplies on page 315) and place the sieve over a medium-sized bowl.

2. Put the butter in a heavy saucepan and warm it over medium heat. When the butter begins to foam and splutter, lower the heat and allow it to simmer gently for 20 to 30 minutes. When it begins to brown around the edges, it's ready.

3. Pour the hot mixture through the cheesecloth or butter muslin, and then discard the strained milk solids. What remains in the bowl is ghee.

4. Store ghee covered, either in the refrigerator or at room temperature. As with butter, protecting it from light will preserve its flavor and keep it fresher longer, for up to several months on the countertop or longer in the refrigerator.

GOMASIO

Makes ¼ cup

Gomasio is an Asian condiment that is good sprinkled over cooked grains, vegetables, or pasta in lieu of salt.

¼ cup brown sesame seeds
1 teaspoon coarse sea salt

1. Warm a cast-iron skillet over medium heat and add the sesame seeds. Toast them, stirring frequently, until the seeds darken, 7 to 10 minutes. You might hear them make a popping sound as they finish toasting.

2. Place the sesame seeds into a suribachi—a Japanese earthenware mortar with grooves inside for grinding seeds, nuts, and other ingredients. As an alternative, transfer the seeds to a spice grinder. With either approach, add the salt, and grind into a coarse meal.

3. Cool and store covered at room temperature or, for lasting freshness, in the refrigerator, where it will keep for 2 months.

TAMARI TOASTED PUMPKIN SEEDS

Makes 3 cups

These seeds are good by the handful as a snack. They are good over brown rice or other steamed grains. They are good sprinkled over salad. They are good, period.

3 cups raw pumpkin seeds
2½ tablespoons tamari, divided

1. Place pumpkin seeds into a cast-iron skillet and cook them over medium heat until they are well toasted and emit a pleasing aroma. The seeds will "pop" and crackle, and when this slows, they are ready. Turn off the heat.

2. Leaving the seeds in the hot skillet, pour 2 tablespoons tamari over them and mix well with a wooden spoon. Taste the seeds. If you prefer a stronger flavor, add the remaining tamari.

3. Transfer the seeds to a cookie sheet or plate, spreading them in a single layer to cool and develop their crunch. Stored covered in the refrigerator, they will keep for months.

MAYONNAISE

Makes about ⅓ cup

Homemade mayonnaise is so superior that once you get used to having this particular luxury, you may not want to compromise on store-bought mayonnaise again. It's easy to be scared off by a recipe like this one, but there are a few tricks that will ensure your success. First, make sure your ingredients are at room temperature; it can help to warm the mixing bowl if it feels cold to touch. Second, start off by adding the oil very slowly, drop by drop, and keep whisking to emulsify the ingredients. Finally, if you want a double quantity of mayonnaise, there is no need to add an extra egg yolk. Doubling the other ingredients is enough.

- **1 egg yolk**, at room temperature
- **¼ teaspoon Dijon mustard**, at room temperature
- **⅛ teaspoon salt**
- **2 tablespoons plus ¼ cup fine-quality extra-virgin olive oil**
- **¾ teaspoon fresh lemon juice**, at room temperature

1. Place the egg yolk, mustard, and salt into a small bowl and whisk until well blended.

2. Drop by drop, add 2 tablespoons olive oil to the egg mixture. Be sure to add the olive oil slowly, and whisk the egg mixture continually while doing so.

3. Slowly whisk in the lemon juice and then add the remaining ¼ cup oil in a slow, thin stream, again whisking continually. At no point should the mixture become thin or the oil remain unemulsified. If this happens, stop adding oil and whisk until the mixture thickens and emulsifies. Then continue adding oil. When finished,

the mayonnaise will be rich and yellow because of the high-quality egg yolk you begin with.

4. Cover and chill. The mayonnaise will keep for several days.

Notes

- It's a good idea to begin with a really fresh egg from a farmer concerned about quality, and the quality of life for his or her hens. Since poor farming methods and poor animal husbandry account for many cases of salmonella in eggs, a recipe like this one, that requires raw eggs, is not a place to compromise.

- If the mayonnaise fails to come together, place a new room-temperature egg yolk into a small bowl. Then, drop by drop, add the loose mayonnaise mixture to the egg yolk, whisking as before, until the mayonnaise thickens and emulsifies.

- To make aioli, use the side of a heavy knife to mash 1 clove minced garlic into a paste with ⅛ teaspoon fine sea salt. Set the garlic paste aside and make the mayonnaise recipe, minus the salt. Whisk the garlic paste into the finished mayonnaise, and season it with salt and pepper if needed. If the aioli is thicker than you would like, whisk in a drop or two of water.

- To enhance mayonnaise with the flavor of fresh herbs, add finely chopped parsley, chives, tarragon, basil, or dill to the finished mayonnaise in whatever quantity you desire. It's best to allow herbed mayonnaise to sit before serving so the flavors have a chance to meld.

- Making mayonnaise by hand is not hard once you get a feel for it, and the results are superior. But if you want to use a blender, add all the ingredients to the blender except the oil and then, with the blender running on the lowest speed, add the oil as slowly as possible until the mixture is thick and smooth.

- Taste the olive oil you plan to use to be sure you find the flavor pleasing. As with salad dressing, a fine-quality olive oil is called for.

- According to Sally Fallon Morell's book *Nourishing Traditions*, it is possible to extend the shelf life of homemade mayonnaise by adding 1½ teaspoons whey to the full quantity of finished mayonnaise; then let it sit on the counter for 7 hours to allow beneficial bacteria to culture the mayonnaise. This approach will enable you to keep it for about a month. I haven't tried this because I haven't found it necessary. I can always find 10 minutes to make fresh mayonnaise that will then keep for several days. But if you want to experiment, this approach might make a difference for you.

PESTO

Makes ⅔ cup

For decades I have made pesto and enjoyed it, but I used to find it something of a heartache. Every time I made it, the pesto would turn brown before reaching the table, and it turned whatever I put it on brown, too. Persistence, however, granted me a solution: Lightly blanching basil leaves before making pesto prevents them from oxidizing and turning brown. For the price of an extra few minutes added to the preparation time, it's possible to have pesto that remains ever green.

Coarse sea salt for blanching water, plus ¾ teaspoon for pesto
1 bunch fresh basil
2 medium cloves garlic, peeled
2 tablespoons pine nuts
⅓ cup extra-virgin olive oil
Freshly ground pepper
⅓ cup freshly grated Parmesan cheese

1. Bring a small pot of well-salted water to a rolling boil. Add the basil, both stems and leaves, and boil for 30 seconds. Drain, rinse under cold running water, and dry well.

2. Separate the basil leaves and put them into the bowl of a food processor. Discard the stems.

3. To the basil, add ¾ teaspoon salt, plus the garlic, pine nuts, olive oil, and a few grinds of fresh pepper. Process until the pesto is uniformly creamy.

4. Transfer the pesto to a bowl and mix in the Parmesan cheese by hand. Use at once or refrigerate, covered, for up to 3 days. Before adding the cheese, you can freeze the pesto for up to 3 months. In

this case, cover the surface of the pesto with waxed paper or a thin layer of olive oil.

Notes

- For the best results when serving pesto over pasta, before draining 16 ounces of cooked pasta, set aside ½ cup of the hot cooking water. Add the pesto and ¼ cup of the cooking water to the pasta in a serving bowl. Stir and let the pasta absorb the water. Add up to ¼ cup more water, until you have the level of creaminess you desire. It's also nice to add 2 to 3 tablespoons butter, 2 to 3 tablespoons fresh ricotta cheese, or a combination of the two.
- Beyond pasta, pesto is also delicious spooned over cooked fish, tossed with roasted potatoes or cooked vegetables, or slathered over a slice of bread along with goat cheese or sliced tomatoes.

RICOTTA-ALMOND SPREAD

Makes 1¼ cups

This recipe comes from the Canyon Ranch resort in Lenox, Massachusetts. For years I was so enamored of it that I made it almost weekly, and because I often had it on hand, I made a lot of banana bread to go with it. I'll also confess that when I've had no time to bake, I have occasionally enjoyed this spread by the spoonful, like pudding, for dessert. That's how much I like it.

1 cup ricotta cheese, fresh if you can get it
¼ cup unsalted almond butter
1½ tablespoons honey
2 teaspoons vanilla
½ teaspoon cinnamon

1. Put all the ingredients into the bowl of a food processor and puree until smooth.
2. Store in the refrigerator, covered, for up to 1 week.

OLIVE SPREAD

MAKES 1 CUP

Olive spread is not a recipe, per se—it's more precisely a combination of olives and olive oil in a ratio that tastes pleasing. It's especially good on bruschetta (see "Notes") made with Sourdough Wheat and Rye Bread (see page 97), or with Italian or French bread if you have no homemade bread on hand. You can also spread it on bread with a layer of goat cheese, toss it into pasta, put it on pizza, or serve it with crudités or hummus and pita crisps.

1 cup pitted kalamata or green olives
3 tablespoons extra-virgin olive oil, plus extra for covering stored spread

1. Place the olives into the bowl of a food processor. Add the olive oil and puree until smooth.
2. Serve at once, or transfer the spread to a container, cover the surface of with a thin layer of olive oil, and refrigerate, covered, for up to 1 week.

Notes

- To make bruschetta, begin with the bread of your choice, and cut it into ½- to ¾-inch slices. Using a pastry brush, coat the bread slices with olive oil on one side, and place the slices dry side down on a baking sheet. Toast in a 350-degree oven until crisp. Remove from the oven and slice 1 to 2 peeled garlic cloves in half. Rub the cloves, cut side down, over the oiled sides of the bread slices and serve with olive spread.

- There are many ways you can successfully embellish this spread. Consider adding chopped parsley, lemon juice, garlic, capers, anchovies, basil, or any other ingredient that comes to mind as a worthy complement.

MONGOLIAN BARBEQUE SAUCE

Makes 2¼ cups

I always feel good when I have a batch of this sauce on hand; legend has it, Genghis Kahn felt much the same. The story is told that he prepared a version of this recipe to use in conquering China. He marinated meat and vegetables in the sauce and, in an inverted shield, cooked them, sending their aroma into the open air. One whiff and the Chinese soldiers surrendered, choosing food over fight. My hunch is that this story might not be true to the letter, but it does make the recipe more compelling. What follows is my own twist on traditional Mongolian barbeque sauce. It makes an excellent marinade for beef, fish, or chicken, and is equally delicious served warm over grains—brown rice, for example. It's a very good sauce to have in your repertoire, for everyday meals or for vanquishing your foes.

½ cup plus 2 tablespoons tamari, divided
2 tablespoons maple crystals
¼ cup brown rice vinegar
1 tablespoon sesame oil
½ cup mirin
1 star anise
3 whole black peppercorns

⅓ cup tomato sauce
Pinch ground coriander
¼ teaspoon red pepper flakes
¼ cup minced leeks
2 teaspoons minced ginger
2 to 3 cloves garlic, minced

1. In a small saucepan, combine ½ cup of the tamari, maple crystals, brown rice vinegar, sesame oil, mirin, star anise, peppercorns, and ⅓ cup water. Stir to mix and then bring to a boil.

2. Add tomato sauce, coriander, and red pepper flakes; lower the heat and simmer, uncovered, for 10 minutes.

3. Strain into a small bowl and add the 2 remaining tablespoons tamari, 2 tablespoons water, leeks, ginger, and garlic. Stir to combine, and let the sauce cool.

4. Use at once, or refrigerate for up to 1 week.

CREAMY HUMMUS

Makes 3 cups

You can make this recipe using canned chickpeas, which saves time by eliminating the first 3 steps, and you will get a good enough result. But to make exceptional hummus, there is no substitute for starting with chickpeas you cook yourself. Canned beans are left firm enough to be used whole in salads or soups, but to make a creamy hummus it's best to start with tender, well-cooked beans that are more suited to a puree.

1 cup dried chickpeas
1 clove garlic, crushed
1 piece kombu, optional
1 teaspoon coarse sea salt
3 cloves garlic, peeled
¼ cup tahini

⅓ cup fresh lemon juice, plus extra to taste
2 tablespoons extra-virgin olive oil
1 tablespoon fine sea salt, plus extra to taste
1 teaspoon cumin seed, toasted and ground, or 1½ teaspoons ground cumin, optional

1. Rinse the chickpeas and place them in a bowl of cool filtered water. The water should cover them by at least 3 to 4 inches. Soak the chickpeas at room temperature for 8 to 12 hours.

2. Drain and rinse the chickpeas and place them in a heavy pot, discarding the soaking water. Add crushed garlic, kombu (if you are using it), and coarse sea salt. Cover the chickpeas with 3 times their height in water, bring to a boil, and turn the heat to low. Skim and discard any foam. Then simmer, partly covered, for 1½ to 2 hours, checking from time to time to be sure the chickpeas are submerged under water. If they're not, add enough water to cover the chickpeas by at least ½ inch.

3. Toward the end of the cooking time, taste the chickpeas for tenderness. When they're well cooked, drain them, reserving ½ cup of cooking liquid. Discard any extra cooking liquid or save it to add to soup.

4. If your preference is for a textured hummus, proceed to step 5. If you like your hummus smooth, put the cooked chickpeas into a large bowl filled with cool filtered water. Using the palms of your hands, gently rub the chickpeas to loosen their skins, taking care not to crush them. As the skins float to the surface, skim and discard them. Repeat until nearly all the skins are removed.

5. Into a food processor, place the peeled garlic cloves, cooked chickpeas, tahini, lemon juice, olive oil, fine sea salt, ¼ cup of the reserved cooking liquid, and cumin, if using. Run the food processor for about 5 minutes for a smooth hummus, or less time for a textured hummus.

6. Taste to check the flavor, consistency, and texture. If needed, add more cooking liquid, lemon juice, or fine sea salt. Keep tasting and blending until you have the hummus you desire.

7. Store hummus in the refrigerator, covered, for up to 5 days or freeze for 2 to 3 months.

Note

- Many ingredients pair well with hummus. Try adding a sprinkling of smoked paprika, or roasted and pureed red peppers. Garnish a bowl of hummus with chopped or sliced kalamata olives, or fresh herbs like thyme. And serve hummus with carrot, celery, or daikon sticks; pita triangles; or whole-grain crackers.

WHITE BEAN SPREAD

Makes 2½ cups

A spread made from little more than beans is a humble offering, yet it tastes wonderful and makes a beautiful presentation on the table. Try serving this Mediterranean spread on bruschetta (see "Notes," page 301) topped with sprigs of baby arugula, or alongside roasted asparagus, eggplant, or mushrooms. Serve it with fresh sourdough bread and marinated olives, or with toasted pita triangles. Options abound, and with soup or a salad, white bean spread becomes a meal.

1 cup dried white beans (navy, great northern, or cannellini)
2 cloves garlic, crushed
1 piece kombu, optional
1 bay leaf
2 fresh sage leaves
1 teaspoon coarse sea salt
1 head fresh garlic
½ cup olive oil, plus extra for coating garlic
2 tablespoons fresh lemon juice
Fine sea salt

1. Rinse the beans and place them in a bowl of cool filtered water and cover by at least 3 to 4 inches. Soak the beans at room temperature for 8 to 12 hours.

2. Toward the end of the soaking time, preheat the oven to 350 degrees. Drain the beans, discard the soaking water, and place the beans in a heavy pot. Add crushed garlic, kombu (if using), bay leaf, sage leaves, and coarse sea salt. Cover the beans with 3 times their height in water, bring them to a boil, and reduce the heat to low. Simmer, partly covered, for 1 to 1½ hours, checking from time to time to be sure the beans are submerged under water. If they're not, add enough water to cover the beans by at least ½ inch.

3. While the beans are cooking, coat the head of garlic with olive oil; there is no need to peel or separate the cloves. Wrap the garlic in parchment paper and then overwrap it in foil. Place it in the oven and roast for 30 minutes, or until the garlic is soft. Unwrap the cooked garlic and set it aside to cool.

4. When the beans are well cooked, remove the kombu (if you used it), bay leaf, and sage leaves. Then drain the beans, reserving ½ cup of cooking liquid. Discard any extra cooking liquid or save it to add to soup.

5. Into a food processor, place the beans, olive oil, and lemon juice. Cut the top off the cooled roasted garlic and squeeze the pulp from the cloves into the mixture. Run the food processor for about 2 minutes to puree the spread. Add reserved cooking liquid, as needed, to achieve a nice texture, and add fine sea salt to taste.

6. Check the spread for flavor, consistency, and texture. If needed, add more cooking liquid, lemon juice, or salt. Keep tasting and blending until you are happy with the result.

7. Store white bean spread in the refrigerator, covered, for up to 5 days or freeze for 2 to 3 months.

Note

- If fresh sage is not available, substitute 1 to 2 sprigs fresh rosemary or thyme. Dried sage is not a substitute.

ELDERBERRY SYRUP

Makes ½ cup

Every summer, I have more elderberries than I know what to do with—if, that is, I harvest them before the birds do. I try my hardest to do that because I prize these small fruits, as does much of the world, for their power as a traditional folk remedy. Cooked into a syrup, they are said to fight colds and flu, and I have found this to be true. The syrup also tastes delicious, so children beg for it, if you can imagine that.

2 pounds elderberries, large stems removed (cutting the stems off with scissors makes this easy)

¼ cup maple syrup

1 teaspoon honey, optional

1. Clean the elderberries in a large bowl filled with plenty of cool water. Then lift them out, small stems included, and place them into a strainer. Discard the water, rinse the bowl, and clean the elderberries again.

2. After 3 changes of water, clean the bowl and set it aside. Place the elderberries into a large pot. Add 8 cups of water and bring the mixture to a boil. Lower the heat and simmer, covered, until the elderberries begin to break down, about 20 minutes.

3. Line a sieve with cheesecloth and place it over the large bowl. Pour the hot elderberry mixture into the sieve and let it drain into the bowl as it cools. Rinse the pot and set it aside.

4. When the elderberry mixture is cool enough to handle, bring the cheesecloth up and around the berries and use your hands to twist

it closed (you may want to wear rubber gloves for this task). Continue twisting to squeeze any remaining juice out of the berries. You should have about 8 cups of juice.

5. Pour the elderberry juice from the bowl back into the cooking pot. Bring the mixture to an active simmer, skimming any foam that covers the surface. Add maple syrup and gently simmer until the mixture cooks down into a thick syrup. This will take 60 to 90 minutes, depending on the dimensions of your pot (in a wider pot, the cooking time will be shorter). You will know the syrup is ready when it just coats the back of a spoon.

6. If needed, add up to 1 teaspoon honey to balance the flavor. Cool, cover, and refrigerate for up to 1 year.

RED WINE VINEGAR

It's fitting that I end this book with a recipe for making homemade vinegar. For me, it typifies the lot of the home artisan. As I wrote in the early pages of this book, and as I'll repeat here: The learning is ongoing and the journey never ends. With this in mind, here is my red wine vinegar story.

Many years ago, I set out to learn how to make red wine vinegar. Every batch of vinegar begins with a "mother," which is a round of cellulose produced by a harmless vinegar bacteria. But because I keep kosher, I needed a kosher "mother," and these could not be purchased. One day, I came up with the idea to take the mother from another variety of vinegar, one that was kosher, and use it to grow my own mother for making red wine vinegar. I don't know what made me think I could do this, but that's what comes of an obsession. I took a bottle of apple cider vinegar with "live mother of vinegar," drained off the liquid, and took the sludge at the bottom of the bottle, using it to give birth to the mother I needed. And with this new mother, I succeeded at making vinegar.

The whole enterprise worked until, after a couple of years, I concluded that one gallon of red wine vinegar not only met my needs, it exceeded them by about three quarters of a gallon. I had so much vinegar and so many mothers that I could have started a business (but then I wouldn't have been able to write this book). So I decided to wind down my small vinegar operation until I could use up what I had. This was harder than you may think because stored vinegar continues to produce mothers—an inordinate number of mothers. I thought that pasteurizing the vinegar might be a solution, but, to me, that would have defeated the purpose of handcrafting my own. Yet I couldn't slow or stop the process. I tried refrigerating the vinegar; no luck. I tried harvesting all but one mother per jar and

BY YOUR OWN HAND • 311

composting the rest; no matter. I could not rein them in.

One day, I gave up, and acknowledged that I was ill-equipped to wage battle against the reproductive will of a gallon jar of vinegar. The mothers had taken over, and I lost dominion over my creation. So this is where I stand today, and this is as much as I know: how to harvest your own mother and make your own red wine vinegar. Storing vinegar, and making this work over years, is another story. That will be for the next book. Or maybe you will figure it out and write your own book. There is more information available on this topic now than there was when I got started.

For now, we can all make vinegar, a lot of it—and if the mothers stage an uprising, there is power in the compost pile and the possibility, always, of a new beginning. And we can remind ourselves that the fun is really in figuring things out.

1¾ cups red wine, 14% alcohol
Red wine vinegar mother (see Gathering Ingredients and Supplies on page 315)

---

1. Into a ½-gallon glass canning jar (or another jar), place the wine along with a vinegar mother and ½ cup filtered water.

2. Loosely cover the jar with the canning lid and set it in a warm, dark place to ferment.

3. If you observe a circular disk on the surface of the vinegar, this may be a new "mother of vinegar." Do not be afraid of it; just leave it alone and let it work its magic.

4. Approximately every two weeks, reach under the mother to taste the vinegar and assess how it is coming along.

5. Use the vinegar as needed straight from the jar, adding more

diluted wine as you have it. Or transfer the vinegar to a storage jar and use the mother to make a new batch of vinegar. Either way, mothers will continue to grow and you will need to compost them or give them away to adventurous friends.

Notes

- If you keep kosher and want to make vinegar, you might try buying a jar of kosher apple cider vinegar with live mother. Pour the vinegar through a fine mesh strainer and set it aside for another use; then add the sludge you collected in the strainer to the jar with the diluted wine in step 1. Over time, a thick disk should form on top of the wine mixture. This is your kosher red wine vinegar mother. I will say, however, that this worked in my early vinegar-making years, but not in recent years. I suspect Bragg, the brand I used, may have made changes to their cider vinegar.

- When I first made vinegar, I covered the jar with cheesecloth to allow for adequate aeration, but I found that this approach attracted more fruit flies than I was willing to share space with. It has worked better for me to cover the jar loosely and then stir the mixture from time to time for adequate aeration.

- The reason for adding water in step 1 is that the alcohol content of the wine is too high for vinegar making. Water reduces the level of alcohol, allowing wine to become vinegar.

- Some vinegar makers suggest using dry wine with a 12 percent alcohol content and combining that with half as much water. Others suggest an alcohol content and ratio that is closer to what I've listed above. I have had many years of success with the approach I describe here and so I continue to recommend it. As you experiment, however, you might want to try using an initial ratio of 2 cups wine to 1 cup water. During the first 2 weeks after mixing, add 2½ cups undiluted wine 3 different times, or a total of 7½ cups undiluted wine. This alternate approach is one that might work for you.

- If you become as overwhelmed with mothers as I was, try shocking them into submission by adding straight wine to the vinegar. This is said to slow their reproduction.

GATHERING INGREDIENTS AND SUPPLIES

It is a comfort and a relief to have able helpmates in our lives, inspiring us and making the daily task of putting exceptional food on the table easier, more interesting, and a lot more fun. These suppliers are unsurpassed; they help me keep my kitchen stocked with tools and ingredients that work effectively in recipes, taste delicious, and are of the highest quality. While there are many good purveyors, these are the ones who have done well by me. They get my orders right, offer wise counsel, and thoroughly know their products. Even better, they care about sustainability and are careful about excess packaging and waste. I'm glad to share their names with you.

Anson Mills
1922-C Gervais Street
Columbia, South Carolina 29201
803-467-4122
ansonmills.com

A small company dedicated to organically growing, harvesting, and milling near-extinct varieties of heirloom corn, rice, wheat, and other grains. I especially like their Colonial-Style 100% Whole Wheat Flour and their Rustic Red Fife Bread Flour, Einkorn Wheat, and Abruzzi Heirloom Rye Flours, the latter of which I use for baking bread. When I can get it, their Polycrop flour improves my bread in noticeable ways. Anson Mills sells many of their flours to both wholesale and retail customers.

Celtic Sea Salt
4 Celtic Drive
Arden, NC 28704
800-867-7258
celticseasalt.com

An artisan-crafted, sustainably harvested sea salt. It is unprocessed, whole, and gathered from as pristine coastal regions as we have left. I use both coarse light gray salt, and lighter finely ground salt.

Coombs Family Farm
PO Box 117
Brattleboro, VT 05302
888-266-6271
coombsfamilyfarms.com
A seventh-generation family business offering pure maple products of its own and of like-minded small maple farmers. They offer sound advice over the phone about when it's important to buy certified organic maple products and when it may matter less. Many of their products are certified kosher.

Cultures for Health
200 Innovation Ave.
Suite 150
Morrisville, NC 27560
800-962-1959
culturesforhealth.com
Supplies for fermenting dairy products, vegetables, fruits, and beverages. Cultures for Health also sells sourdough starter and yogurt starter, offers online culturing lessons, and dispenses troubleshooting advice online and over the phone. Some of their products are certified kosher.

GetCulture
501 Tasman St.
Madison, WI 53714
608-268-0462
getculture.com
Supplies and cultures for making yogurt, butter, and cheese, as well as supplies like butter muslin (a fine-weave cheesecloth) for straining. I use their ABY-611 yogurt

culture and prefer it to any other. They have a wonderful support team for helping you troubleshoot, and many of their cultures are certified kosher.

Giusto's Specialty Foods
344 Littlefield Ave.
South San Francisco, CA 94080
650-873-6566
giustos.com

A third-generation family business that started as a health-food store. Giusto's mills high-performance specialty flours that are used by many professional bakers. I have used their whole-wheat bread flour, whole-wheat pastry flour, and artisan white flour and like them all.

Gold Mine Natural Food Company
13200 Danielson St.
Suite A-1
Poway, CA 92064
800-475-3663
goldminenaturalfoods.com

An exceptional source for whole grains (including wonderful fresh rolled oats); beans; sea vegetables; tamari, shoyu, and mirin; sweeteners; and dried fruits and nuts. They also sell tools for cooking. Many of their products are certified kosher.

Grow and Behold Foods
888-790-5781
growandbehold.com

A purveyor of certified kosher grass-fed meats from animals raised on small family farms. Grow and Behold adheres to the highest standards for kashruth as well as for animal welfare, worker treatment, and sustainable agriculture.

Kamwo Meridian Herbs
211 Grand St.
New York, NY 10013
212-966-6370
kamwo.com

A source for Chinese herbs. I use their **Huang qi** *(astragalus) to enrich chicken broth and other soups, transforming them into a medicinal tonic.*

King Arthur Flour
135 U.S. Route 5 South
Norwich, VT 05055
800-827-6836
kingarthurflour.com

A producer of consistent, quality baking flour, including some organic flour. They've been in business for 200 years. King Arthur also sells baking supplies through their catalog and website, and if you're in Vermont, they offer classes for professionals, home bakers, and children. Most important, King Arthur staffs a complementary baker's hotline with helpful and knowledgeable bakers who will answer your questions. King Arthur's offerings include sourdough starter.

Kushi Store
800-645-8744
kushistore.com

A good source for natural food products, including sea vegetables, with an Asian, macrobiotic twist. The Kushi Store also has brown rice that is second to none and sells hard-to-find kitchen supplies as an added bonus. Many of their products are certified kosher.

Lehman's
4779 Kidron Road
Dalton, OH 44618

888-438-5346

lehmans.com

Wonderful, old-fashioned cooking, household, and livestock-tending supplies. Lehman's caters to the Amish and to others who appreciate simple, sustainable approaches to managing a home or homestead and putting food on the table.

Lodge Cast Iron

423-837-7181

lodgemfg.com

Long-lasting and affordable cast-iron cookware. Lodge is family-owned and operated and their products truly last a lifetime. I use two different Lodge Dutch ovens for baking sourdough bread.

Northampton Beer & Winemaking

154 King Street

Northampton, MA 01060

413-586-0150

beer-winemaking.com

Sells "mothers" for making vinegar. They also generously dispense kind advice.

Prepara

247 Centre St., 4th Floor

New York, NY 10013

888-878-8665

prepara.com

Makers of the tabletop Oil Mister I use for spraying sourdough bread dough before baking. This mister is a big improvement over ordinary sprayers, which don't do the job as well.

Sproutpeople

sproutpeople.org

A funky online business offering every sprouting seed imaginable, along with detailed instructions for sprouting the seeds on their website. Sproutpeople even sells seed mixes for sprouts that animals enjoy. Their enthusiasm is contagious.

Vital Choice Wild Seafood & Organics

2460 Salashan Loop

Ferndale, WA 98248

866-482-5887

vitalchoice.com

A seller of seafood that is sustainably harvested and endorsed by the Marine Stewardship Council. This endorsement certifies that the company's fish come from abundant wild stocks, a healthy habitat, and carefully managed fisheries. Many of their products are certified kosher.

Weston A. Price Foundation

4200 Wisconsin Ave., NW

Washington, DC 20016

202-363-4394

westonaprice.org

A foundation based on the research of dentist and nutrition pioneer Weston A. Price. With your annual membership, you get a directory each year for sourcing high-quality foods, along with a quarterly journal on healthy lifestyles, nutrition, wellness, alternative medicine, sustainable farming, and more.

"Sit down and feed, and welcome to our table." —William Shakespeare

ELLEN ARIAN is a cooking instructor and health-supportive chef with a specialty in handcrafting traditional farm-to-table cuisine. She completed culinary training at the Natural Gourmet Institute for Health and the Culinary Arts, and at the Lukas Klinik, a cancer hospital in Arlesheim, Switzerland. Arian has studied food and healing for more than twenty-five years, with more than two decades of experience cooking for those with special dietary needs due to health conditions. She teaches cooking in New York City and New Jersey. Visit her website at ellensfoodandsoul.com.